·opean Yearbook of International Economic Law (EYIEL) is a Springer-
ion in the field of International Economic Law (IEL), a field increasingly
›ating itself from Public International Law scholarship and evolving into a
dged academic discipline in its own right. With the yearbook, editors and
er make a significant contribution to the development of this "new" discipline
vide an international source of reference of the highest possible quality.
EYIEL covers all areas of IEL, in particular WTO Law, External Trade Law
r trading countries, important Regional Economic Integration agreements,
tional Competition Law, International Investment Regulation, International
ry Law, International Intellectual Property Protection and International
w.
EL publishes articles following a substantive review by the editors and
l experts as appropriate.
editors have published extensively in the field of IEL and European Law
They are supported by an international Advisory Board consisting of
shed scholars of the highest reputation.

Editors

European Yearbook of International Economic Law (EYIEL) is an annual
ation in International Economic Law, a field increasingly emancipating itself
Public International Law scholarship and evolving into a fully-fledged
mic discipline in its own right. With the yearbook, the editors and publisher
l to make a significant contribution to the development of this "new" discipline
rovide an international reference source of the highest possible quality. The
L covers all areas of IEL, in particular WTO Law, External Trade Law for
r trading countries, important Regional Economic Integration agreements,
national Competition Law, International Investment Regulation, International
etary Law, International Intellectual Property Protection and International Tax
In addition to the regular annual volumes, EYIEL Special Issues routinely
ss specific current topics in International Economic Law.

European Yearbook of International E

Special Issue

Wolfgang Weiß
Albrecht von Graevenitz • Ulrich Soltész
Editors

The Foreign Subsidies Regulation

Assessing Implementation

Springer

Editors
Wolfgang Weiß
German University of Administrative Sciences
Speyer, Rheinland-Pfalz, Germany

Ulrich Soltész
Gleiss Lutz Brussels
Brussels, Belgium

Albrecht von Graevenitz
Federal University of Applied
Administrative Sciences
Department Adminstration of the
Armed Forces
Mannheim, Germany

ISSN 2364-8392 ISSN 2364-8406 (electronic)
European Yearbook of International Economic Law
ISSN 2510-6880 ISSN 2510-6899 (electronic)
Special Issue
ISBN 978-3-032-23414-8 ISBN 978-3-032-23415-5 (eBook)
https://doi.org/10.1007/978-3-032-23415-5

This Springer imprint is published by the registered company Springer Nature Switzerland AG
The registered company address is: Gewerbestrasse 11, 6330 Cham, Switzerland

Contents

Introduction: The Foreign Subsidies Regulation 1
Wolfgang Weiß and Albrecht von Graevenitz

General Concepts

The Notion of Foreign Financial Contribution and of Foreign Subsidy 17
Wolfgang Weiß

'Distortion of Competition' in the Age of Industrial Policy: An Examination of Interpretations Across EU Competition Instruments .. 35
Seppe Maes, Caroline Buts, Robin Vandendriessche, and Marc Jegers

Balancing 63
Albrecht von Graevenitz

Challenges in Implementation

The Role of the Commission in the Public Procurement Tool 83
Elke Zeise

The FSR in Public Procurement: A View from Industry 95
Benjamin Linke

The Role of the European Commission in the Concentrations Tool 115
Sara-Alexandra Raitner and Wolfgang Weiß

The FSR in Concentrations: A View from Legal Practice 135
Harald Weiß

FSR: Fit for Purpose?

International Reactions to the Foreign Subsidies Regulation 159
Jan Wouters

The FSR: A Critical View 167
Wolfgang Weiß, Albrecht von Graevenitz, and Ulrich Soltész

Introduction: The Foreign Subsidies Regulation

Wolfgang Weiß and Albrecht von Graevenitz

Abstract The global economic order is changing drastically and is undergoing unprecedented changes. In order to respond to them and the resulting current global trade turmoil, the EU has adopted several new legal instruments, of which the Foreign Subsidies Regulation (FSR) is not only part, but is the instrument that has been applied the most (in contrast, the Anticoercion Instrument, the Carbon Border Adjustment Mechanism and the amendments to the Trade Enforcement Regulation still await their first implementation). Subject of this volume, therefore, is the exploration of the first implementation experiences after around two years of application of the FSR. This introduction has the aim to set the scene and present the reader with a brief introduction into the FSR, its contents and rationale and the resulting issues for its implementation. It will also introduce the reader into the sequence of the book's analysis of the current prospects and challenges of implementing the FSR and address the approaches taken in the volume. Finally, the contributions to this volume will briefly be outlined.

W. Weiß (✉)
German University of Administrative Sciences, Speyer, Rheinland-Pfalz, Germany
e-mail: weiss@uni-speyer.de

A. von Graevenitz
Federal University of Applied Administrative Sciences,
Department Adminstration of the Armed Forces, Mannheim, Germany
e-mail: albrecht.vongraevenitz@hsbund-fbbwv.de

W. Weiß et al. (eds.), *The Foreign Subsidies Regulation*, European Yearbook of International Economic Law, https://doi.org/10.1007/978-3-032-23415-5_1

1 Introduction

The global economic order is changing drastically and undergoes unprecedented transformation.[1] Escalating trade protectionism puts the existing multilateral trading system under threat and raises serious concerns about the future of international trade law and the principles of WTO law.[2] To respond to the resulting global trade turmoil, the EU has adopted a more assertive approach to trade policy, based on the principle of open strategic autonomy.[3] The EU is increasingly pursuing strategic autonomy also with regard to its trade policy. Formally, this commenced with the European Commission's trade review communication of February 2021 on an open, sustainable and enforceable EU trade policy that engendered a reorientation of trade policy that meets the priority of a stronger EU in the world.[4] Following this redirection of its trade policy, the EU adopted several new legal instruments, one of which is Regulation 2022/2560 on foreign subsidies that distort the internal market (hereafter referred to as the 'FSR').[5] With this regulation the EU responds to the globally increasing subsidisation that also affects the EU's internal market. The granting of subsidies to companies by states is rising, also with a view to their presence on foreign markets. States are not afraid of even subsidising companies abroad.[6] The large volume of foreign investment and the recent proliferation of a geo-economic orientation of trade policy by key players in world trade[7] contribute to further incentives for subsidisation. That the EU takes issue with this development and hence adopted the FSR demonstrates that the redirection of EU trade policy also affects EU competition policy. The FSR is a combination of competition and trade policy that aims to create a level playing field for all economic operators acting in the EU in terms of subsidies.

---

[1] For the multifaceted challenges to the world trading system see Weiß and Furculita (2024), pp. 47 ff; Weiß (2023), pp. 55 f; in the context of the foreign subsidies regulation De Ville et al. (2023), pp. 17 ff.

[2] Vidigal (2018).

[3] For a comprehensive analysis see Steinbach (2023), pp. 973 ff; Weiß and Furculita (2024), pp. 25 ff.

[4] Commission, Communication: Trade Policy Review - An open, sustainable and assertive trade policy, COM(2021) 66 final.

[5] Regulation (EU) 2022/2560 of the European Parliament and of the Council of 14 December 2022 on foreign subsidies distorting the internal market, 2022 OJ EU No. L 330/1, i.c.w. Corrigendum 2024 OJ L 90599, p. 1. For the FSR's legislative history see Basedow et al. (2023), pp. 222 ff; Su (2023), pp. 68 f.

[6] Hufbauer et al. (2008), pp. 3 f; Schaus (2021), pp. 146 f; Tokas (2022), p. 780.

[7] Roberts et al. (2019), p. 655; Adriaensen and Postnikov (2022).

As the FSR has been applied much more frequently than the Anticoercion Instrument,[8] the Carbon Border Adjustment Mechanism (CBAM),[9] and the amendments to the Trade Enforcement Regulation,[10] which are yet to be implemented, the subject of this volume is the critical exploration of the first implementation experiences of the FSR, which came into force on 12 January 2023. The regulation soon became effective as it had to be applied as of 13 July 2023 and its notification requirements as of 13 October 2023 according to Article 54(4) of the FSR. Therefore, the new instrument has been applicable in one way or another for around two years. It is therefore timely to discuss the issues that have arisen during this period of application of this new legislation, particularly as the European Commission is obliged under Article 46 of the FSR to issue guidelines by January 2026 on the criteria for distortion and the balancing test.

The past two years of applying the FSR have demonstrated that the new instrument raises a number of interpretative, conceptual, and practical questions. This book aims to contribute to clarifying these issues. The volume therefore examines the lessons learned and challenges identified during the almost two years of application of the FSR by the Commission, legal practice and contracting authorities, and places them in the context of an assessment of the FSR's conceptualisation, international reactions and the proliferating criticism in the academic literature.

As is well known, the FSR aspires to provide the EU with the necessary tools to counteract distortions to competition in the internal market caused by subsidies from third countries. The aim is to ensure a level playing field for all companies economically active in the EU, i.e. between those that receive foreign subsidies and those that do not. Since foreign subsidies can improve the competitive position of recipients operating in the internal market, they can affect the level playing field, for example by enabling recipients to make unduly favourable offers or merge with or acquire companies at uncompetitive high prices. The FSR applies to potentially unfair competition in situations of concentration or public procurement in the EU with the specific tools enshrined in its Chapters 3 and 4, besides a comprehensively applicable *ex officio* tool under Chapter 2.With these new instruments the

[8] Regulation (EU) 2023/2675 of the European Parliament and of the Council of 22 November 2023 on the protection of the Union and its Member States from economic coercion by third countries, 2023 OJ EU No. L 2023/2675, i.c.w. Corrigendum 2024 OJ EU No. L, 2024/90409.

[9] Regulation (EU) 2023/956 of the European Parliament and of the Council of 10 May 2023 establishing a carbon border adjustment mechanism (CBAM), 2023 OJ EU No. L 130/52.

[10] Regulation (EU) No 654/2014 of the European Parliament and of the Council of 15 May 2014 concerning the exercise of the Union's rights for the application and enforcement of international trade rules and amending Council Regulation (EC) No 3286/94 laying down Community procedures in the field of the common commercial policy in order to ensure the exercise of the Community's rights under international trade rules, in particular those established under the auspices of the World Trade Organization, 2024 OJ No. L 189, lastly changed by Regulation (EU) 2021/167 of the European Parliament and of the Council of 10 February 2021 amending Regulation (EU) No 654/2014 concerning the exercise of the Union's rights for the application and enforcement of international trade rules, 2021 OJ No. L 49.

Commission wants to close a legal gap:[11] Whereas state aid by EU Member States is subject to a principled ban under Article 107 TFEU und to comprehensive Commission scrutiny, with regard to foreign subsidies, there was no comparable review mechanism before the advent of the FSR. The EU proclaims to establish a review of foreign subsidies comparable to that of EU State aid control under Articles 107, 108 TFEU and uses regulatory mechanisms of other EU legal acts in order to remedy the counter-competitive effects of foreign subsidies. The EU defends the FSR as being non-discriminatory also in view of pertinent obligations flowing from WTO law or bilateral trade agreements; it counters discrimination blames by ensuring that the new rules are comparable to EU State aid review.[12]

While the rationale behind this new legislative instrument is perfectly understandable, there are significant doubts as to whether this regulation is the best way for the Commission to counter foreign subsidies and achieve a level playing field. Critics argue that the FSR only achieves its objective of ensuring a level playing field by creating new bureaucracy and granting the Commission extensive powers. This results in considerable legal uncertainty and unpredictability due to the use of undefined legal terms in its normative mechanisms, as well as a wide margin of manoeuvre. As will become clear in this book, the success of the FSR depends crucially on how the Commission applies it and how foreign countries respond.

This introduction provides an overview of the FSR, its contents and rationale, in order to identify the issues that may arise during implementation, emphasising the importance of its judicious application. It will also familiarise readers with the structure of the book's analysis of the current prospects and challenges of implementing the FSR, and the approaches taken within it. Finally, the contributions to this volume will be outlined briefly.

2 The Foreign Subsidies Regulation in a Nutshell

As mentioned, the FSR establishes a framework for combating distortions of competition caused by foreign subsidies by providing for review and investigation procedures and remedial measures, Article 1 FSR. The Commission is tasked with investigating foreign subsidies granted to undertakings operating in the EU and taking remedial action in the form of redressive measures if distortions to competition in the internal market occur, Article 7 FSR.

The FSR's scope is very comprehensive. It covers basically any undertaking (including public ones) engaging in any type of economic activity in the EU that

[11] Commission White Paper on Levelling the Playing Field as regards Foreign Subsidies, COM (2020) 253 final, pp. 9 ff; see also Weiß and Furculita (2024), pp. 329 ff.

[12] Commission Staff Working Document Impact Assessment, Accompanying the Proposal for a Regulation of the European Parliament and of the Council on foreign subsidies distorting the internal market, SWD(2021) 99, p. 57.

benefits from foreign subsidies.[13] This includes acquiring control of or merging with an undertaking established in the Union or an undertaking participating in a public procurement procedure in the Union.[14] The FSR provides for three tools to address competition distortions resulting from foreign subsidies. These tools build upon specific rules and procedures, besides the FSR's general and common procedural provisions in Chapters 1 and 5, Articles 1–8, 34–43.

As a general tool pertaining to any type of economic activity on the internal market and in any market situation, Chapter 2 of the Regulation establishes a general instrument for the review of third country subsidies, which enables the Commission to investigate *ex officio* basically all business activities in basically all market situations in the EU (Articles 9–18, also providing some general rules for review). In contrast to this mainly *ex-post* tool, two special tools exist with regard to mergers, acquisitions and other types of concentrations (Chapter 3, Articles 19–26) and with regard to beneficiaries taking part in public procurement procedures in the EU (Chapter 4, Articles 27–33). These two specific tools are notification-based *ex-ante* instruments. Undertakings are required to notify notifiable concentrations to the Commission and notifiable foreign financial contributions to the pertinent contracting authority or entity,[15] respectively, in order to allow for an *ex ante* review of foreign subsidies' distortive effects, see Article 21 in connection with Article 20 (3) and Article 29 in connection with Article 28 (1) FSR. The notification obligations must be met beyond certain thresholds provided in Articles 20, 28 FSR. Below these thresholds, the general *ex-officio* instrument of Chapter 2 applies.

The powers enshrined in the FSR for redressing competition distortions *ex officio* allow the Commission to adopt decisions that either accept commitments of the subsidized undertakings or impose 'redressive measures' in order to fully remedy an even mere potential distortion on the internal market, Articles 7, 11 (2) FSR. As Article 7 (2) FSR shows, the commitments or redressive measures may take very diverse shapes and can be broad in their substance and requirements. They may comprise both behavioral and structural remedies.[16]

The Commission's review procedures in all three tools (Chapters 2–4) are two-phased as under State aid law (Articles 107, 108 TFEU) or merger control under the EUMR[17] and consist of a preliminary and an in-depth investigation. The Commission enjoys a rather comprehensive decision-making power at the end of the latter, as it may either decide not to raise objections, adopt redressive measures or accept commitments, Article 11 (2) to (4) FSR. In case of procurement or concentration, the Commission under Chapters 3 and 4 FSR can interfere only—besides accepting commitments—by prohibiting the concentration (Article 25 (3) c) Regulation) or

[13] See, however Article 346 TFEU, recital 10, Article 44 (9) FSR.

[14] This is defined in accordance with the award procedures provided for in the EU procurement directives, see Article 2 (3) FSR.

[15] These terms are also taken over from the EU procurement directives, see Article 2 (4), (5) FSR.

[16] For more on the extensive Commission powers under the FSR see Weiß (2024), pp. 32 ff.

[17] 2004 OJ EU L 24/1.

the award of contract (Article 31 (2) Regulation). In addition, the Commission can impose reporting and transparency requirements, Article 7 (5) FSR.

These Commission powers build upon an investigation that has to explore three concepts common to all the instruments: The existence of a foreign subsidy, the (causation of a) distortion in competition in the EU internal market, and potentially the compensation of these negative effects by positive effects for the EU economy and its relevant policy objectives, the so-called balancing-test.[18] If the Commission finally finds a competitive distortion caused by a foreign subsidy which is not offset by its positive effects, the Commission then has to determine whether any commitments (if) offered by the beneficiary are sufficient, in order to fully and effectively remedy the distortion (Article 7 (3) Regulation) and—if not—how the redressive measures have to be shaped (ex officio-tool, Chapter 2 FSR), or whether the Commission issues a prohibition (Chapters 3, 4 FSR), respectively.[19]

As these three concepts set out in Articles 3 to 6 of the FSR—foreign subsidy, distortion of competition in the internal market, balancing test—are most relevant for any foreign subsidies review, they are pivotal for the application of the FSR. Admittedly, balancing will not be an issue in the preliminary review under Article 10 FSR; only phase II decisions at the end of the in-depth investigation require balancing.[20] The Commission's application practice so far demonstrates that the notion of foreign subsidies under Article 3 FSR and the meaning of competition distortion under Article 4 FSR[21] have played important roles, whereas the concept of the balancing test[22] has only been briefly addressed in the only phase II decision publicly available at the time of writing early June 2025, the e& decision.[23] Despite their great importance for the application of the FSR, these three criteria are subject to considerable uncertainty. This is because Articles 3 to 6 of the FSR merely introduce these concepts, remaining silent on important corollaries for their determination. Regarding the notion of foreign subsidies, Article 3 of the FSR presents a broad concept that distinguishes between foreign financial contributions and subsidies, but does not clearly define the criteria for attributing financial support to a foreign government. Unlike the situation under State aid, the requirement of competition distortion is not part of the notion of foreign subsidy and the aspects to be considered are only roughly addressed, resulting in a lack of clarity. The balancing test introduced in Article 6 is even more unclear, as it does not prescribe any details

[18] Ritzek-Seidl (2022), pp. 425 f.

[19] See Schonberg (2022), pp. 143 f.

[20] See the reference also to Article 6 in Article 11 (2), (3) FSR.

[21] For more on the notions of foreign financial contributions and foreign subsidies and on the concept of competition distortion, see the Chapters in this volume written by Weiß and Buts.

[22] For more on balancing see the Chapter written by von Graevenitz.

[23] Commission Decision of 24.9.2024 finding that, with the binding commitments, the foreign subsidies in the concentration do not distort the internal market (Case FS.100011 – e&/PPF Telecom Group), available at https://competition-cases.ec.europa.eu/cases/FS.100011. For a detailed analysis & decision see in this volume Raitner, Weiß, The Role of the European Commission in the Concentrations Tool, section 5.

on the aspects to be considered or the criteria for determining whether a negative competition effect is outweighed by positive effects.

In the two specific tools on concentrations and public procurement procedures, the application challenges relate, first, to the precise determination of threshold values, all the more as they depend on the concept of foreign financial contributions, not on foreign subsidies, and with the practicalities of the notifications and declarations, also with regard to pre-notification contacts with the Commission. Second, the scope of the distortion analysis will be a critical aspect. In the procurement tool, the distortion analysis is limited to the procurement in question (Article 27 FSR), and in the concentration tool, the analysis is equally restrained to the concentration concerned (Article 19 FSR). In addition, in the procurement tool, under Article 27 FSR, the power of the Commission may hinge upon the finding of an unduly advantageous tender which represents a non-defined concept in the FSR and whose relationship to establishing a competition distortion under Article 4 FSR is not clear.[24] Thirdly, the consequences of a notification for the domestic administrative procedures and decision-making are to be observed.

3 The Sequence of the Analysis

As the foregoing has made clear, whether the FSR can truly be considered an instrument that promotes fair competition within the EU's internal market hinges largely on how the Commission applies the rules in practice. In this way the Commission's application of the FSR will be decisive to clarify the implementation challenges identified above. In this regard, it may be an additional layer of complexity that within the Commission, there are two different DG's responsible for the implementation of the FSR. While the FSR's procurement tool is taken care of by the the Directorate-General for Internal Market, Industry, Entrepreneurship and SMEs (DG GROW, which is responsible for EU public procurement law), the other FSR tools are in the file of the Directorate-General for Competition (DG COMP). Second, it will also be important how third countries respond to the application of the FSR. The Commission must ensure that the rules are based on clear and appropriate considerations and theories of harm, respectively, that they provide legal certainty through consistent, principle-based interpretation and that they align with established principles and practices from comparable legal areas, particularly State aid, merger and anti-subsidy law. Given the likely backlash from powerful third countries, there is a risk of new distortions that could harm EU companies' activities in foreign markets.

Therefore, the book is divided into three parts, which attempt to explore the above considerations in more detail and from different perspectives in order to gain a comprehensive view of the FSR. The first part addresses general issues of the FSR and its basic concepts. As analysed, they form the cornerstone of the Commission's

[24] Reindl and Van Damme (2024), p. 67.

assessments when adopting redressive measures against foreign subsidies and arise as a first layer of questions in the Commission's application of the FSR and its enforcement powers. In any FSR case, the meaning of foreign financial contributions and subsidies under Article 3 FSR and the conceptualisation of the distortion of competition as set out in Article 4 and 5 FSR have to be identified. The balancing test under Article 6 may have to be employed by the Commission whenever it intends to adopt redressive measures or accept commitments in order to counteract foreign subsidies distorting the internal market. As these concepts are highly indeterminate, their concretisation deserves careful exploration and analysis.

The second part deals with the challenges of implementing the FSR with regard to public procurement and the concentration tool. These notification-based instruments pose particular implementation challenges with regard to the notification and declaration obligations, their scope and cause, and their consequences for the accompanying procurement or merger control procedures. In order to obtain a comprehensive view, it is necessary to consider not only the Commission's position and view, but also that of legal practice. These two instruments under Chapters 3 and 4 of the FSR also were the most important ones in the context of the Commission's experience of applying the FSR so far. The contributions in this part will present and analyse the Commission's specific role in the two instruments and address the implementing challenges of these two specific FSR instruments. Furthermore, the part adds critical perspectives from legal practice as well as from industry.

Part three will conclude the book by exploring the fitness for purpose of the FSR. First, the international responses and reactions that the FSR has provoked will be scrutinised, as these are crucial for the FSR's ability to achieve its aims, too. The reactions of the EU's trade partners will largely determine whether the FSR is perceived as a success in terms of improving the level playing field for EU companies, both within and outside the EU. These reactions will also contribute to determining the scope available to the Commission for implementing the FSR. Counteractions by trade partners limit the Commission's room for manoeuvre, intensifying the need for judicious application of the FSR and for careful consideration of the FSR's critical concepts and mechanisms.

Finally, the concluding chapter will provide an overall critical assessment of the FSR's ability to create a level playing field, dealing with more general issues relevant to assessing the FSR's success in light of the implementation experiences analysed in previous chapters. This chapter will address the critical reception of the FSR, evaluate the criticism in light of the findings, and adopt a constructive perspective to provide an overall assessment of the FSR's effectiveness and usefulness to pursue its policy objectives. To this end, it will synthesise the various findings from the previous chapters and present final conclusions on the FSR's potential and pitfalls. Proposals for relevant amendments will be suggested.

Overall, the three parts of this book cover the various aspects of the problematic facets of the FSR, which are analysed and contextualised to allow for a comprehensive assessment of its role as an instrument of the EU's new trade policy orientation, as reflected in its implementation practice. The book explores the FSR in light of the most recent application practices and responses and combines analytical approaches from the perspective of the Commission, legal practice and academic research in law, international relations and economics, thus bringing together different fields of research and their different research methods.

4 A Brief Outline of the Chapters

Part I is devoted to the three general concepts in the application of the FSR set out in Articles 3–6 (i.e. foreign subsidy, distortion of competition, balancing test).

Its first chapter written by Wolfgang Weiß will address the notions of foreign financial contribution and foreign subsidy as set out in Article 3 FSR and as considered in the Commission's practical application. The chapter will first recall the difference between the concepts of foreign financial contribution and foreign subsidy, the distinction of which is highly important. The Chapter will then carefully assess the different requirements of the concept of foreign subsidy. This will be done by comparing it with the notion of EU State aid and subsidy under WTO law, and by contextualising the notion of foreign subsidy with the other two general concepts of the FSR. In this way, interpretive and conceptual issues can be clarified and those in need of further clarification by practice and jurisprudence can be identified. The comprehensive assessment of the notions of foreign financial contribution and of subsidy will allow for the formulation of proposals to further clarify their notions.

The subsequent chapter written by Seppe Maes, Caroline Buts, Robin Vandendriessche and Marc Jegers focuses on the second central concept, the notion of "distortion of competition" in the context of the FSR and places it within the broader framework of competition law. The notion of distortion of competition is a central yet variably interpreted concept within EU competition policy. While the term generally implies a deviation from a fair competitive business environment, its legal and operational meaning diverges substantially across different branches of EU competition law. This chapter provides a systematic and comparative analysis of how distortion of competition is defined, interpreted, and applied in the three traditional domains and one more nascent domain, i.e. antitrust, merger control, State aid policy, and the more recent regulation of foreign subsidies. Starting from the respective legal bases, it examines how each area conceptualises competitive distortion, drawing also on decisional practice, milestone cases before the EU Courts, as well as academic literature. Through this cross-pillar examination, the chapter identifies both commonalities and divergences in how the concept is deployed and enforced in the traditional competition areas and reviews its meaning in the more recently introduced regulation on foreign subsidies. The analysis reveals that while all branches aim to ensure fair competition in the internal market, the notion of distortion is neither uniform nor interchangeable. This raises important questions about coherence and legal certainty, and suggests the potential benefits of a more integrated approach.

The third chapter of Part I written by Albrecht von Graevenitz will address the balancing test under the FSR. In this test the European Commission may balance the negative effects of a foreign subsidy in terms of distortion in the internal market against positive effects. This balancing may either lead to a 'no objection decision' or influence the Commission's decision on redressive measures or commitments. So far, in the Commission's practice the concept of balancing seems not to have played more than a minor role. However, it is expected to become one central focus in arguments to be brought forward by the parties and to be dealt with by the Commission in its decisions. The Chapter will first place the balancing test in its over-all context in the FSR. Thereafter light is shed on the very assessment the Commission will need to conduct in this test. Further, the possibilities of stakeholders to bring input as to positive effects of a subsidy and the question of whether the Commission may have a duty to investigate for positive effects *ex officio* is debated. In addition, the scope of the Commission's balancing test is discussed.

Starting Part II on the Implementation Challenges in the specific tools, the chapter The Role of the Commission in the Public Procurement tool written by Elke Zeise explores the functioning and implementation of the FSR with regard to the public procurement instrument that aims to address distortions of competition caused by foreign subsidies in tenders, with a particular focus on the role of the Commission. This chapter provides insight into the challenges faced by the Commission when reviewing bids for large public contracts based on notifications and declarations submitted under the FSR. These challenges concern both the quantity and the quality of the submissions. The chapter presents some striking figures on the application of the FSR in public procurement, notably the receipt of more than 3.400 submissions within the first 2 years, far surpassing initial projections. The article outlines the reasons why the number of cases has been significantly higher than anticipated during the legislative process and presents relevant statistical data. It also describes the cooperation between economic operators, contracting authorities, and the Commission, and identifies specificities in the procurement tool's procedures. The contribution concludes with a brief assessment of the current situation and an outlook on the Commission's plans to make its efforts to ensure a level playing field in public procurement more efficient. The chapter identifies critical lessons learned, such as low awareness of the FSR among contracting authorities and economic operators, poor submission quality, and the need for clearer guidance. By combining practical experience, institutional perspectives, and legal interpretation, this chapter provides valuable insights into the operation of the FSR in public procurement and highlights the challenges and opportunities ahead for improving compliance and enforcement.

The subsequent chapter titled The FSR in Public Procurement – A View from Industry written by Benjamin Linke addresses the challenges and uncertainties faced both by economic operators and contracting authorities/entities in the public procurement tool. The contribution shows that the FSR poses numerous uncertainties for undertakings operating within the EU internal market. Economic operators involved in public procurement procedures must adhere to notification obligations if specific value thresholds are surpassed, which imposes substantial administrative burdens in terms of data collection and assessment. The legal concepts that determine whether and to what extent notification obligations arise are also exceptionally ambiguous. The chapter outlines the requirements of notification obligations in public procurement procedures. From an industry perspective, issues related to notification obligations are subsequently discussed, along with proposed changes. The evaluation is conducted from the standpoint of both an economic operator and a contracting entity. The chapter closes with a call for simplifying notification requirements and increasing legal certainty in order to strike a better balance between market protection and regulatory burdens

Sara-Alexandra Raitner and Wolfgang Weiß then switch to an analysis of the concentrations tool of the FSR. Their chapter on the Role of the European Commission in the Concentrations Tool explores the FSR in the context of concentrations, focusing on the practical application of this notification-based tool since it became effective in October 2023. It outlines the FSR's legal framework enshrined in its chapter 4, in particular the notification thresholds, and review procedures and highlights its parallel role alongside merger and foreign investment control. Drawing on the first months of enforcement and the landmark decision in the *e&/PPF Telecom* case, the chapter analyses how the Commission identifies and addresses foreign subsidies that may distort competition in the internal market. It assesses procedural developments, notification and reporting obligations for foreign financial contributions, and the Commission's evolving guidance. The Chapter concludes that while the FSR has added a layer of complexity to M&A practice, it can be expected to have an emerging role in promoting fair competition in the EU.

The chapter titled 'The FSR in concentrations – A view from legal practice' authored by Harald Weiß offers a practitioner's perspective on the application of the FSR to concentrations, reflecting on early trends, practical experiences and challenges faced by companies and their legal advisors. It starts from the observation that after two years on, there is a huge discrepancy between the case load anticipated by the Commission and the actual numbers. After some introductory reflections on this phenomenon, including its possible causes and implications, the Chapter focuses on the practical aspects encountered in the various stages or "key moments" of a typical FSR case from a legal practitioner's perspective: From assessing the FSR filing thresholds over preparing the FSR filing, assisting undertakings in the FSR data collection, and navigating them through the (pre-)notification and FSR review process before DG COMP. It contrasts FSR procedures with EU Merger Regulation practice, identifying not only several parallels but also important differences, such as the lack of a simplified procedure, the absence of clearance decisions at the end of Phase I, and the possibility for the Commission to decide based on the facts available. The Chapter critically assesses the burdensome data collection requirements, including the broad scope of foreign financial contributions (FFCs) to be detected across global group entities. Drawing on legal practice, the Chapter reflects common industry frustrations and argues for reform. Suggested improvements include the introduction of simplified procedure, clearer guidance on the Commission's call-in powers, and a more consistent approach regarding the exceptions from FFC reporting requirements, e.g. regarding tax measures and financial services. This contribution provides a grounded analysis of how the FSR's concentration tool operates in practice and outlines practical reforms to streamline compliance, increase legal certainty and reduce red tape.

Part III commences with the chapter written by Jan Wouters that explores the international reception of the Foreign Subsidies Regulation, positioning it at the intersection of trade and competition law. Initially conceived in response to perceived distortive subsidies from China, particularly during the post-COVID economic landscape, the FSR has since evolved into a broader instrument—now operating in a world where many major economies, including the EU and US (via the Inflation Reduction Act), deploy significant subsidy schemes. The chapter explores third country's responses to the FSR; it presents some case studies of major trading nations, including the United Arab Emirates as the first country subject to a FSR decision. It concludes by stressing that the FSR became a symbol of the EU's assertive reach beyond its borders, raises legitimate concerns and should be implemented with caution and genuine engagement with third countries.

The final, concluding chapter 'The FSR – a critical view' co-authored by Wolfgang Weiß, Albrecht von Graevenitz and Ulrich Soltész serves to offer an overall assessment of the FSR based on the insights gained throughout the preceding Chapters of the book having explored the FSR's roughly two years of implementation. Thus, this chapter aims to take a constructive and critical look at the question of effectiveness and fitness for purpose and the effects of the FSR compared to the political objectives originally pursued with the FSR. Drawing on the findings of the previous parts of the volume, the contribution explores the FSR's overly broad scope, burdensome notification requirements affecting a wide range of undertakings including many EU based ones, and legal and procedural uncertainties. The chapter will also address largely unresolved issues such as the relationship between FSR and international (trade) agreements and commitments which advocate for a narrower scope of application. With regard to the broader scope, consideration should be given to how this can be restricted in order to reduce bureaucratic burdens imposed on companies and the Commission. Based on this, the Chapter questions the FSR's effectiveness in achieving a level playing field, given its conceptual ambiguities, extensive Commission discretion both in interpretation and enforcement, and potential conflict with international obligations. These weaknesses might give cause for a potential misuse of the FSR as a protectionist tool. Furthermore, the chapter questions the FSR's compatibility with international obligations and warns of possible geopolitical repercussions. The Chapter therefore calls for a judicious application, and for legal and practical reconsiderations and alterations of Commission practice. It develops proposals for remedying the identified challenges for the FSR's application.

References

Adriaensen J, Postnikov E (2022) A geo-economic turn in trade policy? EU trade agreements in the Asia-Pacific. Springer/Palgrave, Cham

Basedow R, Meunier S, Roederer-Rynning C (2023) Fair play? The politics of evaluating foreign subsidies in the European Union. In: Hillebrand Pohl J, Warchol J, Papadopoulos T, Wiesenthal J (eds) Weaponising investments, vol 1. Springer, Cham, pp 219–237

De Ville F, Happersberger S, Kalimo H (2023) The unilateral turn in EU trade policy? The origins and characteristics of the EU's new trade instruments. Eur Foreign Aff Rev Special Issue 28:15–34

Hufbauer G, Moll T, Rubini L (2008) Investment subsidies for cross-border M&A: trends and policy implications. United States Council Foundation Occasional Paper No 2

Reindl A, Van Damme I (2024) The EU Foreign Subsidies Regulation. Concurrences, New York

Ritzek-Seidl S (2022) The regulation on foreign subsidies distorting the internal market – outline of the provisional agreement. Zeitschrift für Europarechtliche Studien ZEuS 25:423–430

Roberts A, Choer Moraes H, Ferguson V (2019) Toward a geoeconomic order in international trade and investment. J Int Econ Law JIEL 22:655–676

Schaus M (2021) EU trade policy in light of the new industrial strategy for Europe. Intereconomics 56:144–149

Schonberg M (2022) The EU Foreign Subsidies Regulation: substantive assessment issues and open questions. Eur State Aid Law Q EStAL 21:143–152

Steinbach A (2023) The EU's turn to 'Strategic Autonomy': Leeway for policy action and points of conflict. Eur J Int Law 34:973–1006

Su X (2023) A critical analysis of the EU's Eclectic Foreign Subsidies Regulation: can the level playing field be achieved? Leg Issues Econ Integr LIEI 50:67–92

Tokas M (2022) Playing the game: the EU's proposed regulation on foreign subsidies. J World Trade 56:779–802

Vidigal G (2018) *Westphalia Strikes Back*: The 2018 Trade Wars and Threat to the WTO Regime. Amsterdam Law School Research Paper 2018/31

Weiß W (2023) The EU's strategic autonomy in times of politicization of international trade: the future of Commission accountability. Global Policy 14(Suppl 3):54–64

Weiß W (2024) The regulation on foreign subsidies distorting the internal market. A path to a level playing field? Springer Nature, Cham

Weiß W, Furculita C (2024) Open strategic autonomy in EU trade policy: assessing the turn to stronger enforcement and more robust interest representation. Cambridge University Press, Cambridge

Wolfgang Weiß is Professor of Law and holds the Chair of Public Law, EU Law and Public International Law at the German University of Administrative Sciences Speyer.

Albrecht von Graevenitz is Professor of Civil Law at the Federal University of Applied Administrative Sciences, Department Administration of the Armed Forces in Mannheim.

General Concepts

The Notion of Foreign Financial Contribution and of Foreign Subsidy

Wolfgang Weiß

Abstract This Chapter addresses the notions of foreign financial contribution and foreign subsidy as set out in Article 3 of Foreign Subsidies Regulation and as considered in the Commission's practical application. The Chapter will first recall the difference between the concepts of foreign financial contribution and foreign subsidy, the distinction of which is highly important. The Chapter will then carefully assess the different requirements of the concept of foreign subsidy. This will be done by comparing it with the notion of EU State aid and subsidy under WTO law, and by contextualising the notion of foreign subsidy with the other two general concepts of the FSR. In this way, interpretive and conceptual issues can be clarified and those in need of further clarification by practice and jurisprudence can be identified. The comprehensive assessment of the notions of foreign financial contribution and of subsidy will allow for the formulation of proposals to further clarify their notions.

1 Introduction

The three basic concepts relevant to the application of Regulation 2022/2560 on foreign subsidies distorting the internal market (hereinafter the 'FSR')[1] are set out in Articles 3 to 6 of the FSR. These concepts are applicable to all three FSR tools. The notions and conceptualisations of 'foreign subsidy', 'competition distortion'

[1] Regulation (EU) 2022/2560 of the European Parliament and of the Council of 14 December 2022 on foreign subsidies distorting the internal market, 2022 OJ EU No. L 330/1, i.c.w. Corrigendum 2024 OJ L 90599, p. 1. Its notification obligations apply since 13 October 2023, see Article 54 (4) FSR. For the FSR's legislative history see Basedow et al. (2023), pp. 222 ff; Weiß and Furculita (2024), Chapter 9.2; see also briefly Su (2023), pp. 68 f.

W. Weiß (✉)
German University of Administrative Sciences, Speyer, Rheinland-Pfalz, Germany
e-mail: weiss@uni-speyer.de

W. Weiß et al. (eds.), *The Foreign Subsidies Regulation*, European Yearbook of International Economic Law, https://doi.org/10.1007/978-3-032-23415-5_2

and the 'balancing test' are pivotal for the application of the FSR. Admittedly, balancing will not be an issue in phase I (i.e. the preliminary review under Article 10 FSR); only phase II decisions at the end of the in-depth investigation require balancing.[2] This chapter will address the first of these three concepts: the notion of a foreign subsidy under Article 3 of the FSR. This is one of the two core concepts of the FSR with which the European Commission (hereinafter the 'Commission'), has had to deal more deeply in its application practice of the FSR so far: Alongside the meaning of competition distortion under Article 4 FSR,[3] the notion of foreign subsidies under Article 3 FSR has played an important role in the decisions of the Commission, whereas the concept of the balancing test has only been briefly addressed so far. The prime example is the only phase II decision publicly available at the time of writing early June 2025: the e& decision.[4] In this decision, the section on balancing was quite brief, whereas those on the existence of a foreign financial contribution, a subsidy and on distortion of competition were rather extensive.[5]

As a preliminary remark, it should be recalled that the concept and meaning of foreign financial contribution is to be distinguished from that of foreign subsidy. This is clear not only from the wording of Article 3 (1) FSR, which distinguishes between the concept of foreign financial contribution and that of foreign subsidy, since a foreign subsidy exists if a financial contribution confers a benefit on an undertaking economically active in the EU internal market. Furthermore, the notification requirements in the concentration and in the public procurement instruments are only dependent on the granting of foreign financial contributions, without the need for the notifying economic operator to identify foreign subsidies. Hence the existence of merely a foreign financial contribution (and not of a foreign subsidy) suffices to instigate the notification obligations.[6]

The subsequent analysis will examine the notions of foreign financial contribution and of foreign subsidies by carefully assessing the different requirements of the broader concept of foreign subsidy which includes the term foreign financial contribution. To this end, the notion of foreign subsidies will be compared in particular to that of EU State aid under Article 107 TFEU, as the former draws heavily on the

---

[2] See the reference also to Article 6 in Article 11 (2), (3) FSR.

[3] For more on the concepts of competition distortion and of balancing, see in this volume Maes, Buts et al, 'Distortion of Competition' in the Age of Industrial Policy: An Examination of Interpretations across EU Competition Instruments, and von Graevenitz, Balancing.

[4] Commission Decision of 24.9.2024 finding that, with the binding commitments, the foreign subsidies in the concentration do not distort the internal market (Case FS.100011 – e&/PPF Telecom Group), available at https://competition-cases.ec.europa.eu/cases/FS.100011. For a detailed analysis & decision see in this volume Raitner, Weiß, The Role of the European Commission in the Concentrations Tool, section 4.

[5] The balancing test is briefly addressed in paragraphs 370 to 378 of the decision, while the assessment of the existence of foreign subsidies and of a distortion of competition takes up most of the decision: pp. 15 to 38 deal with the existence of foreign subsidies, and pp. 40–59 with distortive effects.

[6] Reindl and Van Damme (2024), p. 23. For a comparison of EU state aid to WTO anti-subsidy law see Rubini (2010).

latter, besides its verbatim reflection of formulations in the definition of a subsidy contained in Art. 1 WTO ASCM.[7] Furthermore, the notion of foreign subsidy will be contextualized with the other two general concepts of the FSR, i.e. competition distortion and balancing, in order to draw conclusions in particular from the requirements for establishing a competition distortion for the meaning of foreign subsidy. In this way, interpretive and conceptual issues can be determined and clarified, and the necessity of further clarification of the requirements of the term foreign subsidy by practice and jurisprudence can be demonstrated. The analyses presented here will also include the Commission's practical application of the concept of foreign subsidy and the lessons one can learn therefrom. The comprehensive assessment of the notion of foreign subsidy allows for the formulation of some proposals to further clarify the notions of foreign financial contribution and subsidy, respectively.

2 Foreign Financial Contribution Versus Foreign Subsidy

Before the similarities of the term foreign subsidy under the FSR with EU State aid law will be analyzed in more detail, we will first return to the already mentioned distinction between foreign financial contribution and foreign subsidy. The need for distinguishing them is very clear as the notion of subsidy in Article 3 (1) FSR is a broader concept for which the existence of a foreign financial contribution is only part. As the definition in Art 3 (1) shows, the notion of financial contribution is one element besides the existence of a benefit, of selectivity and other requirements (which will be looked at in more detail in what follows). Therefore, the notion of financial contributions must not be conflated with the notion of subsidy. This distinction becomes relevant when looking at the notification obligations of the specific FSR instruments in concentrations and procurement which refer to financial contributions, not to subsidies. Hence, foreign financial contributions and foreign subsidies are different concepts, and the mere existence of a foreign financial contribution (i.e. of any financial support even without the effect of conferring a selective benefit) suffices for triggering the notification obligation, see Articles 20 f and 28 FSR. As a consequence, any (even mere market-conform) remuneration received for the sale of goods or services to foreign countries represents a foreign financial contribution that contributes to meeting the thresholds for notification in the concentrations or public procurement tools of the FSR and hence might be required to be notified. And the same applies even to purchase of goods or services (see Art 3 (2) subparagraph 1 lit c) FSR). This means that if an EU company buys goods from a foreign country (or other entities attributable to the foreign country), the value of the goods received represents a financial contribution as well. The notion of foreign financial contribution thus is wider than the concept of foreign subsidy or EU State

[7] WTO Agreement on Subsidies and Countervailing Measures, 1994 OJ EU No. L 336/156.

aid as it includes any transaction even at market terms and without benefit, and does not (yet) incapsulate the separate requirements of benefit and of selectivity.[8]

In particular, this means that EU companies are subject to FSR scrutiny much more frequently than might be expected, as the FSR applies not only to foreign companies, but to any company in the EU single market that has received foreign contributions. As a result, any EU company that has done business with companies abroad, either as a seller or a buyer, may be affected by the FSR's notification or declaration requirements if the foreign company is an entity attributable to the foreign country. This broad scope of the FSR, due to the very broad notion of foreign financial contribution to be notified which finally may not represent foreign subsidies (as they neither are beneficial nor selective), can be seen as inconsistent with the currently discussed promise of reducing the administrative burden on EU companies. It is therefore reasonable to ask whether there will be any relief—apart from an exemption in reporting[9]—in the foreseeable future in the form of a reduction in the scope of the FSR so as not to include normal cross-border business activities. One solution would be to exempt trade in goods and services on market terms from being counted in calculating the notification thresholds by amending Article 20 (3) and Article 28 (1) to this effect.

3 The Notion of Foreign Subsidy Versus the Notion of State Aid

Under Art 3 (1) FSR we can read[10] that a foreign subsidy is deemed to exist where

- a third country provides directly or indirectly
- a financial contribution
- which confers a benefit on an
- undertaking engaging in economic activity in the internal market
- and which is limited in law or in fact to one or more undertakings or industries.

While this definition takes up some elements used in Article 1 WTO ASCM (financial contribution, confer a benefit),[11] this definition of Article 3 (1) FSR reflects even

[8] Reindl and Van Damme (2024), p. 26. Likewise, the concept of subsidy in Article 1 WTO ASCM is to be differentiated from the notion of foreign financial contribution as only the former includes the requirements of benefit and selectivity, in the same way as under the FSR.

[9] With respect to this see in this volume Raitner, Weiß, The Role of the European Commission in the Concentrations Tool, section 4.2. This exemption from reporting, however does not alter their relevance for counting them to see whether the notification threshold have been met.

[10] The wording of the rules is reproduced here in a structured and subdivided manner that is not contained in the rules themselves. This is done to enable easier comparison of the constituent elements at a glance in graphical form.

[11] Under Article 1.1 ASCM, a subsidy is deemed to exist if there is a financial contribution and a benefit is thereby conferred.

more concepts well known from the notion of state aid under Article 107 (1) TFEU. In Article 107 (1), the prohibition of Member State aid is based on some similar but also on some different requirements. There must be an

- aid
- granted by a Member State or through State resources in any form whatsoever
- which distorts or threatens to distort competition
- by favouring
- certain undertakings or the production of certain goods
- in so far as it affects trade between Member States.

Comparing the formulations, one can easily discern obvious differences which are fully understandable: Whereas Article 107 TFEU addresses state aid coming from EU Member States, the FSR concerns third country subsidies, i.e. subsidies granted by non-EU countries. Another difference, however, is important and may be striking at first glance: Whereas the concept of foreign subsidies in Article 3 (1) does not contain the requirement of competition distortion, in State aid, this requirement is part of the notion of State aid, besides the intra-EU trade effects. We will revert to this also substantially remarkable difference below Sect. 3.3.

The comparison also highlights the functional similarities. The State aid notion of aid is similar to the notion of financial contribution under the FSR. The requirement of conferring a benefit corresponds to the favouring effect of State aid. And the benefit must be limited to one or several undertakings, which in State aid law is reflected in the requirement of selectivity or specificity.

3.1 "Aid granted … in any form whatsoever" versus "provides directly or indirectly a financial contribution"

That the notion of financial contribution is based on concepts from State aid can first of all be derived from the examples set out in Art 3 (2) FSR's non-exhaustive list of foreign financial contributions which reflect the examples of subsidies indicated in Article 1.1 WTO ASCM, but also typical cases of an EU State aid: transfer of funds or capital injections, granting of loans, tax exemptions, or the price paid for the purchase of goods.[12] The term "financial contribution" thus has the same very broad meaning as in EU state aid law the term "aid" also with regard to the forms of grant ("in any form whatsoever"), which covers any type of support granted by reference to its "favouring" effect in competition contained in Article 107 (1) TFEU.

[12] For a more detailed analysis of these types of financial contributions see Reindl and Van Damme (2024), pp. 27 ff.

3.1.1 No Burden for State Resources Needed

However, unlike State aid law which refers to State resources, the FSR does not require the use of State resources. The Regulation applies to subsidies granted directly or indirectly. Article 3 (1) FSR covers financial contributions indirectly provided by the state. As Article 3 (1) subparagraph 2 clarifies, the indirect provision of a financial contribution refers to those contributions granted by foreign public entities or private ones attributable to the foreign state. Consequently, contributions that are merely authorised by or attributable to the foreign state are covered, irrespective of a burden on State resources. This demonstrates that the decisive aspect is the benefit granted to an undertaking that can be attributed to a foreign state. This is in line with the WTO ASCM as also there the benefit for the undertaking counts (see Article 1.1 WTO ASCM), not the issue of whether this is combined with cost to government.[13] Even under State aid law, there are cases where the CJEU held that it may not be necessary to establish that there has been a transfer of State resources, in particular if public or private bodies were designated to grant aid by the State.[14] In the e& decision, however, the Commission surprisingly noted that the unlimited guarantee granted to the company by the UAE creates the "serious and concrete risk of imposing an additional burden on the UAE",[15] which raises the question whether the use of state resources may have any relevance also for the assessment of whether a foreign financial contribution was granted. May an effect on state resources form a necessary requirement for a foreign financial contribution also under the FSR? When one looks at the wording of Article 3 FSR, there is nothing that hints towards such a requirement, in contrast to State aids, where State resources are explicitly mentioned in Article 107 (1) TFEU. Therefore, it appears more likely that the Commission made this reference to the burden for the UAE as a mere confirmation of the financial contribution being provided by the UAE, instead of wanting to introduce a new additional requirement. The wording of Article 3 FSR provides greater flexibility with regard to the provision of a financial contribution, which would be undermined if the e& decision were understood to require greater parallelism with State aid law with regard to the need to use State resources.

3.1.2 The Different Contexts of Attribution

This leads to a further difference with the concept of aid in State aid law: In State aid law, the CJEU jurisprudence requires, besides granting of an advantage through State resources, the imputability of the measure to an EU Member State.[16] The

[13] Su (2023), p. 77.

[14] CJEU, Case C-405/19 P, ECLI:EU:C:2019:268, para. 55 – EEG 2012.

[15] See Commission Decision of 24.9.2024 (fn 4), para. 117.

[16] CJEU, Case C-405/16 P, ECLI:EU:C:2019:268, para. 48 – EEG 2012. See Commission Notice on the Notion of State aid, 2016 OJ EU No. C 262/1, para. 38.

criteria for imputability, however, differ depending on the circumstances of the case. For imputability of the aid, an overall control over an entity or over the provision of the resources may not suffice. As an additional condition for the existence of State aid, the CJEU may also require that public authorities have the power to dispose of the financial benefits in order to confirm the use of State resources by the contested measure under review.[17] As regards public funding schemes, for example, attribution requires a control over the use of the resources in order to turn them into State resources.[18] With regard to the imputability of resources granted by a private or public entity under EU State aid law, the Court held that for this the mere State control over or dominant influence in an entity does not suffice; beyond, proof of an actual exercise of control is required which means that the Commission must examine whether public authorities have been "involved, in one way or another, in the adoption of the measures in question".[19] We will revert to the issue of imputability under the FSR below in Sect. 3.2. For the notion of financial contribution it is sufficient to state here that, as the use of State resources is not a requirement under the FSR, there can neither be room for a requirement of imputability of resources in order to turn them into State resources under the FSR. Nevertheless, the issue of attribution does exist under the FSR, but within a somewhat different context: Attribution under the FSR is not related to attributing the resources to the State (as there is no requirement of State resources under the FSR), but to attributing the financial contribution (wherever it comes from, as the provision of the contribution may also be made indirectly) to a foreign country.

Consequently, although the concept of foreign financial contribution has a comparable breadth to that of State aid, the former is not entirely similar to the latter.[20] The definition of subsidy in the FSR insofar appears more in line with the term subsidy under Article 1 ASCM or Article 2 of the EU Basic Regulation on Subsidised Imports 2016/1037 (BASR).[21] What is highly relevant under Article 3 FSR is the attributability of the provision of a financial contribution to the third country, as a financial contribution can be provided by a foreign country "directly or indirectly". This requirement of attribution will be explored in more detail now.

---

[17] See CJEU, Case C-379/98, ECLI:EU:C:2001:160, paras. 59–66 – PreussenElektra; Case C-405/16 P, ECLI:EU:C:2019:268, paras. 57 ff, 75 f – EEG 2012. See also the Notion of State aid (fn. 16), para. 57.

[18] CJEU, Case C-83/98, ECLI:EU:C:2000:248, para. 50 – Ladbroke Racing; Case C-206/06, ECLI:EU:C:2008:413, para. 70 – Essent Netwerk.

[19] CJEU, Case C-425/19 P, ECLI:EU:C:2021:154, para. 59 – Commission v Italy. See also Notion of State Aid (fn. 16), paras. 40 f.

[20] Commission White Paper on Levelling the Playing Field as regards Foreign Subsidies, COM(2020) 253 final, p. 41; Blazek and Hegener (2022), pp. 457 f; Koenig and von Wendland (2017), pp. 174 f; Schonberg (2022), p. 145; Tokas (2022), p. 782; Trapp (2020), p. 967.

[21] Regulation (EU) 2016/1037 of the European Parliament and of the Council on protection against subsidised imports from countries not members of the European Union, 2016 OJ EU No. L 176/55. See also Hornkohl (2023), p. 141; Su (2023), pp. 76 f.

3.2 *"Third Country" or "Foreign Public Entity": The Attribution of the Financial Contribution*

3.2.1 The Term Foreign

The terms "third" and "foreign" refer to any country outside the EU, thus any third country except EU Member States. The second subparagraph of Article 3 (2) FSR clarifies that the requirement of a foreign country providing a subsidy does not only refer to the central government authorities of third countries, but also to all manifestations of the public sector and to attributable private entities. As Article 3 (1) FSR states, the Regulation covers financial contributions granted directly or indirectly, i.e. by using intermediaries. Thus, it is not only subsidies granted directly from the central State level that come under the FSR's review, but also those granted directly or indirectly from any public institution or private entity as long as the financial contribution is attributable to the third country. The requirement of "foreign", insofar only pertains to public entities, not to private ones. Consequently, even support provided by domestic i.e. EU private entities may come under the scope of application of the FSR review of foreign contribution, if their actions in the form of subsidization can be attributed to a foreign country. Such private entities might, for example, be undertakings established within an EU Member State but owned or controlled by a third State.

3.2.2 Scope of Attribution: Public Authorities Versus Public or Private Entities and Bodies

According to Article 3 (2) second subparagraph lit c) FSR, "all relevant circumstances" may be taken into account in order to establish attribution of the providing private entity, and thus of the financial contribution granted by it, to a foreign State. Lit b) lists some elements which might be taken into account in the attribution of foreign public undertakings (but which in no way are exhaustive), i.e. characteristics of the entity, the legal and economic environment prevailing in the State in which the entity operates, and the government's role in the economy, as confirmed in recital 12 of the FSR. This difference between lit b) and c) prompts the question whether the elements listed in lit b) may also represent relevant circumstances for attribution of private entities under lit c).

Before we turn to the criteria of attribution, one insight into the scope of attribution must be made: As regards the requirement of attribution, one has to differentiate central governments and public authorities at all other levels (Article 3 (2) subparagraph 2 lit a) FSR) from foreign public entities or private entities, with regard to which the requirement of attributability is enshrined in Article 3 (2) subparagraph 2 lit b) and lit c) FSR. This indicates that as regards central government and sub-central public authorities, attribution has not to be specifically examined, but can be taken for granted as it results from the fact that the internal law of the foreign country determines the public authorities. This can be inferred from public international law rules on state responsibility, according to which a state organ is any person or entity which has this status in accordance with internal law[22] (see Article 4 (2) Draft Articles on Responsibility of States for Internationally Wrongful Acts 2001[23]).

Hence, attribution must be examined with regard to a financial contribution provided by foreign public entities (not being authorities) or private ones as such contribution may be perceived as a financial contribution by a foreign country only under the condition of attributability to the foreign country. The differentiation between public authorities (not requiring attribution) and other public or private entities conforms to the situation in State aids: "where a public authority grants an advantage to a beneficiary, the measure is by definition imputable to the State, even if the authority in question enjoys legal autonomy from other public authorities".[24]

3.2.3 Concept of and Criteria for Attribution

As mentioned, Article 3 (2) FSR does not define the relevant circumstances for attribution, but gives only some hints in Article 3 (2) second subparagraph lit b) and recital 12 FSR with regard to public entities. The vague hints in Article 3 (2) second subparagraph FSR point to the fact that attribution of contributions provided by public entities or private ones depends on the individual circumstances of the case and are subject to a case-by-case examination. The same applies to imputation of State aid coming from public or private entities. Hence, one might consider applying the criteria developed in State aid law, as attribution of private conduct or of public entities such as public undertakings, even if designated or established by the State, is also an issue in the application of EU State aid law.[25] In the Court's pertinent case law, the mere control of a private entity such as a public undertaking by the State is not sufficient for confirming attribution, even though it may allow the State to exercise a dominant influence over its operations. For, "the actual exercise of that control in a particular case cannot be automatically presumed. A public undertaking may act with more or less independence."[26] Hence, as already alluded to above in Sect. 3.1.2, what is required in addition to an overall control of the State over a private or public entity is the States' interference in this entity in such a way that the decision to grant an aid can be attributed as well. Therefore it must be examined whether the public authorities must be regarded as having been involved in the

[22] Reindl and Van Damme (2024), p. 35 f.

[23] See UN General Assembly Resolution A/RES/56/83 of 12 December 2001.

[24] Notion of State Aid (fn. 16), para. 39.

[25] Cf. already CJEU, Case C-379/98, ECLI:EU:C:2001:160, para. 58 – PreussenElektra; Case C-482/99 ECLI:EU:C:2002:294, paras. 51 ff – Stardust Marine.

[26] CJEU, Case C-482/99 ECLI:EU:C:2002:294, para. 52 – Stardust Marine.

adoption of the measure.[27] While it is not required to prove that public authorities "specifically incited the public undertaking to take the aid measures" or adopted them on the instructions of the public authorities,[28] imputability of an aid by a public undertaking is inferred from a set of indicators arising from the circumstances of the case and the context in which that measure was taken.[29] Insofar, the factors to be considered are such as the fact that the entity could not take the contested decision without taking account of the requirements of the public authorities or their directives, the integration of the public undertaking into the structures of public administration or the nature of its activities, e.g. as a public development bank, the supervision of public authorities over the management, or any other involvement of public authorities in adopting the measure.[30] The relevant circumstances must allow to establish the involvement by public authorities in granting the aid through the entity.[31]

As already mentioned, the criteria for attribution in Article 3 (2) subparagraph 2 FSR are not clearly spelled out. The hints given there are vague, also with regard to their interrelation, and they neither reflect the criteria spelled out above with regard to establishing the involvement of public authorities in the adoption of the aid measure.

Therefore, it is unclear whether the same conditions apply for the attribution of financial contributions provided by public or private entities under Article 3(2) FSR as under EU State aid law. In fact, one could infer from the different wording in Article 3(2) subparagraph 2 FSR—which only relates to general aspects of the entity's characteristics, the legal and economic environment, and the government's role in the economy, and not to the degree of public authorities' control over and influence in the public or private entity under consideration, not to mention the intensity of supervision actually exercised by public authorities and their involvement in the contested measure—that the requirements for attributing the conduct of private or public entities are considerably lower than those requested under EU State aid law.

In its Questions and Answers to the FSR, the Commission stated that a subsidy granted by a private entity is attributed to a third country "when, for example, the private entity is directed or entrusted by the third country to undertake a certain action"[32] which appears to again hint to a more relaxed, looser concept in comparison to EU State aid law.

Indeed, in the e& decision, the Commission made reference to the legislation of the UAE which formed the basis for the unlimited guarantee, and which is clearly

---

[27] CJEU, ibid. See also Su (2023), p. 78.

[28] CJEU, Case C-482/99 ECLI:EU:C:2002:294, paras. 53 f – Stardust Marine.

[29] CJEU, Case C-482/99 ECLI:EU:C:2002:294, para. 55 – Stardust Marine.

[30] CJEU, Case C-482/99 ECLI:EU:C:2002:294, paras. 55 f – Stardust Marine; Case C-425/19 P, ECLI:EU:C:2021:154, paras. 61 f – Commission v Italy. Notion of Aid (fn. 16) para. 43.

[31] CJEU, Case C-425/19 P, ECLI:EU:C:2021:154, para. 65 – Commission v Italy.

[32] Answer to question 4 of the European Commission's Q&A on the Regulation, available at https://single-market-economy.ec.europa.eu/single-market/public-procurement/foreign-subsidies-regulation/questions-and-answers_en.

attributable. Furthermore, the Commission referred to the decision of the shareholder meeting, controlled by the Emirates Investment Authority (a public authority of the UAE) to make use of the exception from the normal application of bankruptcy law.[33] In other parts of the e& decision, the Commission refers to state ownership of the banks, to government seats in their boards and to their role in decision-making, and to the government role in banking sector generally[34] to confirm the attribution of the revolving credit facility to the UAE. At least, those circumstances allow the Commission to state that these criteria taken together make it unlikely that the UAE were not involved.[35] It can be concluded from this decision practice of the Commission that the high threshold in EU state aid law, according to which an aid can only be attributed to the state if the state not only exercises general control over an entity, but if there is also evidence of the exercise of the control powers with regard to the granting of the aid, cannot be applied to the concept of attribution under the FSR. Thus, the threshold for attribution of aid to the State is considerably higher under EU State aid rules, whereas it is lower under the FSR. Under the FSR, it is sufficient that the foreign country has a more general control and power to intervene in the activities of the entity. This difference can be clearly explained and justified by the fact that the FSR requires clarification of facts that have taken place in a foreign country and in the context of the exercise of public authority there. Setting the bar too high for proving attribution would make the application of the FSR difficult. Therefore, it seems clear that the requirements for attribution cannot be as demanding as for internal EU situations. One might, however, contend, that also under WTO anti-subsidy rules, foreign situations have to be examined in order to reason attribution of the provision of a financial contribution to a government. It may be striking, therefore, that also when comparing the FSR to WTO anti-subsidy law, differences occur: Article 1 (1) a) ASCM provides that a financial contribution may also stem from "any public body". So, no private bodies are mentioned there, which, however, does not mean that contributions made by them are not covered by WTO ASCM. For, under Article 1(1) a) iv), the contribution made by a private entity is attributed to the government, if the government entrusts or directs a private body to transfer funds, make payments or transfer goods, and in this way to exercise functions normally vested in the government. Thus, subsidies granted by a foreign government using private entities for their disbursal are still covered also by WTO ASCM disciplines. However, the notion of public body in Article 1 (1) a) WTO ASCM appears more restrained compared to Article 3 (2) FSR. The notion of "public body" in Article 1 (1) a) ASCM is interpreted by the Appellate Body to be "an entity that possesses, exercises or is vested with governmental authority".[36] Thus, it is the governmental authority that counts, not the formal legal status. And insofar it

[33] See Commission Decision of 24.9.2024 (fn 4), paras. 119–122.

[34] Ibid. paras. 219 ff.

[35] Ibid. para. 231.

[36] See for the attribution of subsidization to the foreign country in case of public undertakings under the WTO ASCM Appellate Body, WT/DS379/AB/R, para. 317 – US – Definitive Anti-Dumping and Countervailing Duties on Certain Products from China.

appears that there is a remarkable difference compared to Article 3 (2) FSR, as the latter broadly refers to considering a foreign "government's role in the economy". Compared to this, the Appellate Body stresses the flexibilities but also complexities inherent in its assessment of whether an entity exercises governmental authority in its interpretation of Article 1 (1) a) ASCM: "that a government exercises meaningful control over an entity and its conduct may serve, in certain circumstances, as evidence that the relevant entity possesses governmental authority and exercises such authority in the performance of governmental functions. We stress, however, that, apart from an express delegation of authority in a legal instrument, the existence of mere formal links between an entity and government in the narrow sense is unlikely to suffice to establish the necessary possession of governmental authority. Thus, for example, the mere fact that a government is the majority shareholder of an entity does not demonstrate that the government exercises meaningful control over the conduct of that entity, much less that the government has bestowed it with governmental authority".[37] "Thus, the mere ownership or control over an entity by a government, without more, is not sufficient to establish that the entity is a public body" in the sense of Article 1 (1) ASCM.[38] Hence, government control must go beyond mere formal ownership; it must be examined whether the control was actually exercised by the government.[39] Accordingly, the Commission in its application of Article 2 BASR confirmed attribution of State-owned banks to China by referring to government guarantees and their instructions for them to grant loans in accordance with government plans and objectives.[40] A later WTO Appellate Body decision confirmed that attribution of a private entity requires establishing a link between government and the conduct in the form of entrustment or direction.[41] This burden is met when the Commission can prove that the government intervened to extend a credit ceiling to facilitate lending to an indebted company.[42]

By contrast, the attribution under Article 3(2) of the FSR allows for a much broader approach in attributing private conduct to foreign countries. This is because there is no need to identify the exercise of governmental authority in the decision-making process regarding the provision of the financial contribution in question, as can be inferred from the e& decision.[43] Once again, this difference in standards is perfectly reasonable. Under the FSR, companies must assess whether they have received financial contributions from a foreign state. The companies' initial assessment is relevant for determining whether the notification thresholds for foreign financial contributions have been met. Therefore, companies are under an obligation

[37] WTO Appellate Body, WT/DS379/AB/R, para. 318 – US – Definitive Anti-Dumping and Countervailing Duties on Certain Products from China.

[38] WTO Appellate Body, WT/DS436/AB/R, para. 4.10 – US – Countervailing Measures on Certain Hot-Rolled Carbon Steel Flat Products from India.

[39] See also Reindl and Van Damme (2024), p. 38 f.

[40] Reindl and Van Damme (2024), p. 40 with further references.

[41] WTO Appellate Body, WT/DS437/AB/RW, para. 5.103 – US - Countervailing Measures (China).

[42] See Reindl and Van Damme (2024), p. 42 with further references.

[43] Commission Decision of 24.9.2024 (fn 4), paras. 216 f.

to self-assess whether they have received financial contributions from a foreign state, which requires clarity on attributability. By contrast, the Commission carries out EU anti-subsidy investigations and has investigative powers to establish whether the conduct of public or private entities is attributable to a foreign state, in order to determine the existence of foreign subsidies. This enables the Commission to scrutinise the relationship between foreign states and private or public entities much more deeply. The difference between a foreign financial contribution and a foreign subsidy under the FSR—already pointed out above Sect. 2—is therefore relevant also in this regard, as companies operating in the EU must determine the attribution of an entity to a foreign state themselves, without investigative rights. Consequently, to ease the burden on them, the attribution threshold is lower under the FSR.

3.3 *"Which Confers a Benefit" (But Not Yet Distortive to Competition)*

As one can learn not least from recital 13 of the FSR, the requirement of the financial contribution conferring a benefit can be interpreted similar to State aid law's favouring effect of an aid. The effect of the foreign financial contribution to grant a benefit is determined, according to recital 13, by analyzing whether a benefit could be obtained under normal market conditions, considering comparative benchmarks. Accordingly, a benefit does not exist if the financial contribution reflects investment practice of "private investors, financing rates obtainable on the market, a comparable tax treatment, or the adequate remuneration for a given good or service". It is normal market conditions that represent the benchmark for assessing the existence of a benefit. As recital 13 continues: "If no directly comparable benchmarks are available, existing benchmarks could be adjusted or alternative benchmarks could be established based on generally accepted assessment methods. Benefits can, for example, be conferred in the context of the relationship established between public authorities and public undertakings, if such a relationship, and in particular any financing by the public authorities to public undertakings does not comply with normal market conditions. The provision or purchase of goods or services carried out following a competitive, transparent and non-discriminatory tender procedure, is presumed to be in line with normal market conditions. A financial contribution to an undertaking engaging in an economic activity in the internal market should not be considered as conferring a benefit when the benchmark assessment shows that the undertaking would have obtained that benefit under normal market conditions. Transfer pricing in the context of goods and services exchanged within an undertaking can confer a benefit if that transfer pricing is not in line with normal market conditions." These explanations given in recital 13 remind of EU State aid practice so that, insofar as the notion of benefit is concerned, there appears be no difference to State aid law's favouring effect.[44] Of particular relevance insofar might be the market economy operator test.[45]

The e& decision also demonstrates that under the term "benefit", the Commission may assess whether the benefit was paid for or remunerated by the company,[46] lack thereof proves the benefit.

As already mentioned, not part of the definition of subsidy, however, is the *financial contribution's distortive effect on competition*, which is addressed separately in Article 4 FSR. According to Article 7 FSR, the distortive effect is a requirement for adopting redressive measures or accepting commitments. Hence, the assessment of a distortive effect is not part of assessing the existence of a foreign subsidy, but is a precondition for the Commission's exercise of its power to adopt redressive measures. In contrast, in State aid law, the capacity of the aid to distort competition is part of the notion of state aid and thus part of the pertinent analysis of the Commission in its review whether a State aid exists. In State aids the competition distortion usually is inferred from the favouring effect of the aid. Thus, the distortion of competition can be established as a regular consequence of a State aid granted to an undertaking which has a beneficial effect as it strengthens its position in competition compared to normal market conditions.[47] There is a presumption that an aid causes a distortion of competition through its favouring effect. Such presumption does not exist under the FSR (apart from the categories of foreign subsidies listed in Article 5 FSR which provides for rebuttable presumptions for the existence of a competition distortion, reflecting severe cases of prohibited state aid). Thus, the difference of the FSR to State aid law is obvious: For the foreign subsidy review and the required assessments under the FSR it is a decisive and a question to be assessed separately whether a subsidy is "liable to improve the competitive position of an undertaking in the internal market", see the first requirement in Article 4 (1) FSR.

It is, however, striking, that the subsidy element of a "benefit" under Article 3 (1) FSR has to be determined, as just mentioned, already on an assessment whether the benefit could not have been obtained under normal market conditions, which actually, at least under State aid review, regularly conflates with finding a competition distortion. For, subsidies in themselves intervene in the normal functioning of the market so that inherently they have the capacity to distort competition.[48] But in foreign subsidies review under the FSR, both assessments (i.e. existence of benefit under Article 3 (1) FSR and liability to improve competitive position under Article 4 (1) FSR)) have to be separated, even though they may not be easily distinguishable.

---

[44] See also Reindl and Van Damme (2024), p. 44 ff.

[45] Insofar see Notion of State Aid (fn 16), paras. 86 ff.

[46] Commission Decision of 24.9.2024 (fn 4), paras. 129 ff.

[47] See e.g. CJEU, Case C-39/94, ECLI:EU:C:1996:285, paras. 60–62 – Syndicat français de l'Express international (SFEI) and others v La Poste and others.

[48] See Hornkohl (2023), pp. 138 f with further references.

In the e& decision, the Commission even though it addressed the existence of a benefit resulting from the foreign financial contribution (the unlimited guarantee), referred to the unlimited guarantee to be "liable to improve the conditions" of transactions and to allow for easier access.[49] The closeness of this formulation to the wording used in Article 4 (1) FSR's distortion requirement confirms the view adopted here that both requirements run in parallel, at least usually.

Despite this parallelism, the notion of benefit and the concept of competition distortion must be differentiated and have to be separated in foreign subsidy review, as the assessment of a distortion of competition also requires the second condition in Article 4 (1) FSR to be met, i.e. that the capacity of a foreign subsidy to improve the competitive decision has actually or potentially negatively affected competition in the internal market. The latter requirement appears to be the actual core of the assessment of a distortion of competition under Article 4 FSR.

Another issue one might raise with regard to the requirement of benefit is the possible interaction between Article 5 FSR and the requirement of benefit. As Article 5 FSR lists some presumptions of competition distortion, one might use them also in the assessment of the benefit criterion. If these cases of foreign financial contributions listed in Article 5 most likely distort competition, one might even more infer that these cases without a doubt also confirm the most likely existence of a benefit resulting from the foreign financial contribution. The e& decision shows that the presumptions of Article 5 are used also in the context of balancing under Article 6: The Commission states that where foreign subsidies fall under the categories of Article 5 FSR, it is also less likely that the negative effects on competition can be outweighed by the positive effects of the subsidy. In the Commission's words: "positive effects are less likely to outweigh its negative effects under Article 6 FSR".[50] Hence, there is no presumption of a negative outcome of the balancing test, but an indication that in order to outweigh the negative effects, the undertaking concerned must meet a high standard of proof. Likewise, one might use the presumptions under Article 5 also to establish the high likeliness of a benefit under Article 3 (1) FSR flowing from the financial contribution.

3.4 *"Specificity"*

As in EU state aid law and also in Article 1.2 WTO ASCM, only specific subsidies, i.e. subsidies granted to an individual company or economic sector ("one or more undertakings or industries"), are covered by the FSR, see its Article 3 (1). Similar to state aid, specificity can be assessed either by analyzing merely the legal rules, or factually, i.e. by exploring who actually is the beneficiary of a financial

[49] Commission Decision of 24.9.2024 (fn 4), paras. 123 f.

[50] Commission Decision (fn 4) para. 374: foreign subsidies falling under one of the categories of Article 5 "so that positive effects are less likely to outweigh its negative effects under Article 6 FSR".

contribution, as confirmed by recital 14 of the FSR. The concept of undertakings borrows from EU competition law[51] and includes any company economically active in one way or another in the EU.[52]

One has to bear in mind again, that for the existence of a foreign financial contribution which might have to be notified, the criterion of specificity does not have a relevance. It is for the determination of a foreign subsidy that a selective benefit resulting from a foreign financial contribution has to be examined. As a consequence, even generally applicable, non-selective financial contributions have to be taken into account as regards the FSR notification or declaration obligations.[53]

4 Conclusion

Due to the closeness of the notion of foreign subsidy to that of State aid, and despite the above-mentioned differences, it can be expected that the Commission will be very much guided by the concept of State aid and hence by most of the pertinent application practice and CJEU case law when applying the FSR with regard to the concept of foreign subsidy.[54] The Commission has clarified that subsidies within the meaning of the WTO ASCM are also covered by the concept of a financial contribution under the FSR, which is important for the fulfilment of the notification and declaration obligations under the special tools for concentrations and procurement,[55] but from which market conform trade should be excluded in order to ease the bureaucratic burden on EU companies flowing from the difference between the notion of foreign financial contribution and the concept of foreign subsidy, as the former does not contain the requirement of a benefit and of selectivity.[56]

Despite the parallelisms with the notion of state aid, significant differences remain, first with regard to the genuine role of assessing competition distortion under the FSR, which is not part of the notion of foreign subsidy (the first requirement provided in Article 4 (1) FSR, however, has an overlap with the notion of benefit), and second with regard to the seemingly lower threshold for attribution of a financial contribution to a foreign country. There is need for further guidance on the exact criteria for attribution. As demonstrated above,[57] a lower threshold is apt given the difficulties in assessing the relationship and concrete interferences of State actors in public or private entities, due to lack of transparency of third country

[51] Reindl and Van Damme (2024), p. 52.

[52] Weiß (2024), pp. 23–25.

[53] Reindl and Van Damme (2024), p. 53.

[54] Laprévote and Lin (2022), p. 447.

[55] See the answer to question 7 of the European Commission's Q&A on the Regulation, available at https://single-market-economy.ec.europa.eu/single-market/public-procurement/foreign-subsidies-regulation/questions-and-answers_en.

[56] See Sect. 2 and the proposal made there.

[57] See Sect. 3.2.3.

processes, and due to the fact that under the FSR, the companies are bound to self-assess whether the notification thresholds are met and to report the foreign financial contributions. Therefore, it should suffice for attribution that a foreign authority has effective powers of control over an entity. Another difference related to the lower threshold for attribution is the lack of relevance of State resources. In the view presented here, the financial contribution to an undertaking does not require as a corollary a cost for the foreign country or the involvement of state resources. The further course of the decisional practice of the Commission may have to be observed insofar. As mentioned, a brief statement of the Commission in the e& decision might give cause for uncertainties in this regard.[58]

Finally, the contextual approach to the requirement of benefit in Article 3 (1) FSR raised the question posed above[59] whether contributions in the form of those listed in Article 5 FSR necessarily imply the presence of a benefit in the sense of Article 3 (1) FSR, at least in the sense of a high probability or even a reputable presumption. The benefit analysis has at least some overlap with the first part of the competition distortion analysis under Article 4 (1) FSR.

References

Basedow R, Meunier S, Roederer-Rynning C (2023) Fair play? The politics of evaluating foreign subsidies in the European Union. In: Hillebrand Pohl J, Warchol J, Papadopoulos T, Wiesenthal J (eds) Weaponising investments, vol 1. Springer, Cham, pp 219–237

Blazek S, Hegener C (2022) Substantive and procedural parallels and overlaps between Art. 107, 108 TFEU and the (Draft) Regulation. Zeitschrift für Europarechtliche Studien ZEuS 25:453–466

Hornkohl L (2023) Protecting the internal market from subsidisation with the EU state aid regime and the Foreign Subsidies Regulation: two sides of the same coin? J Eur Compet Law Pract JECLAP 14:137–151

Koenig C, von Wendland B (2017) The art of regulation competition in Europe – wealth and wariness. Edward Elgar, Cheltenham

Laprévote F-C, Lin W (2022) Between state aid, trade and antitrust: the mixed procedural heritage of the Foreign Subsidies Regulation and the overarching principle of non-discrimination. Zeitschrift für Europarechtliche Studien 25:443–452

Reindl A, Van Damme I (2024) The EU Foreign Subsidies Regulation. Concurrences, New York

Rubini L (2010) The definition of subsidy and state aid: WTO and EC law in comparative perspective. Oxford University Press, Oxford

Schonberg M (2022) The EU Foreign Subsidies Regulation: substantive assessment issues and open questions. Eur State Aid Law Q EStAL 21:143–152

Su X (2023) A critical analysis of the EU's Eclectic Foreign Subsidies Regulation: can the level playing field be achieved? Leg Issues Econ Integr LIEI 50:67–92

Tokas M (2022) Playing the game: the EU's proposed regulation on foreign subsidies. J World Trade 56:779–802

[58] See Sect. 3.1.

[59] See Sect. 3.3.

Trapp P (2020) Das Weißbuch der Kommission zur Gewährleistung fairer Wettbewerbsbedingungen bei Subventionen aus Drittstaaten – Eine erste Analyse. Europäische Zeitschrift für Wirtschaftsrecht EuZW 31:964–970

Weiß W (2024) The regulation on foreign subsidies distorting the internal market. A path to a level playing field? Springer Nature, Cham

Weiß W, Furculita C (2024) Open strategic autonomy in EU trade policy: assessing the turn to stronger enforcement and more robust interest representation. Cambridge University Press, Cambridge

Wolfgang Weiß is Professor of Law and holds the Chair of Public Law, EU Law and Public International Law at the German University of Administrative Sciences Speyer.

'Distortion of Competition' in the Age of Industrial Policy: An Examination of Interpretations Across EU Competition Instruments

Seppe Maes, Caroline Buts, Robin Vandendriessche, and Marc Jegers

Abstract The notion of 'distortion of competition' is a central yet variably interpreted concept within EU competition policy. While the term generally implies a deviation from a fair competitive business environment, its legal and operational meaning diverges substantially across different branches of EU competition law. This chapter provides a systematic and comparative analysis of how distortion of competition is defined, interpreted, and applied in the three traditional domains and one more nascent domain, i.e. antitrust, merger control, State aid policy, and the more recent regulation of foreign subsidies. Starting from the respective legal bases, it examines how each area conceptualises competitive distortion, drawing also on decisional practice, milestone cases before the EU Courts, as well as academic literature. Through this cross-pillar examination, the chapter identifies both commonalities and divergences in how the concept is deployed and enforced in the traditional competition areas and reviews its meaning in the more recently introduced regulation on foreign subsidies. The analysis reveals that while all branches aim to ensure fair competition in the internal market, the notion of distortion is neither uniform nor interchangeable. This raises important questions about coherence and legal certainty, and suggests the potential benefits of a more integrated approach.

AI-assisted tools were employed exclusively for improving the clarity and style of the text. All substantive content, analysis, and interpretation are the work of the authors.

S. Maes · C. Buts (✉) · R. Vandendriessche · M. Jegers
Vrije Universiteit Brussels, Brussels, Belgium
e-mail: Seppe.Maes@vub.be; Caroline.Buts@vub.be; Robin.Vandendriessche@vub.be; Marc.Jegers@vub.be

W. Weiß et al. (eds.), *The Foreign Subsidies Regulation*, European Yearbook of International Economic Law, https://doi.org/10.1007/978-3-032-23415-5_3

1 Introduction

The term 'distortion' generally evokes the idea of an interference or deviation from a natural or ideal state. In everyday use, a distortion may refer to something being bent out of shape, misrepresented, or altered from its original form. Distortion has been formally described as *"a change to the intended or true meaning or appearance of something"*[1] or as *"the act of twisting or altering something of its true, natural, or original state"*.[2] In economic theory, it often signifies a deviation from conditions of (perfect) competition. Within EU competition policy, however, the notion of 'distortion of competition' acquires an even more specific meaning relating directly to the rationale of the policy. Yet even within this competition policy framework, the concept is not applied uniformly.

Different branches of EU competition policy, such as antitrust, merger control, State aid control, and foreign subsidies control, use varying terminology and interpretation to assess when competition is deemed to be distorted, restricted or impeded. These differences reflect not only the distinct legal bases and objectives of each regime, but also the institutional logics and enforcement challenges specific to each domain. As such, the meaning and role of 'distortion of competition' shift depending on the context, making it essential to understand both the common threads and the divergences across these fields. Nevertheless, the concept of distortion of competition is a focal point of EU competition policy.[3] The Treaty on the Functioning of the European Union (TFEU) namely aims to 'prevent restrictions on and distortions of competition'.[4] In general, EU competition law seeks to have a system of undistorted competition in the internal market with an even playing field. This chapter provides a systematic overview of how distortion of competition is conceptualised and enforced under each competition policy pillar, starting from the legal basis, but also including decisional practice and case law, as well as scientific literature.

Understanding how the concept of distortion of competition is defined and applied across the various branches of EU competition policy is essential for both coherence and effective enforcement. While avoiding distortions of competition lies at the heart of EU competition law, its specific terminology, exact interpretation and application vary depending on the area. Yet all these areas aim to preserve or restore fair competition within the internal market.

The remainder of this chapter is organised as follows. Section 2 formulates the research questions and methodology. Section 3 reviews the meaning of competition

[1] Cambridge English Dictionary, 'Meanings & Definitions' (2025) <https://dictionary.cambridge.org/dictionary/english/>.

[2] 'Merriam-Webster: America's Most Trusted Dictionary' <https://www.merriam-webster.com/>.

[3] For a more elaborate explanation on the objectives of competition law, see for example Whish and Bailey (2024).

[4] European Commission Fact Sheets on the European Union - Competition Policy, 2025, available at <https://www.europarl.europa.eu/factsheets/en/sheet/82/competition-policy>.

distortion in each of the main areas of competition policy, ranging from i) antitrust, over ii) merger control, to iii) State aid policy and iv) the regulation of foreign subsidies. Next, Sect. 4 compares the findings per source, covering similarities and differences stemming from legal bases, decisional practice and case law as well as scientific literature.

2 Research Questions and Methodology

This chapter employs a comparative doctrinal research method to analyse and contrast the notion of 'distortion of competition' across four key domains of EU competition policy: antitrust, merger control, State aid law, and the Foreign Subsidies Regulation. Doctrinal research, often referred to as the black letter approach, entails a close examination and systematic interpretation of legal norms as expressed in legislative texts, judicial decisions, and administrative practice. The method is widely recognised and used across different fields of study.[5] As this study focuses on the evolving and multifaceted meaning of a concept within established legal regimes, doctrinal analysis serves as the primary methodological foundation, where we draw on established principles and guidelines.[6]

Because the concept of distortion is not uniformly defined or applied across the fields of competition policy, a comparative legal method is useful to identify points of convergence and divergence in how distortion of competition is operationalised. Comparative legal research enables the investigation of how similar legal concepts function across different but related regulatory frameworks, considering their respective objectives, institutional settings, and enforcement logics. This approach enhances our understanding of whether distinctions in the interpretation of distortion are functionally justified or result in inconsistencies that may undermine coherence in EU competition policy.

At the same time, we recognise that the concept of distortion cannot be fully understood in isolation from its economic underpinnings. Therefore, while the core method remains doctrinal and comparative research, it is interdisciplinary in character, integrating economic logic to the extent that this is embedded and useful in the legal analysis and enforcement practice. This follows the tradition of a law and economics approaches, where legal norms are interpreted considering their economic rationale and effects.[7]

This combined legal and economic comparative method allows for a nuanced understanding of how a seemingly uniform concept diverges in practice, and what this implies.

---

[5] Majeed et al. (2023), p. 559.

[6] Zweigert and Kötz (1998); Örücü and Nelken (2007).

[7] Cooter and Ulen (2012).

More specifically, our analysis aims to answer the following research questions:

RQ1: How is the concept of 'distortion of competition' interpreted and applied within EU antitrust policy?
RQ2: How is the concept of 'distortion of competition' interpreted and applied within EU merger control?
RQ3: How is the concept of 'distortion of competition' interpreted and applied within EU State aid control?
RQ4: What constitutes a 'distortion of competition' under the EU Foreign Subsidies Regulation?
RQ5: What are the main similarities and differences when assessing distortion of competition across these four domains?

To this end we systematically map and compare the different understandings of 'distortion of competition'. Relevance is defined broadly as any passage that clarifies the legal meaning, materiality threshold, or evidential burden associated with distortion of competition or its conceptual proxies and terminology (e.g. significant impediment to effective competition, appreciable restriction, anti-competitive foreclosure, or threat of distortion).

The analysis has three main components. First, we systematically map the legal basis and function of the distortion concept in each domain. Second, we analyse key elements of relevant case law to clarify the operationalisation of what has been documented from the foundational documents, with a focus on how competition distortion is assessed and evidenced. Third, we integrate insights from seminal academic literature and triangulate the findings to further contextualise and highlight areas of scholarly debate or ambiguity. Peer-reviewed articles are identified through bibliographic databases and citation tracking, then assessed for the interpretative frameworks they propose or discuss.

3 Analysis and Results

This section reviews the notion of distortion of competition in four different domains of EU Competition policy, i.e. antitrust policy, merger control, State aid law and the regulation of foreign subsidies. After having analysed each section separately in terms of legal basis, case law and literature, Sect. 4 will proceed with the comparative analysis.

3.1 Distortion of Competition in EU Antitrust Policy

This section examines the concept of distortion of competition in the context of EU antitrust policy. Starting from the wording of Articles 101 and 102 TFEU, alongside relevant Commission guidance, it considers how the concept has been interpreted and applied in case law and policy documents. Unlike in other areas of EU competition policy, where the objective is more explicitly highlighted, the prevention of distortion of competition is more inherently embedded in the spirit and purpose of the Treaty provisions within the field of antitrust.

Article 101 TFEU and Article 102 TFEU form the backbone of EU antitrust. These articles read as follows:

> The following shall be prohibited as incompatible with the internal market: all agreements between undertakings, decisions by associations of undertakings and concerted practices which may affect trade between Member States and which have as their object or effect the prevention, restriction or distortion of competition within the internal market [...].[8]

> Any abuse by one or more undertakings of a dominant position within the internal market or in a substantial part of it shall be prohibited as incompatible with the internal market in so far as it may affect trade between Member States. [...].[9]

Both articles aim to prevent distortion of competition, as is evident from the relevant guidance that explicitly recognises this as their purpose. Nevertheless, they each address fundamentally different types of conduct:

> Articles 101 and 102 of the Treaty on the Functioning of the European Union (TFEU) are a matter of public policy and should be applied effectively throughout the Union to ensure that competition in the internal market is not distorted. Effective enforcement of Articles 101 and 102 TFEU is necessary to ensure fairer and more open competitive markets in the Union, in which undertakings compete more on their merits and without company-erected barriers to market entry, enabling them to generate wealth and create jobs. It protects consumers and undertakings active on the internal market from business practices that keep the prices of goods and services artificially high and enhances their choice of innovative goods and services.[10]

Article 101 TFEU addresses horizontal and vertical agreements between multiple undertakings where cooperation distorts competition, while Article 102 TFEU concerns unilateral conduct by a dominant undertaking. The following section will examine the various forms of conduct targeted under each Treaty provision.

3.1.1 Anticompetitive Agreements

Anticompetitive agreements between competitors provide probably the clearest instance in which competition is prevented, restricted or distorted. When rival undertakings coordinate on prices or allocate markets, for example by agreeing territorial or customer-based divisions, they prevent independent decision-making by colluding and thereby undermine the competitive process.[11] In practice, such

[8] Article 101 2008 (Official Journal 115, 09/05/2008 P 0088 - 0089).

[9] Article 102 2008 (Official Journal 115, 09/05/2008 P 0089 - 0089).

[10] Directive (EU) 2019/1 of the European Parliament and of the Council of 11 December 2018 to Empower the Competition Authorities of the Member States to Be More Effective Enforcers and to Ensure the Proper Functioning of the Internal Market, 2018 OJ EU No. L 11/. 1.

[11] CJEU, Case C-8/08, ECLI:EU:C:2009:343, para. 32 – T-Mobile Netherlands and Others.

behaviour typically results in higher prices, reduced output, diminished choice and quality, weakened innovation incentives, and allocative inefficiency, while also raising or creating barriers to entry.

Under Article 101 TFEU, the Courts treat prevention, restriction and distortion of competition as a unitary notion of an impediment of the competitive process. Distortion of competition can be demonstrated in two ways: by object, and by effect.[12] A restriction by object is an agreement or concerted practice which, judged by its very nature, is harmful to the proper functioning of normal competition so that the (potential) effects do not need to be proven.[13] A restriction by effect applies where such inherent harm is not evident and the authority must demonstrate that the conduct actually or potentially produces appreciable anti-competitive effects in its market context.[14] This division is particularly interesting because it renders certain types of behaviour illegal in theory, without a need to effectively quantify and prove the distortive effect. In practice however, the Courts interpret the by object concept strictly and only where the concerted practices between undertakings reveal, in their content, provisions, objectives or context, a sufficient degree of harm.[15] When the anticompetitive agreement does not, by its very nature, display a sufficient degree of harm, the effects still must be demonstrated to have had a (potentially) preventive, restrictive, or distortive effect on competition.[16] It is also important to note that the anticompetitive conduct must be capable of affecting trade between Member States.[17]

Through Article 101(3) TFEU, the provisions in Article 101(1) can be rendered inapplicable, but only where the undertakings invoking it prove with objective and verifiable evidence four cumulative and exhaustive conditions, namely that i) the agreement improves the production or distribution of goods or promotes technical or economic progress; ii) that consumers on the relevant market receive a fair share of the resulting benefit, for example through lower prices, better quality, choice or innovation, and at least any harm is offset; iii) that the restrictions are indispensable

[12] Guidelines on the applicability of Article 101 of the Treaty on the Functioning of the European Union to horizontal co-operation agreements, 2023 OJ EU No. C 259/1. For an early distinction between a by object and by effect infringement, we refer to: CJEC, Joined Cases 56 and 58/64, ECLI:EU:C:1966:41, para. 7 – Consten and Grundig v Commission; Case C-56/65, ECLI:EU:C:1966:38, p. 248 – Société Technique Minière v Maschinenbau Ulm.

[13] CJEU, Case C-67/13 P, ECLI:EU:C:2014:2204, para. 50 – CB v Commission.

[14] CJEU, Case C-345/14, ECLI:EU:C:2015:784, para. 17 – SIA "Maxima Latvija" v Konkurences padome; Case C-32/11, ECLI:EU:C:2013:160, para. 34 and case law cited; Allianz Hungária Biztosító Zrt and Others v Gazdasági CB v Commission (fn. 13), para. 52; Case C-286/13 P, ECLI:EU:C:2015:184, para. 116 – Dole Food Company Inc v Commission.

[15] CJEU, Case C-307/18, ECLI:EU:C:2020:52, para. 67 – Generics (UK) Ltd and Others v Competition and Markets Authority.

[16] CB v Commission (fn. 13), para. 52; Allianz Hungária (fn. 14), para. 34; Generics (fn. 15), para. 115; Case C-238/05, ECLI:EU:C:2006:734, para. 50 – Asnef-Equifax v Ausbanc; Case C-7/95 P, ECLI:EU:C:1998:256, para. 77 – John Deere Ltd v Commission.

[17] Guidelines on the effect on trade concept contained in Articles 81 and 82 of the Treaty, 2004 OJ No. C 101/81.

to achieving those efficiencies, as regards both the agreement as a whole and each individual clause, with no reasonably available less-restrictive alternative; and iv) that the agreement does not enable the parties to eliminate competition in relation to a substantial part of the relevant products or services.[18] These conditions apply irrespective of market shares unless a block exemption applies.[19]

Table 1 depicts the types of conduct that are (not) likely to distort competition under Article 101 TFEU.

The Commission also adopted several block exemption regulations and safe harbours, which specify categories of conduct that either fall outside the scope of Article 101(1) TFEU or may be exempted under Article 101(3) TFEU. The block exemption regulations set out a number of hardcore restrictions, specific to the type of agreement they cover. These hardcore restrictions are not to be confused with infringements by object, but rather serve to exclude such agreements from the scope of the block exemptions.[20] The block exemptions and their impact on how the notion of distortion is interpreted, are outlined in Table 2.

3.1.2 Abuse of Dominance

This strand of competition enforcement primarily concerns exclusionary as well as exploitative practices stemming from anticompetitive conduct by a dominant undertaking. The Commission's guidance on Article 102 TFEU targets practices such as exploitative and exclusionary behaviour that give concrete meaning to the concept of distortion in situations where a dominant position is abused.[21] It is well established that merely holding a dominant position is not unlawful. It is the abuse of such a position that constitutes an infringement.[22]

First, it is important to note that a dominant position does not exist across all markets in which the undertaking is (potentially) active. In principle, dominance

---

[18] Asnef-Equifax (fn. 16), para. 65; Joined Cases 43/82 and 63/82, ECLI:EU:C:1984:9, para. 61 – VBVB and VBBB v Commission.

[19] Article 101 TFEU.

[20] Maes et al. (2023), p. 189.

[21] Commission Communication (EU) on Guidance on the Commission's enforcement priorities in applying Article 82 of the EC Treaty to abusive exclusionary conduct by dominant undertakings, 2009 OJ EU No. C 45/7; Commission Draft Guidelines (EU) on the Application of Article 102 TFEU, 2025, available at <https://competition-policy.ec.europa.eu/antitrust-and-cartels/legislation/application-article-102-tfeu_en>.

[22] Commission Communication (fn. 34); CJEU, Case 322/81, ECLI:EU:C:1983:313 – Michelin v Commission; Case C-377/20, ECLI:EU:C:2022:379, para. 73 – Servizio Elettrico Nazionale and Others v Autorità Garante della Concorrenza e del Mercato and Others; Case C-333/21, ECLI:EU:C:2023:1011, para. 126 – European Superleague Company v FIFA and UEFA; Case C-209/10, ECLI:EU:C:2012:172, para. 21 – Post Danmark A7S v Konkurrencerådet; Case C-413/14 P, ECLI:EU:C:2017:632, para. 133 – Intel v Commission. Commission Communication (fn. 33).

Table 1 Overview: distortion, no distortion or limited distortion under Article 101 TFEU

Anticompetitive agreements and concerted practices—'distortion of competition within the internal market'		
Legal basis	Stipulations	Result
Article 101(1) TFEU[a]	Agreements, decisions or concerted practices that have as their object or effect the prevention, restriction or distortion of competition within the internal market, and may affect trade between Member States.	Distortion if infringement by object or its effect is demonstrated.
Article 101(3) TFEU[b]	Four cumulative and exhaustive criteria are to be met, in order for Article 101(1) TFEU to be inapplicable: - Improves the production or distribution of goods, or promotes technical or economic progress - Consumers must receive a fair share of the benefit - Does not impose restrictions not indispensable to these objectives - Does not grant the possibility to eliminate competition	Article 101(1) does not apply to these agreements or concerted practices.
De Minimis Notice[c]	Market-share thresholds indicate when restrictions are unlikely to appreciably restrict competition: - ≤10% aggregated market share for agreements between competitors - ≤15% individual market share for agreements between non-competitors Clear exclusion for by object restrictions from the Notice's scope.	Below the applicable thresholds, typically no appreciable distortion. Not applicable to by object conduct.
Effect on Trade Guidelines[d]	Horizontal cooperation agreements in principle do not affect trade between Member States where: - Aggregate market share ≤ 5% - Aggregate annual Union turnover ≤ €40 million	In principle no distortion when below thresholds.

Source: Own composition based on review of the legislation

[a] Ibid. 1

[b] Ibid

[c] Notice on Agreements of Minor Importance Which Do Not Appreciably Restrict Competition under Article 101(1) of the Treaty on the Functioning of the European Union (De Minimis Notice), 2014 OJ EU No. C 291/1

[d] Guidelines on the application of Article 81(3) of the Treaty, 2004 OJ EU No. C 101/97; Guidelines (fn. 12), para. 40

must be established for each relevant product, service or geographical market in which the incumbent operates. A dominant position is defined as:

> [...] a position of economic strength enjoyed by an undertaking, which enables it to prevent effective competition being maintained on a relevant market, by affording it the power to

> behave to an appreciable extent independently of its competitors, its customers and ultimately of consumers.[23]

There are various ways to demonstrate the existence of a dominant position, ranging from conceptual methods based on qualitative factors such as entry barriers, switching costs, etc. to quantitative measures and indices such as market shares and concentration measures, profitability measures, etc.[24]

Once a dominant position has been established, the undertaking bears *“a special responsibility not to allow its conduct to impair genuine undistorted competition on the common market”*.[25] The distortive effect of abusive conduct can lead to various negative outcomes detrimental to the public interest, consumers and other market participants. Such effects may include higher prices, reduced choice, lower quality and/or diminished innovation.

However, as noted above, merely holding a dominant position is not inherently problematic. Gaining and maintaining such a position through competition on the merits can be a natural outcome of competition. As is evident from the ample case law on this topic, undertakings have a right to protect their own commercial interest through proportional and appropriate measures, when deemed necessary.[26] In cases where the conduct can no longer be justified as competition on the merits, it may raise concerns and attract scrutiny regarding its distortive effect on competition through unjustified, exploitative behaviour associated with the dominant position. In such instances, it is necessary to demonstrate the existence of abuse that results in a distortion of the competitive process. Table 3 depicts the legal basis and enforcement priorities under Article 102 TFEU.

Read together, Articles 101 and 102 TFEU frame distortion as a material weakening of rivalry either through coordination that replaces independent decision making or through dominant-firm practices that foreclose or exploit in ways not attributable to competition on the merits.

---

[23] Commission Communication (fn. 33); CJEU, Case 27/76, ECLI:EU:C:1978:22, para. 65 – United Brands v Commission.

[24] A detailed description of these methods falls outside the scope of this article; however, the definition and quantification of market power are extensively discussed by Niels et al. (2023), ch. 4.

[25] Commission Communication (fn. 33).

[26] CJEU (fn. 35), para. 189; Case C-202/07 P, ECLI:EU:C:2009:214, para. 46 – France Télécom SA v Commission; Joined cases T-191/98, T-212/98 to T-214/98, ECLI:EU:T:2003:245, para. 1120 – Atlantic Container Line AB and Others v Commission; (fn. 15), paras. 149–151; Commission Draft Guidelines (EU) (fn. 33).

Table 2 Overview: block exemptions under Article 101 TFEU

Anticompetitive agreements and concerted practices—'distortion of competition within the internal market'		
Legal basis	Stipulations	Result
R&D BER[a]	Exempt under article 101(3), if conditions are met: - Full access to final results for all parties - Aggregate market share ≤ 25% - Hardcore restrictions exclude the whole agreement from the BER	Exempt under Article 101(3) TFEU
Specialisation BER[b]	Exempt under article 101(3), if conditions are met: - Aggregate market share ≤ 20% - Hardcore restrictions exclude the whole agreement from the BER	Exempt under Article 101(3) TFEU
Vertical agreements and concerted practices BER[c]	Exempt under article 101(3), if conditions are met: - Individual market shares ≤ 30% - Hardcore restrictions exclude the whole agreement from the BER (e.g. RPM)[d] - An excluded restriction does not fall under the BER[e]	Exempt under Article 101(3) TFEU
Technology transfer BER[f]	Exempt under article 101(3), if conditions are met: - Aggregate market share ≤ 20% for competitors, Individual market shares ≤ 30% for non-competitors - Hardcore restrictions exclude the whole agreement from the BER - An excluded restriction does not fall under the BER[g]	Exempt under Article 101(3) TFEU
(Soft) safe harbours[h]	A number of safe harbours clarify the conduct to fall under 101(3) or outside the scope of 101(1) - Joint purchasing, aggregate market share in selling and purchasing markets ≤ 15% - Commercialisation agreements: aggregate market share ≤ 15% - Standardisation agreements: unrestricted participation, transparent process, no obligation to comply, access is granted on FRAND terms - Mobile infrastructure sharing: passive access is not restricted, operators keep strategic and investment independence	Exempt under Article 101(3) TFEU Outside the scope of Article 101(1) TFEU

Source: Own composition based on review of the legislation

[a] Commission Regulation (EU) 2023/1066 on the application of Article 101(3) of the Treaty on the Functioning of the European Union to certain categories of research and development agreements, 2023 OJ EU No. L 143/9; Guidelines (fn. 12)

[b] Commission Regulation (EU) 2023/1067 on the application of Article 101(3) of the Treaty on the Functioning of the European Union to certain categories of specialisation agreements, 2023 OJ EU No. 143/20; Guidelines (fn. 12)

[c] Commission Regulation (EU) 2022/720 on the application of Article 101(3) of the Treaty on the Functioning of the European Union to categories of vertical agreements and concerted practices, 2024 OJ EU No. L134/4

(continued)

Table 2 (continued)

[d] See for example the following case, where the concept of resale price maintenance is clearly detailed, as well as the difference between a hardcore restriction and a by object infringement: CJEU, Case C-211/22, ECLI:EU:C:2023:529 – Super Bock; Commission Regulation (EU) 2022/720 on the application of Article 101(3) of the Treaty on the Functioning of the European Union to categories of vertical agreements and concerted practices, 2022 OJ EU No. L 134/4, ch. 4

[e] Commission Regulation (EU) (ibid.) art. 5

[f] Commission Regulation (EU) No 316/2014 on the application of Article 101(3) of the Treaty on the Functioning of the European Union to categories of technology transfer agreements, 2014 OJ EU No. L 93/17

[g] Ibid. art. 5

[h] A safe harbour refers to a legally binding block-exemption following a Commission Regulation, under Article 101(3) TFEU if an agreement meets the specified conditions. A soft safe harbour signals when an agreement is unlikely to appreciably restrict competition, or is likely to satisfy the conditions in Article 101(3) TFEU; Guidelines (fn. 12)

3.2 Distortion of Competition in EU Merger Control

This section reviews distortion of competition in EU merger control. It begins with the wording of the Merger Regulation and the Commission's guidance, and then examines how the notion has been interpreted and applied in mergers and acquisitions.

Merger control is a pillar of competition policy in the EU that was not there from the beginning. The Treaty of Rome did not include a merger control stipulation, despite its commitment to undistorted competition. Initially, before implementing the merger regulation, the initial predecessor of Article 102 TFEU, namely Article 86 EEC could in principle be used as the legal basis to act against acquisitions and mergers that strengthen dominant positions in so far as they substantially impeded competition.[27] However, the Commission deemed this not a sufficiently strong legal basis, and therefore adopted a specific regulation. Strong merger control stems from the same spirit as preventing abuse of dominance. We do not want merging undertakings simply to buy market power and potentially distort competition in the process.[28]

This inherent aim to prevent a distortion of competition can be retrieved from the legal basis for merger control in the EU, namely the Council Regulation (EC) No 139/2004, or so-called merger regulation. Here, it mentions the prevention of a distortive effect on competition quite explicitly:

> In order to ensure a system of undistorted competition in the common market, in furtherance of a policy conducted in accordance with the principle of an open market economy

[27] In 1973, the ECJ confirmed the use of Article 86 EEC as a legal basis for merger control. See: CJEU, Case 6-72, ECLI:EU:C:1973:22, para. 27 – Continental Can.

[28] Niels et al. (2023), p. 169.

Table 3 Overview: notion of distortion and enforcement priorities under Article 102 TFEU

Abuse of dominance—'distortion of competition within the internal market'		
Legal basis	Stipulations	Result
Article 102 TFEU[a]	Prohibits abuse of a dominant position within the internal market, in so far as they may affect trade between Member States.	Distortive if the conduct is found to be abusive.
Guidance on the enforcement priorities[b]	Details the enforcement priorities of the Commission, focus on what is most distortive and harmful to consumers.[c]	Prioritises exclusionary abuses most harmful to consumers, particularly where evidence demonstrates a likely anticompetitive foreclosure.
Updated guidance on the enforcement priorities[d]	Updated the enforcement priorities of the Commission, focus on what is most distortive and harmful to consumers.	The concept of distortion is broadened. An effects-based approach, that prioritises conduct capable of weakening or distorting the competitive structure, not only eliminating rivals.

Source: Own composition based on review of the legislation

[a] Article 102

[b] Commission Communication (fn. 33)

[c] Ibid. paras. 5–6

[d] Commission Communication (EU) on Amendments to the Communication from the Commission – Guidance on the Commission's enforcement priorities in applying Article 82 of the EC Treaty to abusive exclusionary conduct by dominant undertakings, 2023 OJ EU No. C 116/01

> with free competition, this Regulation must permit effective control of all concentrations from the point of view of their effect on competition in the Community.[29]

Furthermore, guidance is provided on what exactly entails an unacceptable concentration resulting from a merger or acquisition:

> A concentration which would significantly impede effective competition, in the common market or in a substantial part of it, in particular as a result of the creation or strengthening of a dominant position, shall be declared incompatible with the common market.[30]

EU merger control translates the Treaty objective of maintaining undistorted competition into a forward-looking appraisal of structural transactions.[31] As opposed to the more traditional approach in antitrust, but more in line with State aid control in the EU, there is a substantive yardstick in the form of the Significant Impediment to Effective Competition test (SIEC). A concentration is generally deemed to be incompatible where it would significantly impede effective competition in the internal market or a substantial part of it. Conversely, a merger is deemed compatible where no such impediment to effective competition is established, or where

[29] Council Regulation (EC) No 139/2004 of 20 January 2004 on the control of concentrations between undertakings (the EC Merger Regulation), 2004 OJ EU No. L 24/1, para. 24.

[30] Ibid. art. 2.

[31] Council Regulation (fn. 45); CJEU Case C-376/20 P, ECLI:EU:C:2023:561, para. 84 – Commission v CK Telecoms UK Investments Ltd.

sufficiently substantiated, merger-specific and verifiable efficiencies are demonstrated that are likely to be passed on to consumers and outweigh the expected competitive harm, resembling in spirit the balancing test applied in State aid control. The balancing test is an exercise in which the positive effects (such as the development of specific regions or sectors) are weighed against the negative effects (such as the crowding out of private investment or the support of less efficient undertakings). In this framework, a distortion is defined not by a general Treaty formula but by whether the transaction is likely to produce a significant weakening of competition post-merger, assessed against the counterfactual of no merger or acquisition.

The Horizontal Merger Guidelines operationalise the SIEC concept for mergers between competitors. They explain how effects arise in differentiated or homogeneous product settings when the merger removes a significant competitive constraint and gives the merged entity an incentive to deprive consumers of the benefits of effective competition.[32] While concentration measures do not create legal presumptions, the guidelines quantify market power through the Herfindahl-Hirschman index (HHI) which is applied together with the assessment of buyer power, entry, efficiencies and failing-firm arguments in the assessment of the distortive effect of a merger or acquisition.[33]

Vertical and conglomerate transactions are addressed in the Non-Horizontal Merger Guidelines.[34] The Commission identifies two main ways a vertical merger can (potentially) foreclose competition: through input foreclosure and customer foreclosure. For conglomerate mergers, portfolio leveraging is identified as the main type of foreclosure. The guidelines also explain how efficiencies that are merger-specific and verifiable can neutralise foreclosure risks, for example by reducing transaction costs, internalising double mark-ups, or enabling quality improvements. These provisions define, for non-horizontal settings, when a concentration is unlikely to distort competition.[35]

In cases where a SIEC is anticipated, through behavioural and/or structural commitments, merger related distortions can be prevented. The Remedies Notice details the different options and sets out the Commission's preference for structural remedies that directly restore competitive structure in the affected markets, such as divestitures creating viable and independent businesses.[36] Behavioural commitments are accepted exceptionally where they credibly remove the identified SIEC and are readily monitorable. In practical terms, the Remedies framework defines how a concentration that would otherwise significantly impede effective competition can

---

[32] Commission Guidelines (EU) on the assessment of horizontal mergers under the Council Regulation on the control of concentrations between undertakings, 2004 OJ EU No. C 31/5, para 8.

[33] Commission Guidelines (EU) (ibid.).

[34] Commission Guidelines (EU) on the assessment of non-horizontal mergers under the Council Regulation on the control of concentrations between undertakings, 2008 OJ EU No. C 265/6.

[35] Ibid.

[36] Commission notice on remedies acceptable under Council Regulation (EC) No 139/2004 and under Commission Regulation (EC) No 802/2004 2008, 2008 OJ EU No. C 267/1.

be rendered compatible by removing the source of the predicted distortion ex ante.[37] Table 4 depicts when, under the merger regulation, a SIEC is found.

In conclusion, EU merger control gives effect to the objective of preventing a distortion of competition by prohibiting concentrations that would significantly impede effective competition, while allowing those that do not, or where verifiable, merger-specific efficiencies are likely to be passed on to consumers such that the overall effect is not harmful.

3.3 Distortion of Competition in EU State Aid Control

This section reviews distortion of competition in State aid control. We start from the wording in Article 107(1) TFEU as well as from the Commission's guidance and subsequently analyse how the notion has been interpreted and applied. The concept has typically been interpreted relatively broadly in State aid control as interventions in the market mechanisms can be presumed to be distortive.[38]

The foundational reference to 'distortion of competition' in EU State aid control can be found in Article 107(1) TFEU which reads as follows:

> Save as otherwise provided in the Treaties, any aid granted by a Member State or through State resources in any form whatsoever <u>which distorts or threatens to distort competition</u> by favouring certain undertakings or the production of certain goods shall, in so far as it affects trade between Member States, be incompatible with the internal market.[39]

From this Treaty article we learn the cumulative State aid criteria that define which measures are considered to constitute 'State aid' within the meaning of EU State aid law. One of those criteria entails that the measure distorts or threatens to distort competition. In other words, the presence or potential of a competition distortion is needed for a measure to qualify as State aid within the meaning of said article.

The criterion is relatively easily fulfilled as we consider it to be met when a measure perpetuates or strengthens the competitive position of an undertaking, i.e. when the measure *"is liable to improve the competitive position of the recipient compared to other undertakings with which it competes"* as is described in the Notice on the Notion of State aid (NoA).[40] It exists when a selective economic advantage is provided to an undertaking in a sector where there is or could be competition.[41] It puts

[37] Ibid.

[38] Werner and Verouden (2016), ch. 4.

[39] Article 107 2008 (Official Journal 115 , 09/05/2008 P 0091 - 0092) 107.

[40] CJEU, Case 730/79, ECLI:EU:C:1980:209, para. 80 – Philip Morris Holland BV v Commission; Joined cases T-298/97, T-312/97, T-313/97 T-315/97 T-600/97 to 607/97 T-1/98 T-3/98 to T-6/98 T-23/98, para. 11 – Alzetta Mauro and Others v Commission; Commission Notice on the notion of State aid as referred to in Article 107(1) of the Treaty on the Functioning of the European Union, 2016 OJ EU No. C 262/1.

[41] CJEU, Case C-280/00, ECLI:EU:C:2003:415 – *Altmark Trans GmbH and Regierungspräsidium Magdeburg v Nahverkehrsgesellschaft Altmark GmbH, and Oberbundesanwalt beim*

Table 4 Overview: Distortion under the merger regulation

Mergers—'Significantly impede effective competition'		
Legal basis	Stipulations	Result
Merger regulation[a]	A concentration which would (not) significantly impede effective competition, in the common market or in a substantial part of it, in particular as a result of the creation or strengthening of a dominant position, shall be declared (in)compatible with the common market.	Distortive where a SIEC is established, not distortive where no SIEC is found
Horizontal merger guidelines[b]	Screens indicate cases unlikely to raise concerns where post-merger HHI is below 1000, or HHI 1000 to 2000 with ΔHHI below 250, or HHI above 2000 with ΔHHI below 150. Market share ≤25% may indicate compatibility. Also sets out buyer power, entry, efficiencies and failing-firm criteria.	Unlikely to be found distortive under the thresholds.
Non-horizontal merger guidelines[c]	Soft safe harbours signal limited concern for vertical and conglomerate cases where relevant market shares are <30 percent and post-merger HHI <2000, subject to case specifics.	Limited or no distortion expected where the soft safe harbours apply. Otherwise, full foreclosure analysis under SIEC
Remedies notice[d]	Structural remedies are preferred over behavioural commitments.	Eliminates distortion where commitments remove the SIEC reliably and durably.

Source: Own composition based on review of the legislation
[a] Council Regulation (EC) (fn. 45)
[b] Commission Guidelines (fn. 48)
[c] Commission Guidelines (fn. 50)
[d] Commission notice (fn. 52)

the beneficiary in a stronger competitive position than it would enjoy in the absence of the aid. This happens from the moment that the measure relieves the beneficiary from costs that it normally would incur.[42] The effect does not have to be significant or material, although it cannot be just merely hypothetical.[43] In short, the criterion is almost always met from the moment that you grant a selective advantage. Therefore, the NoA delineates cumulative criteria to be fulfilled in cases when the criterion on distortion is not met:

- *"a service is subject to a legal monopoly"*
- *"the legal monopoly not only excludes competition on the market, but also for the market"*
- *"the service is not in competition with other services"*

Bundesverwaltungsgerich; Alzetta Mauro (fn. 60), paras. 141–147; Commission Notice (fn. 60).

[42] CJEU, Case C-172/03, ECLI:EU:C:2005:130, para. 55 – Wolfgang Heiser v Finanzamt Innsbruck.

[43] CJEU, Altmark Trans GmbH (fn. 61), para. 79.

– *"if the service provider is active in another (geographical or product) market that is open to competition, cross-subsidisation has to be excluded."*[44]

While the Enabling Regulation does not define the concept of distortion, it provides indications on types of aid where the distortion of competition might be limited.[45] In such cases, and under specific conditions, it allows the Commission to exempt these measures from the notification requirement where the benefits of the measure would outweigh the negative distortive impact. The Regulation lists among others potential exemptions with non-significant impact on competition for small innovation projects, small culture, creation and heritage conservation, damages by natural disasters, certain agricultural products, conservation of marine and freshwater biological resources, (amateur) sports, social character transport, certain types of broadband, specific infrastructure projects.

Consequently, the General Block Exemption Regulation (GBER) exempts measures from the notification obligation provided that general as well as topic specific conditions are fulfilled.[46] Again, this regulation does not define the notion of distortion but lists measures where the distortion of competition is outweighed by the benefits to society resulting from the aid measure. In other words, reviewing the GBER gives an idea regarding aid measures where the impact on competition is limited. Complying with the GBER criteria and ensuring only a limited impact on competition entails diverse limitations for the design of the measures, for instance regarding aid amounts, and intensities.

Additional information on competition distortion is found in the De minimis Regulation, in the sense that it stipulates that aid up to EUR 300,000 over any three years is deemed not to distort or threaten to distort competition.[47] Consequently, such measures do not meet all cumulative State aid criteria and do hence not constitute State aid within the meaning of Article 107(1) TFEU.[48] Table 5 highlights when a state intervention is deemed to be distortive.

We have already established that the criterion on distortion of competition is relatively easily met. There is also no requirement for the European Commission to

[44] Commission Notice on the notion of State aid as referred to in Article 107(1) of the Treaty on the Functioning of the European Union, 2016 OJ EU No. C 262/1.

[45] Council Regulation (EU) 2015/1588 of 13 July 2015 on the application of Articles 107 and 108 of the Treaty on the Functioning of the European Union to certain categories of horizontal State aid (codification), 2015 OJ EU No. L 248/1.

[46] Commission Regulation (EU) No 651/2014 of 17 June 2014 declaring certain categories of aid compatible with the internal market in application of Articles 107 and 108 of the Treaty, 2014 OJ EU No. L 187/1.

[47] Commission Regulation (EU) 2023/2831 of 13 December 2023 on the application of Articles 107 and 108 of the Treaty on the Functioning of the European Union to de minimis aid, 2023 OJ EU No. L series.

[48] Ibid. The SGEI De minimis Regulation follows the same principle for compensation for services of general and economic interest up to EUR 750 000 over any three years. Following a similar logic, de minimis regulations for agriculture and fisheries have been designed.

demonstrate distortion, and it is usually dealt with together with the criterion on affectation of trade between Member States.

3.4 Distortion of Competition Under the FSR

The final part of Sect. 3 reviews distortion of competition under the Foreign Subsidies Regulation. The concept 'distorting the internal market' is mentioned in the title and hence is at the core of the regulation as it aims to address distortions in the internal market caused by foreign subsidies. As the regulation is relatively new, guidance on the meaning of a distortion of competition is still very limited as is apparent from a recent public consultation that has been launched by the European Commission.[49] We start from the wording in the regulation itself, and the explanation provided in the supporting documents. We continue with a review of the distortive effect in the first concluded case with a published decision text. Up to date, case law is not yet available. Most information can be obtained from the FSR[50] itself, the Staff Working Document[51] and the Impact Assessment[52] accompanying the FSR proposal.[53]

> Article 4 FSR addresses the concept 'distortions in the internal market'. The guidance is relatively elaborate and structured in several sections. Article 4(1) FSR reads as follows: *"A distortion in the internal market shall be deemed to exist where a foreign subsidy is liable to improve the competitive position of an undertaking in the internal market and where, in*

---

[49] Executive Vice-President Ribera even mentioned in her LinkedIn post of 24th July 2025 'Are we providing enough clarity as to when foreign subsidies are distortive': Teresa Ribera, 'LinkedIn Feed' (2025), available at <https://www.linkedin.com/posts/teresa-ribera-42a08b340_public-consultations-activity-7354155705664266241-C3c9?utm_source=social_share_send&utm_medium=member_desktop_web&rcm=ACoAADpQfFgB2qmGc9vFQvRweRHdJAiFtB4FRnE>; Commission Guidelines on Foreign Subsidies, 2025, available at <https://competition-policy.ec.europa.eu/public-consultations/guidelines-foreign-subsidies_en>.

[50] Regulation (EU) 2022/2560 of the European Parliament and of the Council of 14 December 2022 on foreign subsidies distorting the internal market, 2022 OJ EU No. L 330/1.

[51] European Commission, Commission Staff Working Document: Initial Clarifications on the Application of Article 4(1), Article 6 and Article 27(1) of Regulation (EU) 2022/2560 on Foreign Subsidies Distorting the Internal Market, 2024, available at <https://competition-policy.ec.europa.eu/document/download/b4c8bb13-839b-4bfb-8863-78b188523d22_en?filename=20240726_SWD_clarifications_on_application_of_FSR.pdf>.

[52] European Commission, Commission Staff Working Document: Impact Assessment Accompanying the Proposal for a Regulation of the European Parliament and of the Council on Foreign Subsidies Distorting the Internal Market, 2021, available at <https://eur-lex.europa.eu/legal-content/EN/TXT/?uri=celex_52021SC0099>.

[53] Unfortunately, the Implementing Regulation does not provide clarification on the notion of distortion of the internal market: Commission Implementing Regulation (EU) 2023/1441 of 10 July 2023 on detailed arrangements for the conduct of proceedings by the Commission pursuant to Regulation (EU) 2022/2560 of the European Parliament and of the Council on foreign subsidies distorting the internal market, 2023 OJ EU No. L 177/1.

Table 5 Overview: distortion, no distortion or limited distortion in State aid control

State aid control—'Distorts or threatens to distort competition'		
Legal basis	Stipulations	Result
NoA	'Improve the competitive position of the recipient compared to other undertakings with which it competes' 'Selective economic advantage to an undertaking in a sector where there is or could be competition'	Distortion
NoA	Cumulative conditions on legal monopoly	Distortion is excluded
GBER	</= EUR 150 Mln per MS per year </= EUR 200 Mln per MS financial products General conditions Specific conditions and ceilings	Limited distortion Potential distortion outweighed by societal benefits
De minimis	</= EUR 300,000 per undertaking per three years	No distortion
De minimis: SGEI	</= EUR 750,000 per undertaking per three years	No distortion

Source: Own composition based on review of the legislation

doing so, that foreign subsidy actually or potentially negatively affects competition in the internal market."[54]

The first part on 'liable to improve the competitive position of an undertaking in the internal market' entails that there is an economic activity in the internal market and that a link between the subsidy and said economic activity can be demonstrated.[55] The second part on 'actually or potentially negatively affects competition in the internal market' requires an actual or potential distortion. In addition, it is relevant for any activity in which the beneficiary is (or is likely to be) active in the internal market.[56] It is said to be further developed by the Commission's case practice. However, also the recent draft FSR Guidelines already provide clarification by addressing the legal standard to establish that a foreign subsidy actually or potentially negatively affects competition in the internal market as well as by detailing steps in the assessment.[57]

Unlike State aid control, the FSR has no presumption of distortion. Non-exhaustive and non-cumulative indicators listed in Article 4(1) FSR are used to assess whether a foreign subsidy can improve the competitive position of an

[54] Regulation (EU) 2022/2560 of the European Parliament and of the Council of 14 December 2022 on foreign subsidies distorting the internal market, OJ EU No. L 330/1, art. 4.

[55] European Commission (fn. 71), para. 1.

[56] Ibid. para. 2.

[57] Communication from the Commission – Draft Guidelines on the application of certain provisions of Regulation (EU) 2022/2560 of the European Parliament and of the Council of 14 December 2022 on foreign subsidies distorting the internal market, available at https://competition-policy.ec.europa.eu/document/download/a0b557e7-96f8-4231-9ed5-522f13de9065_en?filename=FSR_draft_guidelines_application_of_EU_Reg_2022-2560.pdf.

undertaking and whether it then actually or potentially negatively affects competition. These indicators included are the following:

- the amount of the foreign subsidy;
- the nature of the foreign subsidy;
- the situation of the undertaking, including its size and the markets or sectors concerned;
- the level and evolution of economic activity of the undertaking on the internal market;
- the purpose and conditions attached to the foreign subsidy as well as its use on the internal market.[58]

In addition, Article 4 lists subsidies that are unlikely to distort or will not distort the internal market.[59] Specifically, Article 4(2) states that subsidies not exceeding EUR 4 million in three years are unlikely to distort the internal market. In line with the State aid rules, foreign subsidies below the State aid de minimis threshold of EUR 300,000 are considered not to distort the internal market in accordance with Article 4(3). Also, subsidies to compensate for damage caused by natural disasters or exceptional occurrences do not distort the internal market under Article 4(4).

Article 5 provides a list of those subsidies that are likely to distort the internal market.[60] These entail aid to ailing undertakings, unlimited guarantees, non-OECD conform export finance measures, subsidies directly facilitating a concentration or an unduly advantageous tender.

In case we are dealing with a subsidy that is listed in Article 5 FSR, the undertaking may provide information to demonstrate that it does not distort the internal market. Table 6 highlights the likelihood of foreign subsidy to distort the internal market.

Table 6 Unlikely versus likely to distort the internal market

Unlikely or not distort (Art 4 FSR)	Most likely to distort (Art 5 FSR)
< EUR 4 million per three years	Ailing undertaking (unless viable restructuring)
< de minimis aid per third country per three years	Unlimited guarantee
Natural disaster or exceptional occurrence	Non-OECD conform export financing
	Directly facilitating concentration
	Enabling unduly advantageous tender

Source: FSR Articles 4 and 5 (Ibid. paras. 4–5)

[58] Regulation (EU) 2022/2560 of the European Parliament and of the Council of 14 December 2022 on foreign subsidies distorting the internal market, 2022, OJ EU No. L 330/1.

[59] Ibid.

[60] Ibid.

Table 7 Overview: distortion, no distortion or limited distortion under the FSR

FSR—'distorting the internal market'		
Legal basis	Stipulations	Result
FSR Art 4(1)	'A distortion … shall be deemed to exist where a foreign subsidy is liable to improve the competitive position… and actually, or potentially negatively affects competition…'	Distortion
FSR Art 4(2)	< EUR 4,000,000 over three years	Unlikely to distort
FSR Art 4(3)	< EUR 300,000	Shall not be considered to distort
FSR Art 4(4)	Compensate damage natural disasters and exceptional occurrences	May be considered not to distort
FSR Art 5	Aid to ailing undertaking, unlimited guarantee, non-OECD conform export financing, directly facilitating concentration or unduly advantageous tender	Most likely to distort

Source: Own composition based on review of the legislation and supporting documents

The Impact Assessment guidance further helps us to understand the logic and concerns regarding distortion.[61] The distortions caused by foreign subsidies are, in principle, similar regardless of whether they originate from a Member State or a third country.[62] As long as a market exists, subsidies have the potential to distort competition. These distortions can take various forms.

When foreign subsidies facilitate acquisitions, participation in public procurement, or other market activities, several forms of distortion may arise. In the context of acquisitions, foreign subsidies can crowd out potentially more efficient competitors due to soft budget constraints, deter non-subsidised firms from engaging in expansion, and allow subsidised undertakings to grow at the expense of more efficient market players.[63] This can lead to increased market concentration and enable low-pricing or predatory strategies supported by persistent subsidisation.[64]

In the area of public procurement, subsidised firms may offer artificially low prices at the expense of quality and innovation, thereby displacing more innovative or efficient competitors. Such dynamics risk undermining fair competition by awarding contracts to less economically advantageous bids and deterring unsubsidised firms from participating. Moreover, subsidies can lead to unrealistic and false perceptions.[65] More broadly, foreign subsidies can result in general market distortions, including inefficient allocation of resources, uneven growth between

[61] European Commission (fn. 72).

[62] Ibid. para. 7.

[63] Baumann (2020).

[64] Fresard (2010), p. 65; European Commission (fn. 72), paras. 10–12.

[65] European Commission (fn. 72), paras. 17–18.

subsidised and non-subsidised entities, a weakening of EU competitiveness, and the triggering of wasteful subsidy races.[66]

In short, the FSR sets several presumptions as well as safe harbours regarding distortion of the internal market. Table 7 provides an overview of the main principles governing distortion of the internal market under the FSR.[67]

3.4.1 Decisional Practice

Despite the recent nature of the FSR, already 179 cases are recorded on the website of DG Competition.[68] However, there is currently only one published phase II decision that provides extensive information regarding distortion of the internal market: Case FS 100011 e&/PPF Telecom Group.[69] Hence, this section reviews in detail how the Commission has assessed the concept of distortion in that case. Before starting this review, it is important to note that, up to date, there have also been two withdrawals during the preliminary review phase.[70] While no information can be obtained regarding the interpretation of the concept of distortion in these cases, the withdrawals themselves may have had an impact on the competition in the affected markets as neither of the proposed concentrations materialised.

In April 2024, Emirates Telecommunications Group Company (e&), controlled by the UAE's sovereign wealth fund, the EIA, notified the Commission of its intention to acquire PPF's telecom operations in several EU Member States for over EUR 2.15 billion. In September 2024, following a phase II investigation, the Commission cleared the transaction with commitments, marking its first final decision under the FSR. The Commission distinguished two distinct aspects of potential distortion of the internal market, i.e. i) whether the foreign subsidies distorted the acquisition process, and ii) whether this distorted competition post-transaction through the combined entity's activities in the internal market.

In assessing the acquisition process, the Commission acknowledged that certain subsidies, especially an unlimited state guarantee, were likely to fall under the category of those 'most likely to distort the internal market' under Article 5(1) FSR. While it appeared that these subsidies improved e&'s competitive position, the Commission ultimately found no actual or potential negative effects on competition

[66] Albornoz et al. (2009), p. 489.

[67] An extensive analysis of the concept of distortion under the FSR can also be found in Weiß (2024), pp. 40–48.

[68] European Commission, Competition Case Search, 2025, <https://competition-cases.ec.europa.eu/search?caseInstrument=InstrumentFS&sortField=caseLastDecisionDate&sortOrder=DESC>. 169 cases were mentioned, as last verified on 2 September 2025.

This number does not include cases under the public procurement tool nor the ex officio procedure. Numerous public procurement notifications and declarations have been made. To the best of our knowledge, no phase II decision has been taken.

[69] European Commission Decision of 24.9.2024, Case FS. 100011 – e&/PPF Telecom Group.

[70] Project KXL and Project Felix.

Table 8 The four step approach to examining a distortion of the internal market

Step 1
Activities likely to be affected by the identified foreign subsidies: retail mobile telecom service provider
Step 2
Unlimited guarantee classified as 'most likely to distort the internal market'
Step 3
Improvement of the competitive position of the combined entity's economic activities in the internal market
Step 4
Actual or potential negative effects on competition

Source: Own composition based on the decision text of Case FS.100011

during the acquisition. The analysis was rooted in three key findings: First, there were no alternative bidders or interested parties. Second, the purchase price did not exceed market value. Third, e& could have financed the deal even without the foreign subsidies, given its strong cash reserves. Thus, the Commission concluded that the subsidies did not alter the outcome of the acquisition or prevent competitors from entering the bidding process.[71]

However, the Commission took a different view on the post-transaction impact of the foreign subsidies. Applying a four-step test to assess distortion as shown in Table 8, it first identified the activities in the internal market likely to be affected. This concerned e&/PPF's provision of mobile telecom services, a competitive market requiring substantial investment. Second, it confirmed that the unlimited guarantee qualified as a subsidy 'most likely to distort' competition under Article 5(1)(b), as it enabled e& to obtain future financing on preferential terms. Third, it found that the foreign subsidies were liable to improve the combined entity's competitive position by enhancing its access to subsidised financing, enabling it to out-invest or undercut competitors. The lack of any restriction on the use of the guarantee, its scale relative to the target's turnover, and the acquirer's backing by a state fund all heightened the risk of distortion. In the fourth step, the Commission assessed the actual or potential negative effects on competition. It found that the post-transaction entity would likely leverage the financial advantage for aggressive investment and expansion, especially in capital-intensive areas like 5G. The unlimited guarantee would shield it from normal market pressures, reduce its exposure to financial risk, and incentivise riskier strategies, potentially crowding out or disciplining competitors. The Commission thus concluded that the foreign subsidies could enable the combined entity to expand its activities in ways disproportionate to its economic merits, harming fair competition.[72]

The balancing test was not applied, as the Commission found it unlikely that positive effects attributable to the foreign subsidies would outweigh the negative

[71] Commission decision (fn. 90).

[72] Ibid.

Table 9 Checking distortion of the internal market under the FSR

Preliminary Assessment
• Establish a link between the foreign subsidy and the undertaking's activities in the internal market • Determine whether the subsidy is most likely distortive following the list of Article 5(1) FSR
Distortion test in Article 4(1) FSR
• Examine whether the foreign subsidy is liable to improve the competitive position of the undertaking in the internal market • If yes, whether in doing so, the foreign subsidy actually or potentially negatively affects competition in the internal market

Source: Own composition based on review of the legislation

ones. The benefits cited by the parties were related to the transaction itself, not to the financial support from the UAE, thus offering no justification to offset the distortion.

As a remedy, the Commission accepted a series of commitments from e& to neutralise the distortive effects of the foreign subsidies. These included: amending e&'s articles of association to ensure no deviation from UAE bankruptcy law, thereby removing the effect of the unlimited guarantee; a prohibition on further funding of PPF's activities in the EU by EIA or e& post-transaction; and an obligation to notify the Commission of certain future acquisitions, even when not notifiable under the FSR. These commitments will apply for ten years.

The decision also sheds light on the evolving analytical structure of the FSR's general distortion test. While influenced by EU State aid law, the FSR introduces a distinct two-step approach: first, establishing whether the subsidy improves the competitive position of the undertaking; and second, whether this improvement actually or potentially harms competition in the internal market.[73] This second step is a notable departure from the presumption of distortion often found in State aid cases. The preliminary phase of the Commission's inquiry is equally important. Before the two-step test, it must establish a link between the foreign subsidy and the entity's activities in the internal market. Additionally, once a subsidy is classified as 'most likely to distort', the burden shifts to the undertaking to demonstrate that it does not actually distort competition. This presumption streamlines enforcement, while still offering firms an opportunity to rebut the presumption with evidence. This approach is presented in Table 9.

The e&/PPF case also clarifies the Commission's approach to unlimited guarantees. Rather than treating them as automatically distortive, the Commission assessed their effect in context, how they impacted the financing conditions, the incentives of the beneficiary, and the risk of them being used for market expansion. The distortion test is not mechanical but relies on a broad, indicator-based assessment as described in Article 4(1) FSR. Lastly, the decision highlighted that the risk of future distortion is sufficient to trigger intervention, even in the absence of current market harm. This

[73] Regulation (EU) 2022/2560 of the European Parliament and of the Council of 14 December 2022 on foreign subsidies distorting the internal market, 2022 OJ EU No. L 330/1.

aligns with the FSR's forward-looking nature, allowing the Commission to prevent future harm to competition by addressing potentially distortive foreign financial support before it fully materialises.[74]

In conclusion, the e&/PPF decision illustrates how the notion of distortion is operationalised in merger cases. It highlights the regulation's intent to safeguard the EU internal market from unfair competitive advantages arising from foreign public support, even in the absence of conventional State aid rules. By establishing a structured, effects-based framework and confirming its willingness to impose binding commitments, the Commission has laid a strong foundation for future enforcement under the FSR.

4 Conclusion: Comparative Analysis of the Notion(s) of Competition Distortion

This chapter set out to explore the meaning and function of the concept of 'distortion of competition' across the main pillars of EU competition policy: antitrust, merger control, State aid law, and the regulation on foreign subsidies. While the term 'distortion' may intuitively suggest any interference with the free play of market forces, its significance and operationalisation differ substantially across these domains. By examining how the notion is defined, interpreted, and applied in each area, this chapter aims to clarify whether there is a coherent cross-cutting understanding of distortion within EU competition law, or whether each field relies on an own logic shaped by distinct objectives, legal frameworks, and economic methodologies. This is important not only from a legal-theoretical perspective, but also considering growing interaction between these domains, particularly as the FSR regulation is inherently linked to, and borrows from the language and concepts of, State aid control.

We formulated five distinct research questions to investigate the meaning of competition distortion, one for each of the competition policy domains and a final question comparing the results of these different domains.

Table 10 Terminology on competition distortion

Domain	Terminology on competition distortion
Antitrust policy	'competition in the internal market is not distorted'
Merger control	'significant impediment to effective competition'
State aid control	'distorts or threatens to distort competition'
Foreign Subsidies Regulation	'distorting the internal market'

Source: own composition based on a review of the legal bases

[74] Commission Decision (fn. 90).

A first remarkable difference can be found in the terminology used to describe a distortion of competition. Table 10 lists the competition policy domains and their corresponding terminology to point to a distortion.

In antitrust, distortion is anchored in the Treaty's protection of the competitive process. Under Article 101 TFEU, coordination that reveals in its content, aims and context a sufficient degree of harm is condemned by object, while other coordination is assessed by its effects and must produce appreciable adverse impact in its market setting. Under Article 102 TFEU, the inquiry centres on whether a dominant undertaking departs from competition on the merits and is capable of impairing the competitive structure, with no de minimis threshold and with objective justifications and efficiencies considered case by case.

In merger control, the notion of distortion is expressed through the SIEC test embedded in the Merger Regulation, through which a forward looking appraisal of the competitive landscape is made, compared to a counterfactual scenario. It asks whether a transaction will significantly weaken rivalry through unilateral or coordinated effects, or through vertical or conglomerate foreclosure, and then weighs countervailing buyer power, likely and timely entry, verifiable and merger-specific efficiencies with credible pass-on to consumers, and failing firm considerations.

In terms of guidance, the FSR directly includes the definition of a distortion, but also which types of measures will be unlikely as well as most likely to distort competition. Moreover, reference is made to de minimis thresholds below which a measure will not distort the internal market. This is different from State aid control, where such information should be gathered in diverse regulations, guidelines, the NoA and the case law.

The notion of distortion has indeed a different role for State aid control, compared to the FSR. While in the former, a (threat of) distortion must be present for a measure to constitute aid within the meaning of Article 107(1) TFEU, a distortion is not required for a measure to be considered as a foreign subsidy. Notably, in EU State aid law, the assessment of distortions is a necessary condition, but not a central element in determining whether a measure qualifies as State aid. Instead, a more detailed analysis typically takes place during the compatibility assessment, with the depth of scrutiny varying according to the specifics and potential scale of the distortive effects in each case.[75]

Under the FSR, the mere existence of a foreign subsidy does not presume a distortion within the EU internal market. Since distortive effects may occur outside the EU, notifying parties must assess and disclose whether a distortion exists[76] and, where applicable, consider potential balancing against positive effects such as economic development or policy objectives.[77] This is reflected in the FSR notification forms, which require detailed information depending on the nature of the subsidy. Commission case teams are expected to focus on subsidies likely to distort competition within the EU, particularly in sectors prone to subsidisation such as heavy industry,

---

[75] See the analysis in Schonberg (2022), p. 143.

[76] Regulation (EU) (fn. 94), art. 4.

[77] Ibid. art. 6.

infrastructure, and technology. Notifying parties should be especially diligent in disclosing foreign financial contributions, be prepared to justify any exclusions, and note that positive effects only become relevant if an in-depth investigation is triggered.[78]

In short, the comparative analysis of how 'distortion of competition' is conceptualised and applied across the different branches of EU competition policy reveals both similarities and differences. Clearly, the overarching policy goal is an undistorted internal market. However, the specific operationalisation and prominence in the analysis of distortion differs substantially. In antitrust, Article 101 TFEU condemns agreements restrictive by their object or, failing that, by demonstrated effects, whereas Article 102 TFEU addresses abuses of dominance through an effects-focused inquiry into conduct liable to weaken the competitive process and/or to foreclose rivals. Merger control operationalises distortion through the SIEC counterfactual. State aid control generally relies on a broad presumption of distortion once a selective advantage has been detected. Finally, the FSR is distinctive in coupling a definition and calibrated presumptions with activity- and instrument- specific tools.

Future research could build on this chapter, by incorporating empirical studies of enforcement practice, engaging with the economic modelling of distortion across sectors, or examining how other jurisdictions approach comparable notions. An interdisciplinary perspective, combining law, economics, and policy, will be essential to advance towards a more holistic understanding of distortion and its role in sustaining fair and competitive markets in a dynamic global order.

References

Albornoz F, Corcos G, Kendall T (2009) Subsidy competition and the mode of FDI. Reg Sci Urban Econ 39:489

Baumann P (2020) When state enterprises have deeper pockets: ensuring competitive neutrality in cross-border M&A. In: Fach Gómez K, Gourgourinis A, Titi C (eds) International investment law and competition law. Springer International Publishing, pp 73–95

Cambridge English Dictionary, 'Meanings & Definitions' (2025) <https://dictionary.cambridge.org/dictionary/english/>

Cooter R, Ulen T (2012) Law & economics. Prentice Hall

Fresard L (2010) Financial strength and product market behavior: the real effects of corporate cash holdings. J Finance 65:1097

Maes S, Buts C, Jegers M (2023) Brewing control: the case of super bock. Eur Compet Regul Law Rev 7:189

Majeed N, Hilal A, Khan AN (2023) Doctrinal research in law: meaning, scope and methodology. Bull Bus Econ (BBE) 12:559

'Merriam-Webster: America's Most Trusted Dictionary'. <https://www.merriam-webster.com/>

Niels G, Jenkins H, Kavanagh J (2023) Economics for competition lawyers, 3rd edn. Oxford University Press

Örücü E, Nelken D (2007) Comparative law: a handbook. Bloomsbury Publishing

Reinhold P, Weck T (2024) Welcome to the Jungle! Eur State Aid Law Q 23:22

[78] See also the discussion in Reinhold, Weck (2024), p. 22.

Ribera T, 'LinkedIn Feed' (2025) <https://www.linkedin.com/posts/teresa-ribera-42a08b340_public-consultations-activity-7354155705664266241-C3c9?utm_source=social_share_send&utm_medium=member_desktop_web&rcm=ACoAADpQfFgB2qmGc9vFQvRweRHdJAiFtB4FRnE>
Schonberg M (2022) The EU Foreign Subsidies Regulation. Eur State Aid Law Q EStAL 21:143
Weiß W (2024) The regulation on foreign subsidies distorting the internal market: a path to a level playing field? Springer Nature
Werner P, Verouden V (2016) EU state aid control: law and economics. Wolters Kluwer Legal & Regulatory
Whish R, Bailey D (2024) Competition law. Oxford University Press
Zweigert K, Kötz H (1998) An introduction to comparative law

Seppe Maes PhD researcher at the Brussels Centre for Competition Policy of the Vrije Universiteit Brussels.

Caroline Buts professor at the Brussels Centre for Competition Policy of the Vrije Universiteit Brussels.

Robin Vandendriessche PhD researcher at the Brussels Centre for Competition Policy of the Vrije Universiteit Brussels.

Marc Jegers professor at the Brussels Centre for Competition Policy of the Vrije Universiteit Brussels.

Balancing

Albrecht von Graevenitz

Abstract This Chapter addresses the balancing test under the Foreign Subsidies Regulation. In this test the European Commission may balance the negative effects of a foreign subsidy in terms of distortion in the internal market against positive effects. This balancing may either lead to a 'no objection decision' or influence the Commission's decision on redressive measures or commitments. So far, in the Commission's practice the concept of balancing seems not to have played more than a minor role. However, it is expected to become one central focus in arguments to be brought forward by the parties and to be dealt with by the Commission in its decisions. In the following the balancing test will be first put in its over-all context in the Foreign Subsidies Regulation. Thereafter light is shed on the very assessment the Commission will need to conduct in this test. Further the possibilities of stakeholders to bring input as to positive effects of a subsidy and the question of whether the Commission may have a duty to investigate for positive effects ex office is debated. In addition, the scope of the Commission's balancing is discussed.

1 Introduction: Context and Relevance of the Balancing

Regulation 2022/2560 on foreign subsidies distorting the internal market, hereinafter the 'FSR'[1] (accompanied by Commission Implementing Regulation 2023/1441, hereinafter the 'FSRIR')[2] is intended to contribute to the proper functioning of the

[1] Regulation (EU) 2022/2560 of the European Parliament and of the Council of 14 December 2022 on foreign subsidies distorting the internal market, 2022 OJ EU No. L 330/1; i.c.w. Corrigendum 2024 OJ EU No. L 90559.

[2] Commission Implementation Regulation (EU) 2023/1441 2023 on detailed arrangements for the conduct of proceedings by the Commission pursuant to Regulation (EU) 2022/2560 of the

A. von Graevenitz (✉)
Federal University of Applied Administrative Sciences,
Department Adminstration of the Armed Forces, Mannheim, Germany
e-mail: albrecht.vongraevenitz@hsbund-fbbwv.de

W. Weiß et al. (eds.), *The Foreign Subsidies Regulation*, European Yearbook of International Economic Law, https://doi.org/10.1007/978-3-032-23415-5_4

internal market by establishing a harmonised framework to address distortions caused, directly or indirectly, by foreign subsidies, with a view to ensuring a level playing field (Article 1 (1) sentence 1 FSR). The FSR shall cover third-country subsidies that are granted to undertakings that carry out economic activities in the EU internal market, including concentrations and public procurement procedures (Article 1 (2), Article 2 no 3, Article 3 (1) FSR).

The FSR provides for general powers of investigation and intervention ex officio (Chapter 2 FSR) as well as ex-ante review and intervention mechanisms in relation to concentrations (Chapter 3 FSR) and public procurement procedures (Chapter 4 FSR). The central competent authority is the European Commission (hereinafter the 'Commission'), with a Directorate K of the Directorate-General for Competition (DG COMP) and units of the Directorate-General for Internal Market, Industry, Entrepreneurship and SMEs (DG GROW) set up for this purpose.

The material scope of application of the FSR depends on the existence of staged requirements: 'Financial contributions' provided by a third (i.e. non-EU) country, directly or indirectly, above certain thresholds trigger notification obligations and waiting periods under the FSR (Chapter 3, 4 FRS); in this respect, it is not necessary for such contributions to confer a 'benefit'. Measures such as prohibitions or the imposition of redressive measures have further prerequisites. To this end, the foreign financial contributions must constitute a foreign subsidy. Such subsidy is at hand in case of a foreign (non-EU) financial contribution which confers a benefit on an undertaking engaging in an economic activity in the internal market and which is limited, in law or in fact, to one or more undertakings or industries (Article 3 (1) FSR).[3]

However, the Commission can only intervene on the basis of Chapters 2–4 FSR, if the third-country subsidy has led to a 'distortion' of the internal market within the meaning of Art. 4, 5 FSR. Here, the FSR provides for an examination of potential or actual distortions of competition on the basis of categories and indicators[4]—possibly taking into account a balancing test in accordance with Art. 6 FSR with a view to certain positive effects.

The balancing test is not provided for in Phase I, i.e. the preliminary review of a case by the Commission under Article 10 FSR. However, if during an in-depth investigation the Commission finds that the preliminary assessment set out in its decision to open an in-depth investigation is not confirmed or—which is important for this chapter—that positive effects 'outweigh' any distortion of the internal market found by the Commission under Articles 4, 5 FSR, it issues a decision to raise no objections (Articles 11 (4), 25 (1), (3) lit. b, 30 (1),31 (3) FSR), sometimes referred to as a 'clearance decision'.

European Parliament and of the Council on foreign subsidies distorting the internal market, OJ EU L 177; i.c.w. Corrigendum 2023 OJ EU L 2414.

[3] For more details see in this volume Weiß, The Notion of Foreign Financial Contribution and of Foreign Subsidy.

[4] For more details see in this volume Maes, Buts et al., 'Distortion of Competition' in the Age of Industrial Policy: An Examination of Interpretations across EU Competition Instruments.

If the Commission identifies a relevant distortion under Articles 4, 5 FSR and no sufficient 'outweighing' by positive effects, it can respond with measures: Articles 7, 11 (2), (3), 25 (3) lit. a, c, 31 FSR allow the Commission to accept commitments from the undertaking under investigation or to impose redressive measures in the event of ex officio interventions or prohibitions in the case of FSR concentration or public procurement procedures. However, even in these cases balancing under Article 6 (2) FSR may influence the Commission's decision on redressive measures or commitments.

So far, in the Commission's practice the concept of balancing seems not to have played more than a minor role. The exact shape of this test is very much debated.[5] It is expected to become one central focus in arguments to be brought forward by the parties and to be dealt with by the Commission in its decisions. In a Staff Working Document (2024)[6] first thoughts from the Commission's practitioners as to balancing had been brought forward. Further, the Commission services' Draft Guidelines of July 2025[7] included some indications on balancing.

2 Balancing Assessment

2.1 Introduction

Article 6 (1) FSR provides for the aforementioned balancing decision. Based on this provision the 'Commission may, on the basis of information received, balance the negative effects of a foreign subsidy in terms of distortion in the internal market, according to Articles 4 and 5 against the positive effects on the development of the relevant subsidised economic activity on the internal market, while considering other positive effects of the foreign subsidy such as the broader positive effects in relation to the relevant policy objectives, in particular those of the Union.'

---

[5] Weiß (2024), p. 48. During the conference 'The Foreign Subsidies Regulation Two Years On – Assessing Implementation' on 29.4.2025 in Brussels 'Balancing' was one of the issues debated; in this context Martin Rérolle, European Commission, DG COMP, Directorate K, gave his view on balancing, clarifying that his statements do 'not reflect the official opinion of the European Commission'.

[6] SWD(2024) 201 final, 26.7.2024, 9, 10.

[7] Draft Guidelines on the application of certain provisions of Regulation 2022/2560, available at https://competition-policy.ec.europa.eu/document/download/a0b557e7-96f8-4231-9ed5-522f13de9065_en?filename=FSR_draft_guidelines_application_of_EU_Reg_2022-2560.pdf.

2.2 *Starting Point: Negative Effects*

According to the wording of Article 6 (1) starting point of the balancing test are 'the negative effects of a foreign subsidy in terms of distortion in the internal market, according to Articles 4 and 5'.

Here the wording appears clear. On the negative side only 'the negative effects … according to Articles 4 and 5' seem to play a role. This seems not to include other negative effects of a foreign subsidy, in particular non-economic effects.[8] However, subsidies triggering directly non-economic effects, but indirectly effects in the sense of Article 4, 5 FSR, might be deemed relevant by the Commission anyway.

These negative effects according to Articles 4 and 5 FSR need to be balanced against positive effects.

2.3 *Positive Effects on the Development of the Relevant Subsidised Economic Activity on the Internal Market*

Based on the wording of Article 6 (1) FSR, the Commission must include in its assessment 'the positive effects on the development of the relevant subsidised economic activity on the internal market'.[9] Apparently, this addresses economic effects resulting from the subsidy within the EU and specifically in relation to the relevant subsidised economic activity.[10] In this respect only the positive effects of the subsidy of the subsidised economic activity in question on the internal market, but not in third countries, can be taken into account.[11] Positive effects on other undertakings upstream or downstream or on other related activities might be relevant under policy objectives[12] discussed below (Sects. 2.4, 2.5).

This is similar[13] to a concept under the EUMR,[14] mentioned in recital 29 of that regulation, under which for the Commission 'in order to determine the impact of a concentration on competition in the common market, it is appropriate to take account of any substantiated and likely efficiencies' whereby it is 'possible that the efficiencies brought about by the concentration counteract the effects on competition, and in particular the potential harm to consumers, that it might otherwise have and that, as a consequence, the concentration would not significantly impede effective competition, in the common market or in a substantial part of it, in particular as a result of the creation or strengthening of a dominant position.'

[8] Trapp (2023), para. 7; cf. Commission's Draft Guidelines (fn 7), para 41, 48, 55, 58 ff.

[9] Cf. Commission's Draft Guidelines (fn 7), para 104 ff.

[10] Weiß (2024), p. 50.

[11] Trapp (2023), para. 8.

[12] Commission's Draft Guidelines (fn 7), para 106.

[13] Trapp (2023), para. 2.

[14] 2004 OJ EU L 24/1.

Under the FSR interests of consumers are not explicitly mentioned; however, they may be deemed part of the internal market concept and, thus, relevant under the FSR as well.[15] The White Paper (2020) took the view that 'the balancing needs to be based on an appreciation of the various interests, including the need to protect consumers' interest'.[16]

2.4 Relevant Policy Objectives, in Particular Those of the Union

Article 6 (1) FSR clarifies that the Commission may take into account 'other positive effects of the foreign subsidy such as the broader positive effects in relation to the relevant policy objectives, in particular those of the Union'.[17] This is in line with the White Paper (2020)[18] but more than included in the Commission's (later) first proposal of the FSR.[19]

At least at a first glimpse the relationship of this test to the test referred to under Sect. 2.3 above appears unclear. According to the German wording of Article 6 (1) FSR ('und prüft dabei auch andere positive Auswirkungen'), the examination of the relevant 'policy objectives' appears to be limited to the examination of the 'subsidised economic activity concerned in the internal market'. However, the English ('while') and French ('tout en tenant compte') versions of Article 6 (1) FSR make it seem more likely that positive effects in other fields should also be available for consideration. This view is confirmed by recital 21 fourth sentence FSR, where it is clarified that 'other positive effects should be taken into account, where appropriate, in order to avoid that the balancing gives rise to unjustified discrimination.'[20] The Commission's staff seems to have adopted the view that 'in addition' to the test referred to under Sect. 2.3 above other positive effects are to be taken into consideration ('In addition, the Commission also has to 'examine broader positive effects …").[21]

Thus, following the wording of the balancing test that has become law in Article 6 (1) FSR (compared to the original proposal[22]) the assessment is not reduced to economic or competitive aspects.[23]

[15] Trapp (2023), para. 8; cf. Commission's Draft Guidelines (fn 7), para 38, in particular fn 23.

[16] COM(2020) 253 final, 17.06.2020, 4.1.4.

[17] Cf. Commission's Draft Guidelines (fn 7), para 107 ff.

[18] COM(2020) 253 final, 17.06.2020, 4.1.4.

[19] COM(2021) 223 final, 5.5.2021, draft Article 5 (1).

[20] Similarly Weiß (2023a), p. 827 referring to the 'such as' in Article 6 (1) FSR.

[21] SWD(2024) 201 final, 26.7.2024, 9.

[22] COM(2021) 223 final, 5.5.2021, draft Article 5 (1).

[23] Weiß (2024), pp. 50, 51; Weiß (2023a), p. 827 seq.; Trapp (2023), para. 9.

According to recital 21 sentence 6 'those policy objectives can include, in particular, a high level of environmental protection and social standards, and the promotion of research and development.' Other policy objectives relevant for the balancing may be taken from the EU treaties,[24] "policy objectives aiming at promoting or protecting rights guaranteed be the Charter of Fundamental rights"[25] and maybe even non-binding State aid documents.[26] The White Paper (2020)[27] mentioned 'the EU's public policy objectives, such as creating jobs, achieving climate neutrality and protecting the environment, digital transformation, security, public order and public safety and resilience'. This may include (but is not limited to) interests taken into account in EU trade defence instruments.[28]

The last part of Article 6 (1) FSR 'in particular those of the Union' makes it clear by using the word 'in particular' that the 'relevant policy objectives' may relate but are not limited to those of the Union. Thus, objectives of the Member States or even non-EU states may play a role; this may include e.g. third country measures supporting climate protection comparable to those of EU Member States permitted by EU-State aid law.[29] According to the Commission's services positive effects may be "different from those initially intended by the third country providing the subsidy", but should be relevant to the EU.[30]

The provision of Article 6 (1) does not restrict the political objectives that can be taken into account; thus, at least in theory, objectives of third countries that do not coincide with those of the EU could also be taken into account here.[31] However, this only appears to be a theoretical approach and against the ratio of the FSR.

It is debated whether positive effects under Article 6 (1) FSR must occur in the EU.[32] However, it appears quite conceivable that the Commission will even consider positive effects occurring outside the Union if theses positive effects serve its policy objectives.

---

[24] Weiß (2024), p. 51; Commission's Draft Guidelines (fn 7), para 108.

[25] Commission's Draft Guidelines (fn 7), para 108.

[26] Commission's Draft Guidelines (fn 7), para 109.

[27] COM(2020) 253 final, 17.06.2020, 4.1.4.

[28] Weiß (2024), p. 51 seq.

[29] Weiß (2024), p. 51; Weiß (2023a), p. 827; Trapp (2023), para. 9; cf. Commission's Draft Guidelines (fn 7), para 109.

[30] Commission's Draft Guidelines (fn 7), para 103, 111 f.

[31] Trapp (2023), para. 10.

[32] Similarly Rérolle (fn 5).

2.5 *Other Positive Effects*

Further it can be taken from the 'such as' in the wording of Article 6 I FSR ('while considering other positive effects of the foreign subsidy such as') that 'the broader positive effects in relation to the relevant policy objectives' are not the only positive effects outside the test referred to the under Sect. 2.3 above that may be taken into account. This is confirmed by a comparison of sentences four and five of recital 21. Thus, positive effects outside those mentioned in Sects. 2.3 and 2.4 above may be relevant in the context of Article 6 (1) FSR.

In the e&-case[33] the parties argued that the concentration may 'improve the Target's services, in particular in respect of (i) customer value management and improved customer service, (ii) network optimisation, (iii) fraud detection, and (iv) improved roaming services.'

Recital 21 brings up that 'in the context of a public procurement procedure, the Commission should take into account the availability of alternative sources of supply for the goods and services concerned.'[34]

2.6 *Causal Connection*

One may take from the wording of Article 6 (1) FSR (' … the positive effects on the development …, while considering other positive effects of the foreign subsidy …') that there needs to be a causal connection between the foreign subsidy and the positive effects.[35]

In its e&-decision the Commission seems to have adopted this view.[36] Unfortunately, in that case, the Commission did not sufficiently address[37] the question of how its denial of a connection between the subsidy and the positive effects

[33] Commission Decision of 24.9.2024 finding that, with the binding commitments, the foreign subsidies in the concentration do not distort the internal market (Case FS.100011 – e&/PPF Telecom Group), available at https://competition-cases.ec.europa.eu/cases/FS.100011. For a detailed analysis of the e& decision see in this volume Raitner, Weiß, The Role of the European Commission in the Concentrations Tool, section 4.

[34] The like SWD(2024) 201 final, 26.7.2024, 9; cf. Commission's Draft Guidelines (fn 7), para 113 ff.

[35] Commission's Draft Guidelines (fn 7), para 117 ff. discuss the "specificity of positive effects" and para 131 f. the "possibility of cumulative assessment".

[36] Commission decision of 24.9.2024 (fn 33) para. 375: 'Second, the Commission finds that the positive effects alleged by the Notifying Party are not related to any of the foreign subsidies in the Transaction identified by the Commission. Rather, those positive effects, if substantiated, are to be brought about by the Transaction itself, and the subsequent commercial integration between e& and the Target. The foreign subsidies identified are not necessary for those positive effects to occur, nor do they contribute to those positive effects in any way.'

[37] Similarly Šimunović (2024), p. 354.

claimed by the parties for the downstream market[38] fits to its assumption in that very case that the subsidies will have effects on the downstream market.[39]

2.7 *Negative Effects Outside Articles 4, 5 FSR*

As mentioned above under Sect. 2.2, negative effects outside Articles 4, 5 FSR seem not covered by the first half sentence of Article 6 (1) FSR. However, as far as positive effects in the sense of Article 6 (1) FSR are accompanied by negative effects outside Articles 4, 5 FSR, the Commission will need to assess whether theses negative effects outbalance the positive effects. If yes, the Commission may come to the conclusion that no positive effects are left for an assessment under Article 6 (1) FSR.

2.8 *State Aid Concept*

Since the FSR also complements State aid law under Articles 107 seq TFEU,[40] it stands to reason that there are parallels between that State aid law and the FSR in the balancing test.[41] Due to the close links between the FSR and state aid law under Article 107 TFEU, it may be assumed that the decision-making practice of the EU institutions in the latter area may be used as an aid to interpretation when assessing positive effects—at least during the first period of application of the FSR.[42]

2.8.1 Avoid Discrimination

The Commission's Staff Working Document 2024[43] mentions that 'where certain positive effects on the internal market have been acknowledged under the EU State aid rules, such positive effects would likely be taken into account in the assessment under Regulation (EU) 2022/2560.' One may take from this statement that where a balancing under State aid law following Article 107 (3) TFEU led to the conclusion that the aid is permissible, the same might apply for a comparable third country subsidy. This may be underlined by recital 21 fourth sentence FSR, where it is clarified that 'unjustified discrimination' should be avoided ('other positive effects

[38] See above Sect. 2.5 at fn 33.

[39] Commission decision of 24.9.2024 (fn 33) paras. 249, 259 seq.

[40] von Graevenitz (2025), A.IV., I.

[41] Trapp (2023), para. 2; Commission's Draft Guidelines (fn 7), para 109, 123.

[42] Cf. Trapp (2023), para. 6.

[43] SWD(2024) 201 final, 26.7.2024, 9.

should be taken into account, where appropriate, in order to avoid that the balancing gives rise to unjustified discrimination.')

2.8.2 Differences

However, looking at the considerations above under Sects. 2.3–2.7 there seem to be considerable differences between a balancing under Article 107 (3) TFEU and a balancing under Article 6 (1) FSR.

Differences relate to apparent issues such as the source of the aid / subsidy (State aid: EU Member States vs. FSR: foreign governments) or the basic design of the procedure (State aid: notification procedure vs. FSR: ex officio proceeding—if Chapters 3 or 4 are not applicable); further one may argue that the need for fiscal discipline relevant under State aid law does not play the same role for non-EU-subsidies.[44]

Further, the distortion analysis differs significantly.[45] When considering State aid under Article 107 (3) TFEU, the Commission must look at its contribution to the realisation of an objective of common interest (to society in general or its relevance to specific Union policies), the corresponding incentive effect, its necessity, appropriateness, proportionality and transparency; thereby the Commission must limit distortions of competition in a balancing exercise. The positive effects must outweigh the negative ones.[46] Overall, the assessment under Article 107 TFEU may be regarded as a single process.

The test under Articles 4–6 FSR is different.[47] The clear-cut sequence of assessment steps and specific criteria known from Staid aid law seems not mirrored here.[48] Rather the balancing test according to Articles 6, 11 (4) FSR follows the prior identification of competition distortions of foreign subsidies under Articles 4, 5 FSR. The compatibility assessment carried out under Art. 107 (3) TFEU is based on precisely defined exceptions under primary law, block exemption regulations under secondary law and Commission notices; the regulatory environment is therefore structurally different from that of the FSR with its vague wording of Art. 6 I FSR.[49]

Further, as demonstrated above, under Article 6 (1) FSR a broad scope of positives effects may 'outweigh' negative effects whereas state aid measure under Article 107 TFEU must remedy a market failure in order to demonstrate the need for State intervention.[50] In addition, when comparing State aid law and the FSR, there

[44] Rérolle (fn 5).

[45] Rérolle (fn 5).

[46] Cf. e.g. Kreuschitz (2022), paras. 799 seq.

[47] Herrmann and Ellemann (2024), p. 93.

[48] Weiß (2024), p. 49 seq; Weiß (2023a), p. 828 seq.

[49] Herrmann and Ellemann (2024), p. 94.

[50] Weiß (2024), p. 49 seq; Weiß (2023a), p. 828 seq.

may be, under the FSR, an unequal geographic allocation of positive and negative effects.[51]

In the Commission's public consultation[52] for the guidelines expected for early 2026 some commentators hoped for clarifications as to the relationship between the balancing test under the FSR and State aid law concepts and approaches,[53] in particular the question of equal treatment of third country subsidies and State aid within the meaning of Art. 107 TFEU, as well as some kind of block exemption under the FSR.[54]

2.8.3 Block Exemption

With regard to the latter, the idea of a block exemption, it needs to be noted that under the FSR a provision such as Article 108 (4) TFEU does not exist. Thus, the idea of a 'block exemption' under the FSR can only be realised by way of soft law through the Commission or de lege ferenda.

While Articles 107 and 108 TFEU regulate a prohibition with the possibility of a later authorisation, the FSR does not provide for a prohibition or ex ante procedure under Chapter 2. In so far, a 'real' block exemption (in analogy to those under Article 108 (4) TFEU) should not be necessary under the FSR.

This is different for concentrations to be dealt with under Chapter 3 FSR and public procurement procedures to be dealt with under Chapter 4 FSR. Due to the very broad understanding of 'financial contributions' und the current FSR, notification obligations and waiting periods seem easily triggered.[55] The Commission has to deal with significantly more notifications and consultations than initially expected. In fact, it has turned out to be several times the expected number of cases. This administrative burden on the Commission and companies could be significantly reduced by amending the FSR to exempt companies from notification requirements by means of block exemptions through an anticipated balancing assessment in certain constellations.

---

[51] Rérolle (fn 5).

[52] Ref Ares(2025)1757107, 5.3.2025.

[53] Cf. Commission's Draft Guidelines (fn 7), para 109, 123.

[54] Cf. e.g. Cleary Gottlieb (2025) paras 4.b, 17 seq; Baker McKenzie (2025) paras. 24 seq; Clifford Chance LLP (2025) para. 2.1.

[55] See in this volume Weiß, The Notion of Foreign Financial Contribution and of Foreign Subsidy, section 2.

3 Stakeholders' Input

According to the recital 21 (and taking into account Article 35) FSR 'Member States, as well as any natural or legal persons are able to submit information on the positive effects of a foreign subsidy, of which the Commission should take due account when carrying out the balancing test.' The Commission staff emphasizes that 'information which serves to evidence the positive effects may be submitted at any point during the investigation, but at the latest in due time to enable the Commission to adopt a decision closing an in-depth investigation in line with the procedural time limits.'[56] In cases of concentrations (Chapter 3 FSR) and public procurement (Chapter 4 FSR) the parties are invited to bring forward such arguments already with their formal notification.[57]

Undertakings concerned are further encouraged to provide information on positive effects by the Commission's staff clarifying that 'the application of the balancing test cannot, under any circumstances, lead to a less favourable outcome for undertakings under investigation than if the balancing test had not been applied.'[58]

According to recital 21 FSR 'in the case of categories of foreign subsidies that are deemed most likely to distort the internal market', i.e. in cases under Article 5 FSR, 'positive effects are less likely to outweigh negative effects'.[59] This indicates that in order to outweigh the negative effects, the undertaking concerned must meet a high standard of proof; however, there is no presumption of a negative outcome of the balancing test in cases where Article 5 FSR applies.[60]

4 Investigations ex officio

It appears unclear whether the Commission is obliged to investigate for positive effects ex officio.

This is denied in literature.[61] That view appears confirmed by the Commission's staff clarifying that it will 'rely on the information received on possible positive effects'.[62] The position seems further confirmed by the wording of Article 6 (1)

---

[56] SWD(2024) 201 final, 26.7.2024, 9; see in this respect further Commission's Draft Guidelines (fn 7), para 133 ff, 137 ff.

[57] FSRIR Annex I [Form FS-CO] no 2 d), 3, 7.1, Annex II [Form FS-PP] no 8 a) vi), 5.1; SWD(2024) 201 final, 26.7.2024, 9.

[58] SWD(2024) 201 final, 26.7.2024, 10; cf. recital 21 second last sentence FSR.

[59] Cf. SWD(2024) 201 final, 26.7.2024, 9; Commission decision of 24.9.2024 (fn. 33) para. 374.

[60] See in this volume Weiß, The Notion of Foreign Financial Contribution and of Foreign Subsidy, section 3.3.

[61] Trapp (2023), paras. 13, 16.

[62] SWD(2024) 201 final, 26.7.2024, 9; similarly Commission's Draft Guidelines (fn 7), para 99, 118, 133 ff.; cf. Commission decision of 24.9.2024 (fn 33) paras 371 seq.

FSR: The expression 'may' ('peut'/'kann') seems to give discretion to the Commission.[63] The term 'on the basis of information received' may be understood in a way that the receipt of information is a condition sine qua non for a balancing test. The same applies for the first two sentences of recital 21: 'Member States, as well as any natural or legal persons are able to submit information on the positive effects of a foreign subsidy, of which the Commission should take due account when carrying out the balancing test. The Commission should consider the positive effects of the foreign subsidy on the basis of the evidence about such positive effects submitted during the investigation.' These sentences seem to indicate that information on positive effects are to be submitted from outside the Commission if they shall be taken into consideration.

Against this background one may speak of a reversal of the burden of proof to the detriment of the undertakings concerned.[64]

However, the fourth sentence of the recital 21 seems to hint into a different direction stating that 'other positive effects should be taken into account, where appropriate, in order to avoid that the balancing gives rise to unjustified discrimination'. Compared to the first and second sentences of recital 21, this could mean that the Union legislator at least expects that the Commission will not close its eyes to positive effects even if they have not been presented.[65] This position might be deemed underlined by comparing the FSR's wording with the White Paper[66] and a former statement on the Commission's web site looking at the FSR in the version which became law.[67,68] The same applies to the Commission's Staff Working Document (2024) using the wording 'needs to' and 'has to'.[69]

By virtue of the right and duty to good administration and in accordance with general principles of EU law on the obligations for administrative authorities adopting burdensome decisions, the Commission appears to be obliged to investigate for positive effects ex officio.[70]

This view is without prejudice to the last sentence of recital 28 where it is stated that the 'Commission should also have the power to take decisions on the basis of facts available if the undertaking under investigation or the third country that granted the subsidy does not cooperate.' In principle, as mentioned above, the Commission should be deemed obliged to investigate for positive effects ex officio. However, if

[63] Trapp (2023), para. 13.

[64] Weiß (2023), Art. 9 para. 9.

[65] von Graevenitz (2025) E.5.c.

[66] COM(2020) 253 final, 17.06.2020, 4.1.4: 'where there is evidence of a possible positive impact'.

[67] https://competition-policy.ec.europa.eu/foreign-subsidies-regulation/about_en: 'If the Commission establishes that a foreign subsidy exists and is distortive, it will balance the negative effects of the subsidy, in terms of the distortion, with positive effects of the subsidy to determine appropriate redressive measures or to accept commitments.'

[68] Cf. Trapp (2023), para. 5.

[69] SWD(2024) 201 final, 26.7.2024, 9: 'When conducting the balancing test, the Commission needs to take into account … . In addition, the Commission also has to …'

[70] Weiß (2024), p. 49.

in this context it is reasonably necessary for the Commission to direct questions to undertakings or third countries and those do not cooperate, the rules of Articles 14 (3) lit. b, 16, 25 (1), 30 (1) FSR shall apply.

Even if one was of the opinion that there is no principle of ex officio investigations with regard to positive effects, sentences five and six in recital 21 FSR seem to indicate that this should be different for 'the relevant policy objectives, in particular those of the Union'. The Commission should be expected to know, recognise and respect the latter.

In any case, irrespective of the above, insofar as any positive effects have been brought to the attention of the Commission, the latter—for reasons of proportionality (recitals (22), (48), (70), Articles 7 (3), 32 (7) FSR)—appears obliged to enter into a balancing process.[71] This is supported by the wording of recital 21 sentences one and two ('should'/'devrait'/'sollte').

5 Scope of Consideration

The central provision giving relevance to the balancing test is Article 11 (4) lit. b FSR. According to this provision in its assessment the Commission may come to the result that 'a distortion in the internal market is outweighed by positive effects within the meaning of Article 6'.

5.1 The Term 'Outweighed'

This leads to the question, whether the term 'outweighed' means something like 'to be greater or more important'[72] or requires only a 'counterbalance' or 'compensation'.[73]

The German version of Article 11 (4) lit. b FSR ('schwerer wiegen') is more in the former, the French version ('compensée par') more in the latter sense. Looking at Article 7 (3) FSR and the principle of proportionality (Article 5 (4) EU treaty) 'outweighed' should be understood as 'equal'; if distortions are already fully offset by the positive effects, there is nothing left to rule on.[74] This would be in line with the White Paper[75] stating that 'if on balance, the distortion on the internal market caused by the foreign subsidy is sufficiently mitigated by the positive impact of the supported economic activity or investment, the ongoing investigation would not

[71] Weiß (2023), Art. 9 para. 9.

[72] Hornby (2010) "outweigh".

[73] Among the synonyms mentioned on https://www.thesaurus.com/browse/outweigh.

[74] Weiß (2024), p. 54 seq; Weiß (2023), Art. 11 para. 16.

[75] COM(2020) 253 final, 17.06.2020, 4.1.4.

need to be pursued further.' It would also be in line with the Commission's call for evidence[76] referring to the test under Article 6 (1) FSR as 'whether positive effects stemming from the foreign subsidies could offset the negative, distortive, effects'.[77]

5.2 *Article 11 (4) lit. b FSR*

According to Article 11 (4) lit. b FSR, if 'a distortion in the internal market is outweighed by positive effects within the meaning of Article 6' then the 'Commission shall adopt an implementing act in the form of a decision to raise no objection ('no objection decision')'.

In the light of recital 21 using the word 'can' ('The balancing can lead to the conclusion not to impose redressive measures …') one may come to the conclusion that the 'shall' in Article 11 (4) FSR is meant to be a 'can', i.e. leading to a discretion of the Commission.[78] The same applies to the use of the word 'may' in Article 6 (1) FSR.

However, looking at the German ('Die Kommission erlässt') and the French ('La Commission adopte') version of Article 11 (4) FSR it becomes clear that the 'shall' is to be read as a 'must'. This can be deducted as well from the structure of Article 11 (4) FSR where the 'shall' covers not only the balancing test (lit. b) but also the case of lit. a where the Commission finds that the 'preliminary assessment as set out in its decision to initiate the in-depth investigation is not confirmed'. In this latter case it is apparent that the Commission must issue a 'no objection decision'. Thus, the same must apply for lit. b, i.e. the balancing test.[79]

In other words, the outcome of the test in Article 11 (4) lit. b FSR is binary: Either there is an 'outweigh' of the positive and negative effects (as discussed in Sect. 5.1 above)—then a 'no objection decision' must be issued—or there is no 'outweigh'. In the latter case the Commission responds according to Articles 7, 11 (2), (3), 25 (3) lit. a, c, 31 FSR, i.e. with a decision accepting commitments from the undertaking under investigation or imposing redressive measures in the event of ex officio interventions or a prohibition in the case of FSR merger control or public procurement procedures.

Accordingly, the question whether to pursue a balancing according to Articles 6 (1), 11 (4) lit. b FSR is not in the Commission's discretion. It is rather a binding requirement in the decision-making process of the Commission and its results must be respected in its decision-making.[80]

---

[76] Ref Ares(2025)1757107, 5.3.2025.

[77] Similarly Commission's Draft Guidelines (fn 7), para 127: "If the negative effects prevail …", para 135 lit. d: "… positive effects mitigate or outweigh the distortion …".

[78] Cf. Trapp (2023), para. 13.

[79] Cf. COM(2020) 253 final, 17.06.2020, 4.1.1/4.1.4.

[80] Weiß (2024), p. 53; similarly Cleary Gottlieb (2025), para. 15.

Besides the principles set out above, the provision of Article 6 (1) FSR leaves it open as to how the Commission carries out the balancing and by what standards. This seems to give the Commission a broad discretion.[81] However, the Commission is bound by the principle of proportionality as a general principle of EU administrative law, mentioned by the FSR itself (recitals (22), (48), (70), Articles 7 (3), 32 (7) FSR).[82] The assessment might include the test whether the subsidy would have been compatible if granted by an EU-Member State; in this case foreign subsidy might be considered balanced.[83]

The Commission is deemed to give reasons in its decision as regards the balancing;[84] otherwise the EU courts were not in a position to take into account the Commission's considerations.

5.3 *Redressive Measures or Acceptance of Commitments*

According to Article 6 (2) FSR 'the Commission shall take into account the assessment under paragraph 1 when deciding whether to impose redressive measures or to accept commitments, and the nature and level of those redressive measures or commitments.'

Thus, the Commission's staff is right when underlining (referring to recital 21 FSR) 'that even if a subsidy falls under one of the categories of Article 5 of Regulation (EU) 2022/2560 and is considered distortive, the balancing test under Article 6 may still play a role in determining whether any redressive measures or commitments are necessary to address the distortion' as 'the balancing test may lead the Commission to adapt the nature and scope of those redressive measures or commitments, in order specifically to cater for those positive effects, while still ensuring that the negative effects are fully and effectively redressed'.[85]

Unfortunately, it is unclear how or to what extent positive effects need to be taken into consideration in this context. According to the wording of Article 6 (2) FSR the Commission just needs to 'take into account' its balancing under Article 6 (1) FSR. However, as explained in Sect. 5.2 above, Article 6 (2) FSR is only relevant, if there was no 'outweigh' by positive effects, in other words no or not sufficient positive effects.

Thus, what does this mean for the term 'take into account' in case of a non-successful balancing test under Article 11 (4) lit. b FSR? According to recitals (21) 'if the negative effects prevail, the balancing test can help to determine the appropriate nature and level of the commitments or redressive measures.' This is mirrored in

---

[81] Trapp (2023), para. 15.

[82] Weiß (2024), p. 53.

[83] Rérolle (fn 5).

[84] Trapp (2023), para. 19.

[85] SWD(2024) 201 final, 26.7.2024, 5, 10.

the last half-sentence of Article 6 (2) FSR. Accordingly, in the e&-decision the Commission mentioned that 'in case the negative effects prevail, the balancing test can help establish the suitable nature and level of the commitments.'[86]

On its face Article 6 (2) FSR seems to give the Commission a broad discretion in this respect.[87] However, again, the Commission is bound by the principle of proportionality as a general principle of EU administrative law, mentioned by the FSR itself (recitals (22), (48), (70), Articles 7 (3), 32 (7) FSR).[88]

It is important to raise that according to Article 31 (4) FSR 'the assessment under Article 6 shall not result in a modification of the tender or final tender submitted by the economic operator that is incompatible with Union law.'

The Commission is deemed to give reasons in its decision as regards the (non) taking into account of positive effect under Article 6 (2) FSR;[89] otherwise the EU courts were not in a position to take into account the Commission's considerations.

6 Outlook

At the moment the balancing test remains a highly speculative and evolving area with many interpretative questions unresolved; its implementation is to be shaped through the first cases.[90] It will be interesting to see how the European Commission will deal with the issue of balancing in its guidelines, which are expected for January 2026 (recital 73, Article 46 (1) lit. b FSR).[91] According to the Commission's call for evidence[92] these guidelines shall 'clarify the application of the balancing test' and 'provide guidance on which positive effects can be taken into account for that assessment, and the approach to be taken by the Commission in performing this balancing test.'

It is, however, to be expected that the Commission's guidelines can not and will not be conclusive as regards the scope of positive effects to be taken into consideration; soft law such as guidelines must never limit the application of primary and secondary EU law. Rather, it is to be expected that for each and any case to come a detailed assessment of the very circumstances of the case will be necessary as to the question whether relevant positive effects are at hand and how they are to be balanced with the negative effects under Articles 4, 5 FSR.[93]

[86] Commission decision of 24.9.2024 (fn 33) para. 45.

[87] Weiß (2024), p. 53 seq.

[88] Weiß (2024), p. 53.

[89] Cf. Trapp (2023) para 19.

[90] Rérolle (fn 5).

[91] Cf. Commission's Draft Guidelines (fn 7).

[92] Ref Ares(2025)1757107, 5.3.2025.

[93] Cf. Commission's Draft Guidelines (fn 7), para 7 f, 96 ff.

References

Baker McKenzie (2025) Response to the Call for Evidence on the FSR Guidelines, taken from https://ec.europa.eu/info/law/better-regulation/have-your-say/initiatives/14516-Foreign-Subsidies-Guidelines/F3532851_en

Cleary Gottlieb (2025) Submission to the European Commission's Consultation, taken from https://ec.europa.eu/info/law/better-regulation/have-your-say/initiatives/14516-Foreign-Subsidies-Guidelines/F3532856_en

Clifford Chance LLP (2025) Response to the European Commission's Call for Evidence on the FSR, taken from https://ec.europa.eu/info/law/better-regulation/have-your-say/initiatives/14516-Foreign-Subsidies-Guidelines/F3532848_en

Herrmann C, Ellemann T (2024) Die neue Verordnung über den Binnenmarkt verzerrende drittstaatliche Subventionen – Ein Brussels Effect in Zeiten geoökonomischer Subventionswettläufe? Zeitschrift für Europäisches Privatrecht ZEuP 2024:64–104

Hornby AS (2010) Oxford advanced learner's dictionary

Kreuschitz V (2022) Art. 107 AEUV. In: Säcker FJ, Karpenstein U, Ludwigs M (eds) Münchener Kommentar zum Wettbewerbsrecht, Band 5: Beihilfenrecht, 4th edn

Šimunović L (2024) The EU Foreign Subsidies Regulation (FSR): a game changer or impossible mission. UDK 346.546:336.566.2(4-67 EU). In: EU and Comparative Law Issues and Challenges Series ECLIC 8 - Special Issue, pp 342–362

Trapp P (2023) Art. 6 VO (EU) 2022/2560. In: Krenzler HG, Herrmann C, Niestedt M (eds) EU-Außenwirtschafts- und Zollrecht, 21st Supplement

von Graevenitz A (2025) Drittstaatliche Subventionen im Fokus der Europäischen Kommission - Die FSR - Verordnung (EU) 2022/2560 über den Binnenmarkt verzerrende drittstaatliche Subventionen. 2nd edn, urn:nbn:de:hbz:1073-opus-4748, https://doi.org/10.48701/opus4-474

Weiß W (2023) Art. 9, 11 VO (EU) 2022/2560. In: Krenzler HG, Herrmann C, Niestedt M (eds) EU-Außenwirtschafts- und Zollrecht, 22nd Supplement

Weiß W (2023a) Die Verordnung über den Binnenmarkt verzerrende drittstaatliche Subventionen: Ein Weg zu mehr Wettbewerbsgleichheit? Zeitschrift für das Gesamte Handels- und Wirtschaftsrecht ZHR 187:809–850

Weiß W (2024) The regulation on foreign subsidies distorting the internal market. A path to a level playing field? Springer Nature, Cham

Albrecht von Graevenitz is Professor of Civil Law at the Federal University of Applied Administrative Sciences, Department Administration of the Armed Forces in Mannheim.

Challenges in Implementation

The Role of the Commission in the Public Procurement Tool

Elke Zeise

Abstract This contribution outlines the main issues identified in relation to the Commission's review of tenders for large public contracts based on notifications and declarations submitted under Regulation 2022/2560. This analysis addresses both the quantity and the quality of the submissions. The article assesses possible factors contributing to the higher-than-expected number of cases compared with initial projections anticipated during the legislative process and presents relevant statistical data. It also analyses the interaction between economic operators, contracting authorities, and the Commission as an important aspect of the procedure. The article concludes with an overview of the current situation and an outlook highlighting possible avenues for further action to enhance a level playing field in public procurement.

1 Introduction

Regulation (EU) 2022/2560[1] (hereinafter 'Regulation 2022/2560') became applicable on 13 July 2023. It establishes a comprehensive framework of rules and procedures for the investigation of foreign subsidies that may distort competition within the internal market. Particular emphasis is placed on concentrations and public

The views expressed are solely those of the author and do not necessarily represent the views of the European Commission.

[1] Regulation (EU) 2022/2560 of the European Parliament and of the Council of 14 December 2022 on foreign subsidies distorting the internal market, OJ L 330/1, and Corrigendum OJ L 2024/90559.

E. Zeise (✉)
European Commission, Brussels, Belgium
e-mail: Elke.ZEISE@ec.europa.eu

W. Weiß et al. (eds.), *The Foreign Subsidies Regulation*, European Yearbook of International Economic Law, https://doi.org/10.1007/978-3-032-23415-5_5

procurement procedures, for which the obligation to notify foreign financial contributions—subject to specified conditions—entered into force on 13 October 2023.

In light of this dual focus, enforcement responsibilities are divided between the two Directorates-General (DGs) of the European Commission competent in the respective areas. The Directorate-General for Competition (DG COMP) is entrusted with enforcement in relation to concentrations, whereas the Directorate-General for Internal Market, Industry, Entrepreneurship and SMEs (DG GROW) acts as the lead service for enforcement in the field of public procurement.

Although DG GROW's mandate concerning the assessment of foreign subsidies extends more broadly across public procurement, this contribution concentrates on its competences under Chapter 4 of Regulation 2022/2560 (Articles 27 et seq.). To date, these provisions have constituted the primary focus of DG GROW's practical enforcement activities, given the time-sensitive character of the procedures governed by this chapter.

2 Legal Framework for the Obligation to Notify in Public Procurement Procedures

In public procurement procedures, Article 29(1) of Regulation (EU) 2022/2560 establishes an obligation to notify foreign financial contributions where certain conditions are met.

First, the economic operator must be participating in a public procurement procedure as defined in Article 2(3) of Regulation 2022/2560. In principle, this includes public award procedures covered by Directives 2014/24/EU, 2014/25/EU, and 2014/23/EU—namely, any procedure for the award of a public contract for works, supplies, or services, or for the award of works or services concessions by contracting authorities or contracting entities, unless expressly excluded from the scope of the public procurement directives. Certain exceptions apply. Article 2(3) of Regulation 2022/2560 explicitly also refers to procurement procedures in the defense and security sector governed by Directive 2009/81/EC. However, public procurement procedures are exempted from Regulation 2022/2560 where a Member State invokes Article 346 of the Treaty on the Functioning of the European Union (TFEU).

It should be noted that certain exceptions to the notification obligation under Article 29(1) of Regulation 2022/2560 apply even when the procedure in question qualifies as a public procurement procedure within the meaning of Article 2(3). For instance, according to Article 28(3) of Regulation 2022/2560 award procedures in the defense and security sector under Directive 2009/81/EC fall outside Chapter 4 of the Regulation even where a Member State does not invoke Article 346 TFEU. Additional exemptions from the notification obligation exist for procurements conducted under conditions of extreme urgency (Article 28(4)) or where the works, supplies, or services can only be provided by a specific economic operator (Article 28(5)).

A further prerequisite for the notification obligation is that the conditions set out in Article 28(1) and (2) of Regulation 2022/2560 are fulfilled. Pursuant to Article 28(1)(a), the obligation applies where the estimated value of the public procurement or framework contract amounts to at least EUR 250 million (net of VAT). Where the contracting authority or entity decides to divide the procurement into lots, the notification requirement arises if the overall value exceeds EUR 250 million and the aggregate value of the lots for which the tenderer applies reaches at least EUR 125 million (Article 28(2)).

Any economic operator participating in a large-scale public procurement procedure as defined above must notify the aggregate foreign financial contributions received in the three years preceding the notification. This obligation covers financial contributions granted to the economic operator itself, its subsidiaries without commercial autonomy, and its direct and indirect holding companies up to the ultimate holding company. Where relevant, it also extends to the economic operator's main subcontractors and suppliers, provided that the foreign financial contributions received from a single third country equal or exceed EUR 4 million (Article 28(1)(b)).

In all other cases of large-scale procurement meeting the thresholds of Article 28(1)(a) and (2), each participating economic operator that has not received foreign financial contributions of at least EUR 4 million per third country must submit a declaration containing the information specified in the form set out in Annex II to Implementing Regulation (EU) 2023/1441[2] (hereinafter 'Form FS-PP'). Consequently, whenever an economic operator participates in a public procurement procedure exceeding the thresholds laid down in Article 28(1)(a) and (2), a statement on foreign financial contributions—either a notification or a declaration—is always required.

As a general rule, contracting authorities and entities indicate in the contract notice that economic operators are subject to the notification obligation set out in Article 29 of Regulation 2022/2560. Since 1st June 2024, contracting authorities may indicate in a designated field in all contract notices published on Tenders Electronic Daily (TED) whether the notification obligation under Regulation 2022/2560 applies. If so, the contracting authority will be required to indicate the outcome of the procedure under Regulation 2022/2560 in the contract award notice.

However, the absence of such a statement does not affect the legal obligation to submit a notification or declaration where the relevant conditions are met. Economic

[2] Form FS-PP relating to the notification of financial contributions in the context of public procurement procedures pursuant to Regulation (EU) 2022/2560 as Annex II to Commission Implementing Regulation (EU) 2023/1441 on detailed arrangements for the conduct of proceedings by the Commission pursuant to Regulation (EU) 2022/2560 of the European Parliament and the Council on foreign subsidies distorting the internal market.

operators are required to submit Form FS-PP even in cases where the contract notice omits any reference to this obligation.[3]

3 Statistics

From the entry into application of the notification obligation under Chapter 4 of Regulation (EU) 2022/2560 on 13 October 2023 until 25 April 2025,[4] DG GROW received a total of 2.112 submissions from economic operators participating in public procurement procedures subject to the requirement to submit a Form FS-PP.[5]

These submissions correspond to approximately 400 public procurement procedures conducted within the European Union above the thresholds set out in Article 28(1) and (2) of Regulation 2022/2560 during the same period.[6] It is noteworthy that certain procurement procedures have attracted the interest of more than 100 candidates or bidders.

The following Fig. 1 illustrates the types of submissions received during the roughly eighteen months following the Regulation's entry into force. The vast majority—1.734 cases, representing 82%—were declarations, followed by 322 notifications (15%) and 56 pre-notifications, accounting for approximately 2% of all submissions.

The overview of notifications and declarations presents a certain degree of inaccuracy, as instances have occurred where an economic operator submitted a declaration when, in fact, a notification would have been required. It is conceivable that this might stem from persistent misinterpretations of the concept of a "foreign financial contribution" to be considered for calculating the threshold under Article 28(1)(b) of Regulation (EU) 2022/2560 during the period covered by this overview.

According to Article 3(2)(c) of Regulation 2022/2560, such contributions include, inter alia, the provision of goods or services to public authorities or public entities of third countries, as well as the purchase of goods or services from those authorities or entities. In other words, whenever goods or services are sold to third-country public authorities or entities, the turnover generated from such sales constitutes a foreign financial contribution that must be taken into account when determining whether the thresholds laid down in Article 28(1) are met.[7] This aspect

[3] For more details regarding the notification process see in this volume the chapter written by Linke, section 2.

[4] Date of completion of presentation for the conference on the Foreign Subsidies Regulation.

[5] On 22 October 2025, the number had already increased to some more than 3.000 cases (presentation of García Porras, Commission/DG GROW, at the PWC EUFSR Conference in Brussels on 23 October 2025).

[6] On 22 October 2025, the number of public procurement procedures for which the Commission received submissions already reached over 600 (presentation of García Porras, Commission/DG GROW, at the PWC EUFSR Conference in Brussels on 23 October 2025).

[7] Form FS-PP, recital (7).

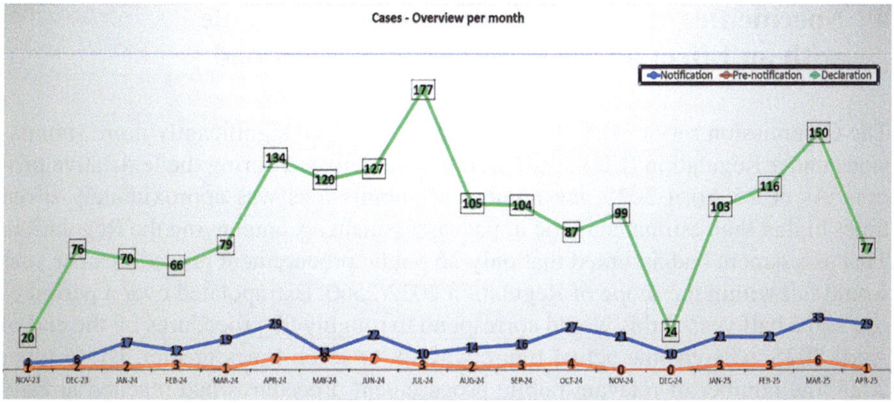

Fig. 1 Types of submissions received during the months following the Regulation's entry into force

has not been immediately apparent to all economic operators submitting declarations. It can therefore be assumed that an economic operator whose principal area of activity is located in a third country and whose product or service portfolio primarily targets the public sector (for example, civil engineering companies involved in infrastructure such as tunnels, roads, or hospitals) is generally under the obligation to submit a notification rather than a declaration.

During the roughly eighteen months in which the notification obligation has been in effect, most public procurement procedures meeting the threshold of an estimated value of at least EUR 250 million—and thus falling within the scope of Regulation 2022/2560—originated from France. One possible explanation lies in the relatively centralized nature of the French public procurement system: the aggregation of demand often results in procurements of greater scale. Germany ranked second in terms of the number of affected procedures, despite its comparatively fragmented procurement structure, which operates across federal, regional, and local levels with fewer central purchasing bodies. Italy followed in third place.

The majority of all submissions were received from economic operators whose headquarters, or the headquarters of their ultimate holding company, were located within the European Union. The sectors most frequently involved were information technology, construction, transport, energy, and health, with various other sectors only playing a minor role.

4 Specificities of the Public Procurement Module with an Effect on the Commission's Workload

The Commission services of DG GROW have received significantly more submissions under Regulation (EU) 2022/2560 than anticipated during the legislative process. As of 25 April 2025, the number of submissions was approximately seven times higher than estimated in the impact assessment accompanying the Regulation. That assessment had assumed that only 36 public procurement procedures per year would fall within the scope of Regulation 2022/2560. Extrapolated over a period of one and a half years,[8] this would correspond to roughly 60 procedures by the end of April 2025, whereas the actual figure was six to seven times greater. By October 2025, the number of relevant public procurement procedures had reached already 600, confirming this trend.

The initial projections anticipated during the legislative process were based on contract notices published on Tenders Electronic Daily (TED) and limited to those tenders where an estimated contract value was explicitly disclosed. In practice, however, the contract value is often not specified in the notice or is indicated merely as EUR 1—a phenomenon observable, for instance, in Germany. This has led to a substantial underestimation of the number of procedures falling within the scope of the Regulation. The actual number (more than 600 as of October 2025) would likely be even higher if all contracting authorities and entities were fully aware of their obligations under the Regulation—particularly the duty set out in Article 28(6) to state in the contract notice, or in the procurement documents where no prior publication occurs, that economic operators are subject to the notification obligation under Article 29.

Moreover, a single tender may involve multiple notifying parties, each of which must be examined individually. Consequently, the total number of undertakings potentially affected by foreign financial contributions exceeds the number of cases. Under the procedural framework, all notifying parties submitting a joint request to participate or a joint tender must use a single Form FS-PP for their joint submission. Where at least one of the notifying parties has received a notifiable foreign financial contribution, they are required to submit a joint notification. Conversely, if none of the notifying parties has received such contributions, they must submit a joint declaration using one Form FS-PP. Accordingly, one submission may necessitate the examination of several—sometimes up to ten—undertakings.

For statistical purposes, submissions in a given procurement procedure are counted only once, although in multi-stage procedures, the notification or declaration shall be submitted twice, first with the request to participate and then as an updated notification or declaration with the submitted tender or final tender. Both submissions are reviewed by the Commission services under the same case number. The number of submissions per procedure is, however, limited to two pursuant to Article 29(1) of Regulation 2022/2560. Determining the appropriate moment to

[8] Thus, approximately corresponding to the period of 13 October 2023 to 25 April 2025.

request an update is not always straightforward for contracting authorities or entities. While the decisive point in open and restricted procedures is the submission of the tender, identifying the relevant stage in negotiated procedures can be more complex. Such procedures often involve several negotiation rounds following the initial tender, although in some cases the contracting authority reserves in the contract notice or in the invitation to confirm interest the possibility to award the contract on the basis of the initial tenders. This then becomes the final tender, often called the Best and Final Offer (BAFO). As a general rule, the update must be made with the final tender. Where additional negotiation rounds occur, the Form FS-PP must be updated and submitted together with the request to submit the final tender. If the contract is awarded on the basis of the initial tender, however, the form may not yet have been updated, as further negotiations had appeared possible at the time of submission. In such cases, the Form FS-PP must be updated retrospectively and the preliminary review shall be closed before the contract is awarded.

If an economic operator submits tenders in several public procurement procedures falling within the scope of Regulation 2022/2560, it is required to complete and submit a separate Form FS-PP for each tender. Each submission constitutes a distinct case, even if the information provided is largely identical. The assessment itself depends on the specific procurement procedure, the procurement at issue and the competing economic operators.

The public procurement module under the Regulation requires extensive interaction with representatives of both economic operators and contracting authorities. The Forms FS-PP are frequently prepared by the same practitioners responsible for drafting and submitting the tenders themselves. Many of these practitioners are unfamiliar with the legal framework of Regulation 2022/2560 and with the precise definitions of its key concepts. For instance, information is often provided only for the economic operator itself, without including all group entities that control or are controlled by it. Similarly, the requirement to take into account transactions with third-country authorities or public institutions when calculating the relevant foreign financial contributions is not always known. In such instances, requests for additional information are common.

It also occurs that contracting authorities, with the good intention of simplifying the reporting process, design their own reporting templates. However, this approach often neglects that certain information in the Form FS-PP is mandatory and essential for the completeness of a notification or declaration. Where such information is missing, the procedural deadlines established under Article 30(2) and (6) of Regulation 2022/2560 will not be set in motion.

5 The Role of the Commission and of the Contracting Authority in the Procedure to Enforce Regulation 2022/2560

Unlike in the concentration module of Regulation (EU) 2022/2560, where undertakings interact solely with the European Commission, in the public procurement module economic operators must deal with both the Commission and the contracting authority responsible for the procurement procedure in which a notification or declaration of foreign financial contributions is required.

5.1 Pre-Notification Contacts

Notifying parties may initiate discussions with the Commission prior to submitting a notification or declaration under Regulation 2022/2560. These discussions should take place well in advance of the deadline for submitting the tender or—where applicable, in multi-stage procedures—the request to participate. This is because the period available for such exchanges is constrained by the deadline set by the contracting authority, as the Form FS-PP must be submitted together with the tender or request to participate. To initiate pre-notification contacts, notifying parties are required to submit a "case team allocation request," available on DG GROW's website.[9] As the name implies, discussions during this stage are confined to the pre-notification period and concern the amount and type of information to be included in the Form FS-PP.

As noted in Sect. 3 above, the number of pre-notification contacts in the public procurement module remains relatively limited. This contrasts with the concentration module, where a pre-notification contact is generally a standard step preceding every notification.

The possibility of pre-notification is also highlighted in Form FS-PP. The Commission offers this service to notifying parties on a voluntary basis to facilitate the preparation of the preliminary review of foreign subsidies in the context of a published public procurement. Although the Form FS-PP describes pre-notification contacts as beneficial for both notifying parties and the Commission—particularly in clarifying the amount of information required—the limited number of pre-notification contacts shows that this option is not of great practical relevance. Its main benefit seems to lie in clarifying the scope of information to be provided in the FS-PP form. They rarely result in a reduction of the information required, as the information obligations in the public procurement module are already limited in scope.

[9] https://single-market-economy.ec.europa.eu/single-market/public-procurement/foreign-subsidies-regulation/guidance-economic-operators_en.

Pursuant to Article 28(1)(b) of Regulation 2022/2560, the notification obligation is confined to the economic operator itself, including its subsidiaries lacking commercial autonomy, its direct and indirect holding companies up to the ultimate holding company, and, where applicable, its main subcontractors and suppliers participating in the same tender. For main subcontractors and suppliers, information is required only for the individual company, excluding its subsidiaries and holdings. While the Commission may, where necessary, request additional information concerning foreign subsidies granted to other entities outside the scope of Article 28(1)(b) of Regulation 2022/2560 and within the broader corporate group—particularly where such subsidies could confer a benefit on the economic operator—such information is not required ab initio and need not be included in the Form FS-PP.[10] As the reporting requirements are already restricted to certain entities within the corporate group, pre-notification contacts seldom lead to waivers of information.

Nonetheless, pre-notification procedures can be particularly useful in cases where a large number of notifiable foreign financial contributions are expected. In such situations, the Commission may, during the pre-notification phase, indicate what supplementary information it will likely require. This allows economic operators additional time to prepare and collect the necessary data, thereby avoiding the considerable time pressure that might otherwise arise once the notification has been formally submitted, and the review deadlines start.

The option to engage in pre-notification contacts is used primarily by legal practitioners familiar with this instrument from merger control proceedings before DG COMP.

5.2 *Submission and Review Process*

In the submission process of foreign financial contributions based on the Form FS-PP under Regulation 2022/2560, the initial addressee of the economic operator is the contracting authority or contracting entity. Pursuant to Article 29(1), economic operators must notify the contracting authority or entity of all foreign financial contributions as defined in Article 28(1)(b). The contracting authority must then transmit the notification or declaration to the Commission without delay, thereby triggering the preliminary review—provided that the submission is complete—pursuant to Article 30(2).

Notifications or declarations under the public procurement module must be submitted using a single Form FS-PP covering all notifying parties related to the tender procedure, as stipulated in Article 5(1) of Implementing Regulation (EU) 2023/1441. The online version of the Form FS-PP, available on DG GROW's website, is the

[10] See point 2.5.1 of the draft Guidelines on the application of certain provisions of Regulation (EU) 2022/2560 of the European Parliament and of the Council of 14 December 2022 on foreign subsidies distorting the internal market, published for public consultation in summer 2025.

most efficient means for both economic operators and the Commission to manage and assess the required information. It is available in all EU languages.

It happens that either contracting authorities, with the good intention of simplifying matters, or economic operators themselves, design their own forms for notifications or declarations which do not, however, contain all the mandatory information. As specified in recitals (16) and (17) of the Form FS-PP, information requested in Sections 1–3, 6, and 8 is required for a complete notification, while Sections 1, 2, 7, and 8 are required for a complete declaration. Failure to use the official Form FS-PP, or to provide the required information, prevents the initiation of the preliminary review period under Article 30(2) and (6) of Regulation 2022/2560.

Economic operators should be aware that a separate submission of the relevant information on foreign financial contributions, covering the entities referred to in Article 28(1)(b) of Regulation 2022/2560 for the three years preceding the submission, is required for each tender. There indeed exists the risk that submissions—particularly from operators within larger corporate groups—may sometimes be inconsistent. For instance, a notification may be submitted in one procurement, while a declaration is submitted in another. This might occur where the person responsible for preparing the Form FS-PP within the economic operator is not fully aware of the scope of Article 28(1)(b). Consequently, information may be provided only for the economic operator itself, whereas information for subsidiaries and holding companies is also required. Some corporate groups have addressed this issue by involving their legal departments at the holding level to coordinate and align information and organize the information-gathering process.

The contracting authority or entity receives the Form FS-PP together with the request to participate or the tender. Under Article 29(2) of Regulation 2022/2560, the contracting authority must then transfer the notification or declaration to the Commission without delay. The Regulation does not impose on the contracting authority an obligation to verify the completeness of the information submitted. However, where it is immediately apparent that the submission is incomplete—for example, if self-created forms are used or the Form FS-PP is unsigned—it is in the interest of the contracting authority to request the missing information from the economic operator to ensure that the preliminary review can commence without unnecessary delay.

When the information is submitted in the required form, the contracting authority must transfer it to the Commission without delay. In practice, however, the Commission often receives submissions some time after the deadline for the request to participate or the tender. While it is preferable for contracting authorities to forward submissions as early as possible to trigger the preliminary review under Article 30(2), it is common practice to submit all Forms FS-PP as a package once all economic operators have provided them. This approach ensures that the same preliminary review deadlines apply to all participants. Some authorities wait to forward Forms FS-PP accompanying requests to participate until after assessing exclusion grounds and selection criteria, submitting the documents only for selected candidates. Although this deviates from the strict wording of Article 29(2), it may reduce unnecessary work for the Commission. The drawback is that the Commission may not have a complete overview of all requests to participate, which could be relevant for potential procedures based on Article 9 of Regulation 2022/2560.

Contracting authorities should use EU-Send[11] for transmitting Forms FS-PP received from economic operators. While submission via DG GROW's functional mailbox[12] is technically possible, EU-Send offers higher security standards and reduced vulnerability to cyber-attacks. Separate registration is required for EU-Send accounts for DG COMP and DG GROW.

If a notification or declaration is missing from the request to participate or tender, the contracting authority may request that the economic operator submit the relevant documents within ten working days. Pursuant to Article 29(3), tenders or requests to participate from economic operators subject to the obligations of Article 29 that are ultimately not accompanied by a notification or declaration, despite the contracting authority's request, must be declared irregular and rejected. Although the wording of Article 29(3) uses "may", it would be essential that contracting authorities act in accordance with this provision, as Member States and their authorities are obliged to cooperate effectively with the Commission in implementing Regulation 2022/2560.[13]

Upon receipt of the Forms FS-PP, the Commission initiates a twenty-working-day preliminary review. Unlike in the concentration module, the Commission cannot "stop the clock" if an economic operator fails to provide complete information as required under Article 13.[14] This renders the preliminary review particularly challenging, especially when requests for additional information are necessary. The theoretical possibility to extend this period by ten working days in duly justified cases may be regarded as being largely academic. In open procedures, the preliminary review closes at the end of the twenty-day period, absent sufficient indications of an actual or potential distortion of the internal market. In multi-stage procedures, the Commission examines the complete notification or declaration submitted with the request to participate within twenty working days. Article 30(6) provides that upon expiry, the preliminary review is suspended rather than closed, until the submission of a final or restricted tender. Once the final tender containing a completed and updated notification or declaration is submitted, the preliminary review resumes, with the Commission having twenty working days to finalize it.

Even during the suspension of the preliminary review, the Commission may request supplementary information between stages, as envisaged in Recital (44).

---

[11] EU Send provides a safe and secure communication channel with DG GROW/G.3 to ensure the maximum level of confidentiality. To request access to EU Send, a message needs to be sent to GROW-FSR-PP-NOTIFICATIONS@ec.europa.eu. Furthermore, an EU-Login is required for every user belonging to the entity using EU Send to access the platform (see the EU Login Tutorial, available at https://single-market-economy.ec.europa.eu/document/6e7182cc-271e-4801-a785-431cf802375f_en). While the use of EU Send is not mandatory, the Commission cannot guarantee confidentiality through non-secured email communications.

[12] GROW-FSR-PP-NOTIFICATIONS@ec.europa.eu.

[13] Recital 58 of Regulation 2022/2560.

[14] See Article 24(5) of Regulation 2022/2560 for the concentration module.

The contracting authority or entity may continue with all procedural steps in the procurement, except for the award of the contract. In multi-stage procedures, authorities can select candidates and advance the process following the request to participate without having to wait for the twenty-day assessment period of the preliminary review to be suspended (Article 30(6)).

6 Lessons Learned and Way Forward

The first eighteen months following the introduction of the reporting requirement for foreign financial contributions have demonstrated that significantly more public procurement procedures have entailed the obligation to submit notifications or declarations than originally anticipated. Not all Member States are equally familiar with Regulation 2022/2560; contract notices for procurement procedures exceeding the threshold specified in Article 28(1) are repeatedly published without reference to the Regulation. Moreover, the quality of submitted notifications and declarations frequently generates queries and necessitates corrections. While large international corporations have often established organizational mechanisms to systematically collect the required data, this is by no means the case for all economic operators subject to the reporting obligation.

It remains important to raise awareness among public contracting authorities in Member States of the need to highlight the reporting obligation under Regulation 2022/2560 and certainly, to strictly enforce compliance with formal requirements. Answers to frequently asked questions should be published more regularly in the form of a Q&A on the Commission's website. Regular meetings with designated contact points in Member States should further enhance the exchange of information, increase awareness of the Regulation, and clarify questions raised by contracting authorities regarding its application.

To ensure a more coherent and focused enforcement of the FSR-PP module within DG GROW and to better address the issues outlined above, a dedicated unit, G.3 Foreign Subsidies, within 'Directorate G - Compliance and Responsible Business Conduct' was established on 1st May 2025. In line with its legislative mandate, the Commission's guidelines pursuant to Article 46 of Regulation 2022/2560 have been published on 6 January 2026. These guidelines are intended to clarify key concepts of the Regulation and enhance transparency. In conjunction with the first report on the application of Regulation 2022/2560, scheduled for July 2026, legislative proposals may be submitted based on the experience gained in implementing the Regulation. In particular, undertakings, economic operators, and public contracting authorities will have the opportunity to contribute proposals aimed at achieving a more efficient and less bureaucratic application of the rules.

Elke Zeise works as legal and policy officer at the European Commission, Directorate-General GROW, in the Unit G.3 - Foreign Subsidies, which is responsible for enforcing the Foreign Subsidies Regulation in the context of public procurement.

The FSR in Public Procurement: A View from Industry

Benjamin Linke

Abstract The Regulation on third-country subsidies continues to pose numerous uncertainties for undertakings operating within the EU internal market. Economic operators involved in public procurement procedures must adhere to notification obligations if specific value thresholds are met. This results in challenges and uncertainties for both economic operators and contracting authorities/entities. Not only do the notification requirements impose substantial administrative burdens in terms of data collection and assessment, but the legal concepts that determine whether and to what extent notification obligations arise are also exceptionally ambiguous. The following chapter outlines the requirements of notification obligations in public procurement procedures. From an industry perspective, issues related to notification obligations are subsequently discussed, along with proposed changes. The evaluation is conducted from the standpoint of both an economic operator and a contracting entity, as Deutsche Bahn acts in both roles.

1 Introduction

Since 13 October 2023, notification requirements under the Foreign Subsidies Regulation (EU) 2022/2560[1] (hereinafter referred to as 'FSR') have been applicable to large-scale procurement procedures. In procedures with a procurement value of at least EUR 250 million, Chapter 4 of the regulation mandates that economic operators submit data and information regarding foreign financial contributions. The FSR also impacts contracting authorities or entities. For procurements with a value

[1] Regulation (EU) 2022/2560 of the European Parliament and of the Council of 14 December 2022 on foreign subsidies distorting the internal market, OJ L 330/1, i.c.w. Corrigendum 2024 OJ L 90559.

B. Linke (✉)
Deutsche Bahn AG, Frankfurt am Main, Germany
e-mail: Benjamin.Linke@deutschebahn.com

W. Weiß et al. (eds.), *The Foreign Subsidies Regulation*, European Yearbook of International Economic Law, https://doi.org/10.1007/978-3-032-23415-5_6

of at least EUR 250 million, these authorities or entities receive notifications and declarations from companies and are required to forward them, along with potentially other documents, to the European Commission (hereinafter: Commission). The awarding of contracts is thus constrained and may be contingent upon the findings of the Commission's examination. The Commission assesses, within specific deadlines, whether the financial contributions represent foreign subsidies that distort competition within the procurement process.

The issuance of the FSR has already elicited intense criticism from the business sector. A larger number of companies had approached the Commission due to the effort and practical difficulties in implementing the FSR, demanding easements concerning the legal framework. With the enactment of the Implementing Regulation[2] (hereinafter referred to as 'IR') on 10 July 2023, the Commission subsequently improved the notification obligations for economic operators. Nevertheless, challenges remain, as evidenced over the past two years.

2 Notification Obligations in Public Procurement Procedures

The FSR establishes notification obligations for economic operators regarding financial contributions from third countries (Articles 28, 29 FSR). In the procurement procedures concerned, notifications or declarations must be submitted to contracting authorities or entities. The contracting authority or entity, in turn, is required to forward the submissions to the Commission for examination during the ongoing procurement procedure (Article 29 (2) FSR).

Affected are public procurement procedures in the sense of the European procurement directives (see Sect. 2.1), which have an estimated procurement value equal to or greater than EUR 250 million, where in the case of division into lots, the value of the lot or the aggregate value of all the lots to which the tenderer applies is equal to or greater than EUR 125 million (see Sect. 2.2). If the FSR is applicable to the respective procurement procedure, economic operators must take action: They must assess whether they have received foreign financial contributions within the meaning of Article 3 (2) FSR over the past three years (see Fig. 1 for the examination sequence). Depending on the sum of the foreign financial contributions, they are required to submit either a notification or declaration (see Sect. 2.3).

[2] Commission Implementing Regulation (EU) 2023/1441 of 10 July 2023 on detailed arrangements for the conduct of proceedings by the Commission pursuant to Regulation (EU) 2022/2560 of the European Parliament and of the Council on foreign subsidies distorting the internal market, OJ L 177/1, i.c.w. Corrigendum 2023 OJ 2414.

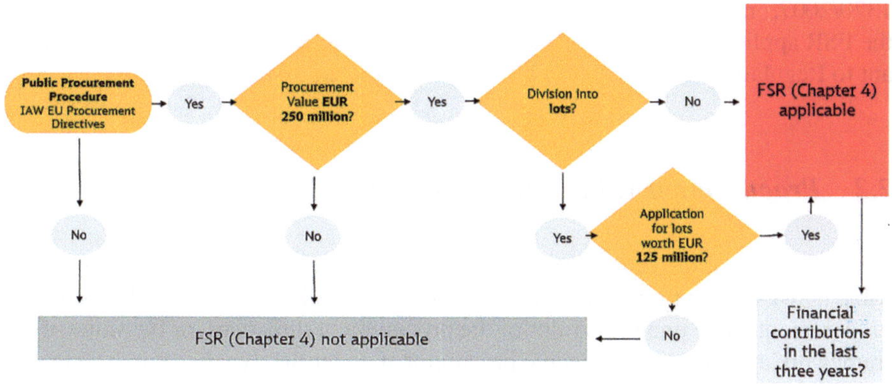

Fig. 1 Examination sequence

2.1 Public Procurement Procedure

Prerequisite for the application of the provisions in Chapter 4 FSR regarding public procurement procedures is the existence of a public procurement procedure pursuant to Article 2 No. 3 FSR. Chapter 4 of the FSR primarily applies to procurement procedures in the area of general procurement law (Directive 2014/24/EU), sectoral procurement (Directive 2014/25/EU), and concession procurement (Directive 2014/23/EU), see Article 2 No. 3 a, b FSR. Essentially, all types of procedures are affected, from open and restricted procedures, negotiated procedures (with or without prior publication or call for competition), through the competitive dialogue to innovation partnership. Excluded are in the context of negotiated procedures without prior publication/call for competition only urgency procurements and procurements where works, supplies or services can only be supplied by a particular economic operator (Article 28 (4), (5) FSR).[3] The FSR also encompasses the awarding of framework agreements (see Article 28 (1) lit. a FSR).

However, the FSR does not apply to individual call-off orders under a framework agreement, as understood from recital 42 FSR. Also not covered by the notification and declaration obligations of Chapter 4 FSR are procedures for the award of contracts falling within the scope of Directive 2009/81/EC in the defense and security sector (Article 28 (3) FSR). Moreover, Chapter 4 of the FSR does not apply to procurement procedures that do not fall under the directives mentioned in Article 2 No. 3 FSR. This affects, for example, public passenger transport services by rail or metro (see Article 10 lit. i Directive 2014/24/EU, Article 21 lit. g Directive 2014/25/EU, Article 10 (3) Directive 2014/23/EU). In this area, Regulation (EC) No

[3] In the latter case, however, a direct information obligation of the economic operator towards the Commission applies according to Article 28 (5) sent. 1 FSR. Here, the economic operator must—deviating from the otherwise necessary transmission of notifications or declarations to the contracting authority or entity—directly inform the Commission about foreign financial contributions.

1370/2007, not listed in the definition of procurement procedures to which the FSR applies, constitutes special procurement law. In conclusion, awards pursuant to Regulation (EC) No 1370/2007 are not affected by the FSR.[4]

2.2 Procurement Value and Division into Lots

The provisions of the FSR regarding public procurement procedures are only applicable above certain thresholds. According to Article 28 (1) lit. a FSR, the estimated procurement value under the rules of the procurement directives, or the value of the framework agreement or a specific procurement under the dynamic purchasing system, must be at least EUR 250 million for the notification and declaration obligations to apply.

In the case of awarding in lots, an economic operator must additionally apply for a lot or lots with a total value of at least EUR 125 million (Article 28 (2) FSR). In contrast to the procurement value, which is relevant for all economic operators equally, reaching the threshold value in Article 28 (2) FSR depends on the economic operator's individual interest in different lots. In the same public procurement procedure, some economic operators might apply for lots with a value of at least EUR 125 million, while others do not exceed the threshold and are, therefore, exempt from the notification requirement. The discretion of the contracting authority or entity in dividing lots might even open up the possibility to legally avoid the emergence of notification obligations through clever lot design.[5]

2.3 Notification and Declaration

If a procurement procedure as defined in the aforementioned Sects. 2.1 and 2.2 exists, the respective economic operator in the public procurement procedure is either obliged to submit a notification or provide a declaration. In a single-phase procedure (notably in the open procedure), the submission of the notification or declaration occurs only once with the offer. If the chosen procurement procedure is a multi-stage procedure as defined in Article 2 (6) FSR, i.e., with a preliminary request to participate, the notification or declaration must be submitted twice to the contracting authority or entity—once with the request to participate and then again (updated) with the submitted tender or final tender (Article 29 (1) sent. 4 FSR). In practice, it happens that submissions occur more than twice. This is the case when the contracting authority or entity conducts rounds of negotiations in a negotiated procedure (potentially multiple times) and reserves the right to award the contract

[4] Delcuvé and von Donat (2024), p. 271; Linke (2023), p. 428.

[5] Osseforth et al. (2025), p. 786.

based on the initial bids (without entering negotiations).[6] In this case, each new binding bid is potentially a 'final tender,' thus, for practical reasons, necessitating the contracting authority or entity to request submission of a notification or declaration with each of these subsequent tenders.

A notification requirement arises if the economic operator, including its subsidiary companies without commercial autonomy, its holding companies, and, where applicable, its main subcontractors and suppliers involved in the same tender in the public procurement procedure was granted aggregate financial contributions in the three years prior to the (updated) notification equal to or greater than EUR 4 million per third country. If this threshold is not reached, a declaration must be submitted. In both scenarios, however, the economic operator must act and transmit the completed Form FS-PP (Annex II IR) to the contracting authority, regardless of whether the threshold in Article 28 (1) lit. b FSR is exceeded.[7]

2.3.1 Entities Affected by the Obligations

Not only the financial contributions of the economic operator must be considered, but according to Article 28 (1) lit. b FSR, also those from its subsidiary companies without commercial autonomy, from its holding companies, and, where applicable, its main subcontractors and suppliers involved in the same tender in the public procurement procedure. If the economic operator is a consortium, the obligation extends to all members of the consortium (Article 29 (5) FSR). Unfortunately, the aforementioned terms in their legal application pose significant risks. A legal definition (also fraught with interpretation issues) only exists with regard to main subcontractors and suppliers in Article 29 (5) sent. 2 FSR.

Subsidiaries and Holding Companies

Especially in the assessment of whether subsidiary companies without commercial autonomy of the economic operator exist, there is unfortunately a lack of binding criteria for determining the dependence or independence of the subsidiary. By 13 July 2026, the Commission will review its practice of implementing and enforcing the FSR, and present a report to the European Parliament and the Council, accompanied, where the Commission considers it appropriate, by relevant legislative proposals (Art. 52 (2) FSR). It is to be hoped that the Commission will thoroughly clarify the problematic delimitation.

---

[6] See Article 29 (4) Directive 2014/24/EU for details.

[7] Cf. Commission, DG GROW, FSR Q&A point 11, https://single-market-economy.ec.europa.eu/single-market/public-procurement/foreign-subsidies-regulation/questions-and-answers_en; Reindl and van Damme (2024), p. 115; Reinhold and Weck (2024), p. 27; Stas and Geisel (2023), p. 368.

'Holding companies' of the economic operator, according to the wording, are only companies that in a straight line (directly or indirectly) hold shares of the economic operator, such as parent or grandparent companies.[8] Other group companies like sister or aunt companies are not comprised. Nothing different results from the reference in Article 30 (1) FSR to the provisions of Article 23 FSR in conjunction with Article 22 (4) FSR.[9] This is because, according to the heading, Article 30 FSR provides '[p]rocedural rules applicable to the preliminary review and the in-depth investigation of notified financial contributions in public procurement procedures' addressed to the Commission. Hence, Article 30 (1) FSR does not extend the notification obligation of Article 29 in conjunction with Article 28 FSR directed at economic operators. The provisions on the notification obligation do not contain any reference to Article 23 FSR. Article 30 (1) FSR explicitly applies to already 'notified financial contributions in public procurement procedures' solely. The provisions have no relevance before the initial notification. The reference to Article 23 FSR in Article 30 (1) FSR merely clarifies that the Commission could also extend its review to certain affiliated group companies.[10]

Main Subcontractors and Main Suppliers

The distinction between main subcontractors/suppliers and simple subcontractors/suppliers can also be challenging. Although the definition in Article 29 (5) sent. 2 FSR refers to the achievement of an objective threshold value of more than 20% of the value of the submitted tender for the existence of a main subcontractor or main supplier, the legal definition also includes a general clause. Companies whose participation in the tender ensures key elements of the contract performance are thus main subcontractors or main suppliers. The contract specific situation is likely decisive for categorizing contributions as ensuring key elements of the contract performance. According to recital 54 FSR, such elements can include, for example, specific know-how, special technology, specialized staff, patents, or similar advantages. Particularly relevant are elements on which the economic operator relies to fulfil the majority of at least one of the selection criteria in a public procurement procedure.

The assessment of whether and when key elements of the contract performance are given is highly case-dependent and thus prone to error. Therefore, the general clause of 'key elements of the contract performance' in Article 29 (5) sent. 2 FSR should be viewed critically. This is especially true because it is likely to become relevant only for activities that do not reach the threshold of more than 20% of the value of the submitted tender. The economic impact of such performance

---

[8] Delcuvé and von Donat (2024), p. 275; Linke (2023), p. 430; Reindl and van Damme (2024), pp. 118 f, p. 152; Stas and Geisel (2023), p. 368; van Weelden et al. (2024), p. 149.

[9] Of different opinion: von Graevenitz (2025), p. 35.

[10] Cf. Linke (2023), p. 430.

contributions on the tender price is limited. Against this background, it would be appropriate for the European legislator to consider, in a future revision of the FSR, eliminating this general clause part of the legal definition entirely for reasons of legal certainty.

2.3.2 What Must Be Submitted?

If the threshold of EUR 4 million in Article 28 (1) lit. b FRS is reached by the relevant entities, the economic operator or (if a submission is required for multiple entities) the main contractor/concessionaire must submit a notification to the contracting authority (Article 3 (2) IR). In a notification, all sections of Annex II IR (Form FS-PP) must generally be completed, except for Section 7. Third-country financial contributions must be specified individually if they fall into one of the four categories of Article 5 (1) lit. a–c, e FSR. These are third-country financial contributions that have the potential for significant market distortion. Only financial contributions that as individually granted contributions amount to at least EUR 1 million must be considered (Section 3.1 Form FS-PP). If none of the categories of Article 5 (1) FSR apply, Table 1 in connection with Section 3.3. Form FS-PP must be filled out. This table only requires an 'overview' of the foreign financial contributions equal to or in excess of EUR 1 million granted to the notifying parties in the three years prior to the notification. Certain financial contributions can be disregarded when filling out the table according to the exceptions in No. 6 of Table 1 Form FS-PP. Foremost, these involve 'provision/purchase of goods/services (except financial services) at market terms in the ordinary course of business'. Given this context, if all financial contributions of a company have been received at market terms in the ordinary course of business, a transmissioned notification may, in individual cases, omit details of financial contributions altogether, even though the threshold specified in Article 28 (1) lit. b FSR has been exceeded. The third-country financial contributions remaining after applying the exceptions can be estimated for the overview. The estimation must be conducted per third country and then entered as a range in Table 1 Form FS-PP.

Below the threshold of EUR 4 million per third country according to Article 28 (1) lit. b FSR, a declaration must be submitted. The requirements for a declaration are detailed in Section 7 of Form FS-PP. Sections 1, 2, and 8, as well as, if applicable, Table 2 of Form FS-PP, must be completed. Certain foreign financial contributions must also be specified in the declaration. As the exceptions for specifying financial contributions in notifications (see No. 6 of Table 1 Form FS-PP) do not apply to declarations, the specification of financial contributions may sometimes even go further than in notifications. However, only individual granted contributions of at least EUR 1 million must be listed separately (see Section 7.2, 7.3 Form FS-PP). Individual granted contributions under EUR 1 million can be declared as aggregate in Table 2 Form FS-PP without particularising individual amounts. A 'brief description of the financial contributions' must be provided, without the FSR expounding what this includes. It seems reasonable to provide details regarding the form and purpose of the financial contributions. The wording does not necessarily require the indication of the total amount of financial contributions granted or the grant dates. If the total amount of financial contributions in the last three years per third country does not reach the amount of de minimis aid as defined in Article 3 (2), first subparagraph, of Regulation (EU) No 1407/2013,[11] no further details are required (Section 7.4 Form FS-PP).

2.3.3 Challenges for Economic Operators

With regard to the threshold in Article 28 (1) lit. b FSR, economic operators in large public procurement procedures must thoroughly examine their business relationships to determine whether these qualify as foreign financial contributions within the meaning of Article 3 (2) FSR. This can entail significant effort and carry substantial legal risks (see detailed discussion below in Sect. 5). Not only can missing or incorrect information in notifications or declarations be sanctioned with fines (Article 33 FSR), but exclusion from the procurement procedure may also be threatened (see e.g., Article 29 (3), 4 FSR). The problematic aspect for economic operators is the breadth of the concept of 'foreign financial contributions', which encompasses every business transaction with a non-EU state or its public enterprises.[12] The legal term includes concepts such as tax exemptions or the granting of special or exclusive rights without adequate remuneration (Article 3 (2) lit. b FSR). Neither does the FSR provide criteria for assessing when a measure falls under such terms, nor is the legal evaluation (even if criteria exist) straightforward. The latter can be illustrated by looking at European state aid law, where the question regarding the aid quality of tax measures[13] or the mitigation of charges[14] in the context of awarded rights is often problematic. In the context of the deadlines set within the procurement procedure, economic operators may have to make assessments within short timeframes. Overall, there is significant scope for error.

---

[11] The regulation is no longer in force. It is disputed whether the reference automatically extends to the successor Regulation (EU) 2023/2832, which in Article 3 (2) issues an increased de minimis threshold of 300,000 EUR. In favour of a reference to the successor regulation: van Heezik et al. (2024), p. 25; Weiß (2023), p. 826. Of the opposite opinion: Werner et al. (2024), p. 33; Hornkohl (2023a), p. 143: '€200 000 threshold in Article 4(3) FSR'.

[12] For details see in this volume Weiß, The Notion of Foreign Financial Contribution and of Foreign Subsidy; von Graevenitz (2025), p. 15; Van Heezik et al. (2024), p. 25.

[13] See Jaeger (2016), mn. 5.

[14] See Arhold (2016), mn. 111.

3 Review by European Commission

Within the framework of the procedural rules of Article 30 FSR, the Commission exclusively[15] examines whether a foreign subsidy exists. If a foreign subsidy is present, the Commission assesses possible distortions in the public procurement procedure based on Articles 4, 5, 6[16] in conjunction with Article 27 FSR. Article 27 FSR modifies the assessment standard of distortions in the internal market concerning public procurement procedures. According to Article 27 FSR, foreign subsidies that cause or risk causing a distortion in a public procurement procedure 'shall be understood' as foreign subsidies that enable an economic operator to submit a tender that is unduly advantageous in relation to the works, supplies, or services concerned. Article 27 FSR is a special provision in relation to Article 4 (1) FSR. Hence, the indicators listed in Article 4 (1) FSR alone cannot substantiate distortion in the context of public procurement procedures. It must always be determined whether the economic operator was enabled to submit a tender that is unduly advantageous. An assessment of whether a third-country subsidy has affected the bid can be performed based on the bid calculation (specifically in comparison with the calculation of competitors and the procurement value estimate of the contracting authority/entity). If individual parts of the bid calculation are particularly favourable, the price advantage must be economically explainable. According to recital 53 FSR, such factors that can be adduced by the economic operator may concern, in particular, the elements referred to in Article 69 (2) Directive 2014/24/EU or Article 84 (2) Directive 2014/25/EU to justify abnormally low tenders, e.g., the particular cost-effectiveness of a production process, innovations or novel technical solutions, or exceptionally favourable conditions from which the economic operator benefits in the supply of goods or services. Where the Commission finds that an economic operator benefited from a foreign subsidy distorting the internal market, it adopts decisions in accordance with Article 31 (1), (2) FSR.

4 Role of the Contracting Authority or Entity

The contracting authorities or entities play only a limited role within the framework of Chapter 4 FSR. Any notifications or declarations received from the economic operators must be forwarded to the Commission without delay (Article 29 (2) FSR). Apart from this, the contracting authorities or entities only have certain other obligations:

---

[15] Refer to Sect. 4.2 below for more information.

[16] Regarding the balancing test, see in this volume von Graevenitz, Balancing.

4.1 Publication

According to Article 28 (6) FSR, the contracting authority or entity must highlight the notification obligations under the FSR, either in the contract notice or (if such notice is not published) in the procurement documents. If such a reference is missing, it does not affect the obligations of the economic operators to provide data according to the FSR (Article 28 (6) sent. 2 FSR). Article 28 (6) FSR does not specify substantive requirements for the publication. This is at the discretion of the contracting authority or entity. A simple indication that 'the economic operators are under the notification obligation as set out in Article 29 [FSR]' suffices. Therefore, a general reference to the existing obligations under Article 29 FSR within the current public procurement procedure is sufficient.[17] An exact quotation of Article 29 FSR in the contract notice or procurement documents can be advantageous but is not obligatory.

4.2 Obligation to Review?

Contracting authorities or entities are not authorized themselves to determine whether an economic operator has received third-country subsidies or not.[18] The assessment of whether a third-country subsidy exists is an exclusive responsibility of the Commission.[19] The same applies to the assessment of whether the tender is unduly advantageous, which is also within the exclusive competence of the Commission.[20] Consequently, the FSR does not generally impose any obligations on the contracting authority or entity to review the submitted documents.

However, contracting authorities or entities must monitor the receipt of a declaration or notification. Otherwise, the Commission would not be informed that a participant in the tender procedure has not submitted anything. If a declaration or notification from an applicant or bidder is missing, the contracting authority or entity must report this to the Commission. This can be derived from Article 4 par. 3 TEU, according to which the Union and the Member States assist each other in carrying out their tasks (in the implementation of European law).[21]

If an economic operator does not submit anything, Article 29 (3) FSR grants the contracting authority or entity the option to request a missing notification or declaration with a deadline of ten working days. The clause is designed as a discretionary

---

[17] The FSR does not specifically require the publication of the estimated contract value or the values of individual lots.

[18] Delcuvé and von Donat (2024), p. 283; Ebrecht (2022), p. 493; Linke (2024), p. 261; Reindl and van Damme (2024), p. 126.

[19] Cf. recital 8 FSR; von Graevenitz (2025), p. 22; Hornkohl (2023b), p. 9.

[20] Van Heezik et al. (2024), p. 24.

[21] Linke (2024), p. 260.

rule. Therefore, the contracting authority or entity is not obliged to request the documents but must exercise its discretion dutifully.[22] However, if it issued a request under Article 29 (3) sent. 1 FSR and no notification or declaration is submitted within the set deadline, the contracting authority or entity must exclude the economic operator from the procedure (see Article 29 (3) sent. 2 FSR). Still, the contracting authority or entity cannot complain about any substantive deficiencies in the notification or declaration itself to the economic operator based on the FSR, since this falls in the sole responsibility of the Commission.[23]

4.3 Transmission of Information

The contracting authority or entity has various information obligations towards the Commission. For instance, according to Article 29 (7) sent. 1 FSR, where the contracting authority or entity suspects that third-country subsidies exist, even though the economic operator has submitted a declaration. Furthermore, the contracting authority or entity must inform the Commission without undue delay of any decision relating to the cancellation of the public procurement procedure, the rejection of the tender or request to participate by the economic operator concerned, the submission of a new tender by the economic operator concerned, or the award of the contract (Article 32 (6) FSR).

Article 11 (2) IR further requires the contracting authority or entity to provide (copies of) the documents used in preparing the procurement documents when forwarding a notification. If the applicant submits information according to Section 4 of Form FS-PP, the contracting authority or entity must also forward copies of all bids submitted in the respective public procurement procedure. The Commission needs the tenders to assess, for example through a benchmark comparison, whether the notifying party's calculation has been influenced by third-country subsidies.

5 Practical Difficulties in the Implementation of FSR Notification Obligations

The effects of the FSR with regard to public procurement procedures have been heavily underestimated by the European legislator. In the EU, there are more than 250,000 contracting authorities.[24] The total volume of public procurement in the

[22] Delcuvé and von Donat (2024), p. 282; Linke (2023), p. 430.

[23] See above in this section.

[24] European Commission, DG GROW, https://single-market-economy.ec.europa.eu/single-market/public-procurement_en.

European Union amounts to around EUR 3 trillion a year.[25] Despite this volume, the Commission assumed during the legislative process that only 36 procurement procedures per year would reach the relevant threshold of EUR 250 million and thus be subject to notification obligations.[26] However, this estimate was based on insufficient data.[27] In reality, far more procurement procedures are subject to notification obligations than anticipated. Since the notification obligations came into force in public procurement procedures (on 13 October 2023), submissions for more than 400 procedures have been received by the Commission (as of the end of April 2025).[28] The Commission had to process over 2100 submissions in total.[29] It must be noted that this only reflects the visible part of the affected procedures. It can be assumed that due to still missing awareness,[30] there are even more procedures that actually fall under Chapter 4 of the FSR.

Based on the euphemistic estimation, the European legislator assumed that the burden on companies would be 'reasonable and proportionate'.[31] It was concluded that

> [i]n view of the limited administrative burden on undertakings and the clear framework that this proposal establishes, the risk that the new instrument will negatively impact trade and investment flows is deemed low.[32]

The practical experiences of the past two years demonstrate that the effort for companies and contracting authorities or entities is by no means small (refer to Sect. 5.1). Not only are more procedures subject to notification obligations than assumed. There are also scenarios affected, which the European legislator considered outside

[25] European Parliament, Public procurement contracts, https://www.europarl.europa.eu/factsheets/en/sheet/34/vergabe-offentlicher-auftrage. See also European Commission, DG GROW, https://single-market-economy.ec.europa.eu/single-market/public-procurement_en: 'around 14% of EU GDP'.

[26] Commission Staff Working Document – Impact Assessment, Accompanying the Proposal for a Regulation of the European Parliament and of the Council on foreign subsidies distorting the internal market, SWD (2021) 99 final, point 6.2. See also van Weelden et al. (2024), p. 146.

[27] In the calculation, only the published contract values in the contract award notices were evaluated. It was ignored that a large portion of contracting authorities or entities do not provide any indication of the contract value, as the specific price is classified as confidential information. Therefore, the evaluation was done on an incomplete data basis. The overall number of affected procedures has also been increased due to high inflation in recent years. See also Weiß (2024), pp. 97 f.: Between 2015 and 2021, there were 936 procurement procedures with an estimated value of EUR 250 million or more. Thus, it is assumed that at least 130 procurement procedures per year will be affected.

[28] See in this volume Zeise, The Role of the Commission in the Public Procurement tool, Sect. 3.

[29] Ibid.

[30] Cf. in this volume Zeise, The Role of the Commission in the Public Procurement tool, Sect. 4.

[31] See Proposal for a Regulation of the European Parliament and the Council on foreign subsidies distorting the internal market, COM(2021) 223 final, point 2 on Proportionality.

[32] Proposal for a Regulation of the European Parliament and the Council on foreign subsidies distorting the internal market, COM(2021) 223 final, point 3 on Regulatory fitness and simplification.

the notification obligations, such as the involvement of small and medium-sized enterprises (refer to Sect. 5.2). It is these companies, in particular, that face challenges with the notification obligations as well as with the rather complex contents of Form FS-PP (refer to Sect. 5.3). Overall, it can certainly be critically questioned whether the current design of the notification obligations is still proportionate.[33]

5.1 Considerable Administrative Burden for Companies and Contracting Authorities/Entities

Instead of grounding its notification system on the legal concept of 'foreign subsidy', the FSR relies on the notably broad concept of 'foreign financial contribution'. Existing financial contributions must be aggregated with regard to meeting the thresholds specified in Article 28 (1) lit. b FSR. Consequently, the economic operator must possess a clear understanding of the inventory of financial contributions, even if they need not initially be disclosed in a notification or declaration.[34] However, the concept of a 'foreign financial contribution' lacks contours.[35] All business transactions can potentially fall within its scope. Consider, for instance, the purchase of stamps issued by a third country or a postal company under its control. Similarly, the purchase of a ticket on a business trip from a public transport company owned by a non-EU country qualifies as a financial contribution.[36] The breadth of the term creates not only legal uncertainty[37] but also leads to a high administrative burden in collecting data. Undertakings must gather an enormous amount of information, which is not readily available in the accounting systems.[38] The Federation of German Industries (Bundesverband der Deutschen Industrie e.V.) refers in this context to a large multinational company identifying millions of individual received financial contributions.[39] Given the high number of such business transactions, it is hardly practicable to conduct a case-by-case examination regarding single booking entries.[40] However, the FSR expects such an examination. The relevant data cannot be automatically extracted from the systems regarding the features of Article 3 (2) FSR. Instead, booking entries must be manually assessed.[41] This is particularly true

---

[33] Disputing proportionality: Business Europe (2025), p. 1.

[34] Refer to Sect. 2.3.2 above for more information.

[35] As explicitly stated by Osseforth et al. (2025), p. 785 ('konturenlos'). Cf. also Business Europe (2025), p. 2.

[36] For further details on the notion of financial contribution see in this volume Weiß, The Notion of Foreign Financial Contribution and of Foreign Subsidy.

[37] See above Sect. 2.3.3. Legal uncertainty is all the more serious because companies are exposed to the risk of being fined or being excluded from the tender process for incorrect information.

[38] Business Europe (2025), p. 1.

[39] Bundesverband der Deutschen Industrie (2023), p. 3.

[40] van Weelden et al. (2024), p. 147.

[41] Business Europe (2025), p. 1.

concerning the attribution of business transactions to third countries (Article 3 (2) sub(2) FSR). The accounting systems do not indicate whether a business partner is a third country. All the more, it is not readable whether a company can be attributed to a third country. In the worst case, information about a third country's influence on a company is not accessible to economic operators at all. Therefore, there is already a lack of a readable data basis for evaluation, which has to be generated by economic operators with great effort. With regard to the legal evaluation of third-country financial contributions, it adds to the uncertainty factor that reliable criteria for assessing an attribution to a third country do not yet even exist.[42]

Additionally, economic operators certainly do not have their own stock of data from subcontractors or suppliers (see Article 28 (1) lit. b FSR), thus creating further risks.[43] To minimize such risks, in practice, subcontractors/suppliers are already occasionally selected with regard to their compliance capabilities with FSR notification obligations and not solely based on their economic merits. This can be detrimental to small and medium-sized enterprises,[44] which tend to struggle more with adhering to the obligations.

Although most of the burdens fall on economic operators, negative effects are also noted at awarding authorities or entities. Implementing the FSR requires additional steps in procedure design and continuous checks during the award phase of the procurement procedure.[45] Moreover, contracting authorities or entities rarely have an interest in artificially reducing the supplier market through bidder-side errors in FSR implementation, which lead to exclusion from the procedure. Larger procurement procedures are already often characterized by a small circle of tenderers.[46] If individual bidders must be excluded, it can swiftly undermine the intended competitive process. Ultimately, the deadline regime of the FSR burdens the awarding authority, especially in the case of urgent procurements outside Article 32 (2) lit. c Directive 2014/24/EU and Article 50 lit. d Directive 2014/25/EU, as they must consider the significant time needed for review by the Commission (see Article 30 FSR).[47]

5.2 *Small and Medium-sized Enterprises Are Affected*

The notification obligations in public procurement procedures sometimes lead to highly undesirable side effects. For example, the impact of the obligations on small and medium-sized enterprises (SMEs) presents a practical problem. The European

[42] Cf. Reindl and van Damme (2024), p. 36.

[43] See also van Weelden et al. (2024), p. 149.

[44] Provided these qualify as main subcontractors and suppliers pursuant to Article 29 (5) sent. 2 FSR.

[45] Regarding the obligations of the awarding authorities or entities, see Sect. 4.

[46] Cf. Van Heezik et al. (2024), p. 24.

[47] Cf. von Graevenitz (2025), pp. 41 f.

legislator assumed that because of the high notification thresholds, SMEs would not be affected by the notification obligations.[48] This assumption has proven incorrect. SMEs can be subject to reporting obligations, for example, as part of a bidding consortium or as main subcontractors and suppliers pursuant to Article 29 (5) sent. 2 FSR. More practically relevant is the impact on the tendering of framework[49] agreements. For the notification obligation in the context of a framework agreement, it is not the value an individual contractual partner can monetize from the framework agreement (see recital 42 FSR), but the value of the framework agreement itself that matters, leading to procurement procedures above threshold values in which SMEs participate. This mainly affects framework agreements intended to be concluded with many contractual partners, thus distributing the total contract value among many contractors (cf. Article 33 (1) Directive 2014/24/EU: 'one or more economic operators'). In practice, it is observed that small enterprises are overwhelmed by the notification obligations, resulting in them not being able to continue participating in the procedure due to non-compliance with FSR requirements. SMEs lack the resources and internal structures to independently manage the legal and bureaucratic complexity of compliance with the FSR.

5.3 Challenging Form FS-PP

Notifications and declarations must be submitted using the official Form FS-PP (Article 5 (1), (2) IR). Practical experiences show that even using the form can become a challenge for economic operators.[50] Compared to customary forms in procurement procedures, the Form FS-PP is extremely detailed. For example, it requests information that is likely to play a major role only in the in-depth investigation, such as possible positive effects of the foreign subsidies in Section 5.1 Form FS-PP. Such information on positive effects has not yet played a role in any public procurement case assessment since the FSR came into effect. Additionally, there are confusing references to other legal acts that must be considered when completing the form (see, for example, Sections 1.2.–1.5. or 2.1.–2.4. of Form FS-PP). Overall, the form could indeed be simplified for the purposes of a preliminary examination by the Commission. The Commission still can request additional information at any

[48] Proposal for a Regulation of the European Parliament and the Council on foreign subsidies distorting the internal market, COM(2021) 223 final, point 3 on Regulatory fitness and simplification. See also Commission Staff Working Document – Impact Assessment, Accompanying the Proposal for a Regulation of the European Parliament and of the Council on foreign subsidies distorting the internal market, SWD(2021) 99 final, point 6.2.

[49] See Article 33 (1) Directive 2014/24/EU: 'A framework agreement means an agreement between one or more contracting authorities and one or more economic operators, the purpose of which is to establish the terms governing contracts to be awarded during a given period, in particular with regard to price and, where appropriate, the quantity envisaged.' See also Article 51 (1) Directive 2014/25/EU.

[50] See in this volume Zeise, The Role of the Commission in the Public Procurement tool, Sect. 6.

time (see Article 13 FSR). The need for more streamlined forms is demonstrated by various divergent FSR forms specifically designed by contracting authorities.[51] However, with respect to Article 5 paras. 1, 2 IR, these well-meaning initiatives are noncompliant with FSR requirements.

6 Potential for Changes

The practical challenges in implementing the notification obligations fuel demands for a future legislative[52] adjustment of the FSR. Especially, mandatory notifications should be avoided in situations where there is little potential for distortion of competition due to third-country subsidies. Despite more than 2100 submissions[53] so far, there have only been a handful of cases where the Commission has had an initial suspicion of competition-distorting third-country subsidies.[54] The reliance on a rigid threshold (of EUR 250 million) is only partially helpful, as both cases with potential for distortion are excluded, and cases without sufficient distortion potential are included. Particularly in the aforementioned[55] instances of awarding framework agreements, in which almost exclusively small and medium enterprises participate, there is little potential for influence through third-country subsidies regardless of a high value of the framework agreement.

In the current legal framework, the expertise of contracting authorities/entities and competitors is hardly utilized. While they can (or must) supply information to the Commission (see Article 29 (7) FSR), they have limited influence on the FSR-procedure itself. Competitors, in particular, could be valuable sources of information regarding whether a notification requirement in the planned procurement procedure is truly sensible, for example, because advantages due to third-country subsidies are suspected among other market participants. By better involving stakeholders, notification obligations could be selectively applied to 'vulnerable'

[51] See, for example: https://www.vergabe.nrw.de/system/files/media/document/file/524_eu-eigenerklarung-subventionen_0.docx.

[52] With regard to Article 47 (1) lit. b FSR, the Commission, too, should be encouraged to streamline notification requirements for the future.

[53] Refer to Sect. 5 above for this.

[54] As far as is known until July 2025, the Commission has initiated merely three in-depth investigations (cf. Article 11 FSR): Summary notice concerning the initiation of an in-depth investigation in case FSP.100147 pursuant to Articles 10(3)(d) of Regulation (EU) 2022/2560, OJ C 1913, 29.2.2024; Summary notice concerning the initiation of an in-depth investigation in Case FSP. 100151, pursuant to Articles 10(3)(d) of Regulation (EU) 2022/2560, OJ C 2830, 22.4.2024; Summary notice concerning the initiation of an in-depth investigation in Case FSP. 100154, pursuant to Articles 10(3)(d) of Regulation (EU) 2022/2560, OJ C 2832, 22.4.2024. In two more cases, bids have been declared irregular under the FSR due to incomplete notifications: https://www.mlex.com/mlex/state-aid/articles/2318527/bidders-blocked-from-edf-polish-tenders-under-eu-s-foreign-subsidy-rules.

[55] See Sect. 5.2.

procurement procedures rather than indiscriminately applied to large-scale procurement procedures—irrespective of whether third-country subsidies are likely to play a role in such procurements. It must be taken into account here that, based on available[56] statistical evaluations, the proportion of procurement procedures in which bidders from third countries actually participate is overall likely to be small. For instance, during the 2016–2019 period, only around 7 percent of all EU public procurement authorities received an offer from a non-EU bidder.[57] The main share of winning bidders from third countries originated from the United Kingdom, followed by Switzerland and finally the United States.[58] Against this backdrop, the scope of Chapter 4 of the FSR appears to be excessively broad. Instead of a blanket application of the notification obligations to all procurement procedures above certain thresholds, the notification obligations could be considered for procedures where participating economic operators, responsible contracting authorities/entities, or the EU Commission request such a notification (switch-on mechanism).[59] Since competitors would likely regularly demand a notification in cases of initial suspicions, it is not expected that tenders favoured by third-country subsidies would escape control. Instead, for such a switch-on mechanism to limit the number of notifications, a minimum procurement value might also be required.

Furthermore, the requirement to submit notifications or declarations with each affected procurement procedure (sometimes repeatedly)[60] is considered unnecessary bureaucratic effort. To enable effective control by the Commission while simultaneously reducing the burden on companies, it is proposed to establish a system whereby future tenderers could submit information on received financial contributions once at the beginning of each year (or even every two years) through a centralized platform instead of submissions in every large-scale procurement procedure (one-time abstract notification).[61]

It is also worth considering whether maintaining the linkage to financial contributions for notification obligations is still necessary. Alternatively, economic operators could be required to report third-country subsidies directly to the Commission in accordance with Article 3 (1) FSR. This approach could facilitate targeted processing of benefits from third countries, thus obviating the need for companies to manually examine every business relationship with (companies from) third countries in search for financial contributions.

---

[56] Overall, the data situation still seems to be quite limited. See Cernat (2025), p. 10.

[57] Cernat (2025), p. 9.

[58] Cernat (2025), p. 7.

[59] Here too, the award of the contract in the specific procedure could initially be halted (Article 32 (1) FSR) until the Commission has had sufficient time to examine submissions.

[60] Refer to Sect. 2.3 above for more information.

[61] Business Europe (2025), p. 3.

7 Conclusion

It can be determined that the implications of the FSR notification obligations burden public procurement procedures far more than originally intended. The data collection by economic operators is not only labour-intensive but also highly prone to errors. Additionally, the legal terms underlying the FSR require significant interpretation. Concurrently, available data suggests that more procedures fall under the notification criteria than would be necessary to achieve effective monitoring of third-country subsidy allocations. Consequently, proposals for restricting or simplifying the notification obligations are compelling to avoid disproportionate burdens on economic operators. After two years of experience with the FSR, it should be possible to strike a better balance between the legitimate goal of protecting the internal market and regulatory proportionality.

References

Arhold C (2016) Part II – Article 107 TFEU. In: Säcker FJ, Montag F (eds) European state aid law – a commentary, 1st edn. C.H. Beck and Hart and Nomos, München

Bundesverband der Deutschen Industrie e.V. (2023) Stellungnahme – Konsultation zum Entwurf einer Durchführungsverordnung zur Foreign Subsidies Regulation. 6.3.2023

Business Europe (2025) Foreign Subsidies Regulation – suggestions for improvement. https://www.businesseurope.eu/wp-content/uploads/2025/03/2025-03-03_foreign_subsidies_regulation-_businesseurope_suggestions_for_improvement_and_clarification.pdf

Cernat L (2025) ECIPE Policy Brief – No. 05/2025. The participation of foreign bidders in EU public procurement: too much or too little? https://ecipe.org/wp-content/uploads/2025/02/ECI_25_PolicyBrief_05-2025_LY02.pdf

Delcuvé F, von Donat C (2024) Die Drittstaatensubventionsverordnung im Vergabeverfahren. Vergaberecht, pp 266–292

Ebrecht C (2022) Foreign Subsidies Regulation and EU international procurement – necessity, changes and challenges. Zeitschrift für europarechtliche Studien ZEuS, pp 487–494

Hornkohl L (2023a) Protecting the internal market from subsidisation with the EU state aid regime and the foreign subsidies regulation: two sides of the same coin? J Eur Compet Law Pract JECLAP 14:137–151

Hornkohl L (2023b) The role of third parties in the enforcement of the Foreign Subsidies Regulation: complaints, participation, judicial review, and private enforcement. https://doi.org/10.2139/ssrn.4433639

Jaeger T (2016) Part VII – tax measures. In: Säcker FJ, Montag F (eds) European state aid law – a commentary, 1st edn. C.H. Beck and Hart and Nomos, München

Linke B (2023) Wirkungen der neuen Drittstaatensubventionsverordnung im Vergabeverfahren. Neue Zeitschrift für Baurecht und Vergaberecht NZBau, pp 427–432

Linke B (2024) Anmeldepflichten nach der Drittstaatssubventionsverordnung bei öffentlichen Vergabeverfahren – Welche praktischen Erleichterungen bringt die Durchführungsverordnung? Europäische Zeitschrift für Wirtschaftsrecht EuZW, pp 257–261

Osseforth T, Ackermann C, Sellmeyer M (2025) Meldungen und Erklärungen von drittstaatlichen finanziellen Zuwendungen – Bedeutung und Auswirkung der VO (EU) 2022/2560. Neue Juristische Wochenschrift NJW, pp 783–788

Reindl A, van Damme I (2024) The EU Foreign Subsidies Regulation. Concurrences, New York

Reinhold P, Weck T (2024) Welcome to the Jungle! – Identification of foreign subsidies under the new EU Foreign Subsidies Regulation. Eur State Aid Law Q EStAL 23:22–34

Stas K, Geisel B (2023) The Foreign Subsidies Regulation of the European Union: a new instrument levelling the playing field? Global Trade Customs J GTCJ 18:360–371

Van Heezik G, van Broeckhuijsen D, de Wit O (2024) The FSR: effective tool for fair competition in public procurement procedures or a paper tiger? Mededingingsrecht in de Praktijk MP, pp 23–28

Van Weelden V, Bickel F, Bock L (2024) Die EU-Drittstaatensubventionsverordnung – erste Erfahrungen aus der anwaltlichen Praxis. Corporate Compliance Zeitschrift CCZ, pp 145–153

von Graevenitz A (2025) Drittstaatliche Subventionen im Fokus der Europäischen Kommission – Die FSR-Verordnung (EU) 2022/2560 über den Binnenmarkt verzerrende drittstaatliche Subventionen, 2nd edn, 15 April 2025. https://opus4.kobv.de/opus4-fizbw/frontdoor/deliver/index/docId/474/file/2025-04-15_2te_Aufl_AvG_Verordng_EU_2022_2560.pdf

Weiß W (2023) Die Verordnung über den Binnenmarkt verzerrende drittstaatliche Subventionen: Ein Weg zu mehr Wettbewerbsgleichheit? Zeitschrift für das gesamte Handelsrecht und Wirtschaftsrecht ZHR 187:809–850

Weiß W (2024) The regulation on foreign subsidies distorting the internal market. A path to a level playing field? Springer Nature, Cham

Werner P, de la Barre H, Music K (2024) Untangling the Foreign Subsidies Regulation. Eur Compet Regul Law Rev CoRe 8:23–37

Benjamin Linke Dr. iur., LL.M (Edinburgh) works at the Legal Department of the Deutsche Bahn AG in Frankfurt, Germany.

The Role of the European Commission in the Concentrations Tool

Sara-Alexandra Raitner and Wolfgang Weiß

Abstract This Chapter examines the European Commission's early implementation of the Foreign Subsidies Regulation (FSR) in the field of concentrations. It outlines the FSR's legal framework enshrined in its chapter 'Balancing', in particular the notification thresholds, and review procedures and highlights its parallel role alongside merger and foreign investment control. Drawing on the first months of enforcement and the landmark decision in the *e&/PPF Telecom* case, the chapter analyses how the Commission identifies and addresses foreign subsidies that may distort competition in the internal market. It assesses procedural developments, notification and reporting obligations for foreign financial contributions, and the Commission's evolving guidance. The Chapter concludes that while the FSR has added a layer of complexity to M&A practice, it can be expected to have an emerging role in promoting fair competition in the EU.

1 Introduction

In 2022, the European Union introduced the Foreign Subsidies Regulation ("FSR")[1] as a new instrument to address distortions in the internal market caused by foreign subsidies, i.e. subsidies granted by non-EU States. The FSR became applicable on 13 July 2023[2] and introduced, among other tools, a merger tool for concentrations meeting certain thresholds. Since 13 October 2023, companies engaging in qualifying mergers or concentrations must notify the European Commission under

[1] Regulation (EU) 2022/2560 of the European Parliament and of the Council of 14 December 2022 on foreign subsidies distorting the internal market, 2022 OJ EU No. L 330/1, i.c.w. Corrigendum 2024 OJ L 90599.

[2] For the dates see the Corrigendum 2024 OJ EU No. L 90599, p. 1.

S.-A. Raitner (✉) · W. Weiß
German University of Administrative Sciences, Speyer, Rheinland-Pfalz, Germany
e-mail: Sara-Alexandra.Raitner@uni-speyer.de; weiss@uni-speyer.de

W. Weiß et al. (eds.), *The Foreign Subsidies Regulation*, European Yearbook of International Economic Law, https://doi.org/10.1007/978-3-032-23415-5_7

the FSR and await clearance before closing, which causes a suspensory review process like the EU Merger Regulation (EUMR)[3] but focusing on foreign contributions. This chapter provides an overview of the FSR framework in the context of concentrations and examines the early implementation experiences, including procedural developments, the European Commission's guidance to companies, and insights from the first cases reviewed under the FSR's merger tool.

The chapter is structured as follows: Sect. 2 outlines the FSR framework for concentrations, including the scope of transactions covered, notification thresholds, and the Commission's powers and procedure. Section 3 describes procedural developments and initial statistics from the early implementation of the FSR in merger cases, highlighting the volume of notifications and key trends observed. Section 4 explains the criteria for notifiable and reportable foreign financial contributions (FFCs) in concentration notifications, clarifying what information companies must provide about foreign financial contributions. Section 5 details the first phase II decision under the FSR in a concentration case—the conditional approval of Emirates Telecommunications Group (e&)'s acquisition of PPF Telecom—and its implications. Section 6 then surveys the guidance materials issued by the Commission and upcoming regulatory clarifications, including Q&A documents, policy briefs, and plans for future guidelines. The paper concludes with reflections on the significance of the FSR's concentration tool in preserving a level playing field in EU markets while the Commission continues to refine its approach through ongoing enforcement and guidance.

2 The FSR Framework for Concentrations

In the context of mergers, the FSR (with its Chapter 'Balancing') introduced a new review mechanism for certain concentrations, effectively adding a third layer of approval for some transactions alongside merger control and foreign investment screening.[4] The Commission considers this merger tool to be essential to ensure that companies do not gain undue competitive advantages from financial support from third countries when acquiring EU companies, and that post-merger competition is not distorted by such subsidies.

The FSR's concentration tool applies to transactions that meet specific thresholds. A concentration (such as a merger, acquisition of control, or the

[3] Council Regulation (EC) No 139/2004 of 20 January 2004 on the control of concentrations between undertakings (the EC Merger Regulation), 2004 OJ EU No. L 24/1.

[4] Regarding investment screening see the EU FDI Screening Regulation (Regulation (EU) 2019/452 of the European Parliament and of the Council of 19 March 2019 establishing a framework for the screening of foreign direct investments into the Union, 2019 OJ EU No. L 79I/1). For a most recent reform proposal see Commission document COM/2024/23 final; Börnsen and Pollakowsky (2024), p. 606.

creation of a full-function joint venture)[5] must be notified to the Commission if two cumulative conditions are satisfied (Article 20 (3) FSR):

(i) at least one of the merging undertakings, the acquired undertaking or the joint venture is established in the Union and generates an aggregate turnover in the Union of at least EUR 500 million; and
(ii) the relevant undertakings (Article 20 (3) b) FSR) were granted combined aggregate financial contributions of more than EUR 50 million from third countries in the three years preceding the conclusion of the agreement, the announcement of the public bid, or the acquisition of a controlling interest.

It must be added here, as explained in more detail in Sect. 4.2 that all foreign financial contributions count towards the 50 million threshold, even if not to be reported.[6]

These threshold criteria, set out in Article 20 (3) FSR, ensure that the regulation targets large transactions with significant foreign support. Notably, both conditions must be met. The requirement captures "EU-linked" concentrations of substantial size that have received considerable foreign financial contributions. If a transaction meets these thresholds, notification to the Commission is mandatory and the parties must await clearance under the FSR before completing the deal.

It is important that companies determine whether a prospective deal triggers these thresholds based on a self-assessment of the facts.[7] It can be expected that no "comfort letters" will be issued.[8] It is therefore up to undertakings to assess their EU turnover and foreign financial contributions received. In practice, this means that from the early stages of transaction planning, parties must gather data on any financial contributions from third countries to their group in the past three years. In case of doubt, undertakings are encouraged to engage in pre-notification discussions with the European Commission (addressed in Sect. 3) to verify whether a notification is required.[9] As mentioned above, the merger tool became applicable to transactions where the agreement was concluded, the public bid was announced, or a controlling interest was acquired on or after 13 July 2023 (Article 53 FSR), but the notification requirement started on 13 October 2023, meaning that in-scope

---

[5] Cf. Article 20 (1) and (2) FSR.

[6] Cf. Bauermeister (2022), p. 483; Weiß (2024), p. 83; Reinhold and Weck (2024), p. 25.

[7] For the consequences of the self-assessment see in this volume Weiß, The Notion of Foreign Financial Contribution and of Foreign Subsidy, section 3.2; Commission, FSR Policy Brief of 22 February 2024, available at https://competition-policy.ec.europa.eu/document/download/22197012-2036-4b1e-8b02-0eb8b2d6e666_en?filename=kdar24001enn_competition_FSR_brief_1_2024_100-days-of-FSR-notification-obligation.pdf; Soltész (2023), p. 176.

[8] Kamila Kaukiel, European Commission, DG COMP, during the conference 'The Foreign Subsidies Regulation Two Years On – Assessing Implementation' on 29 April 2025 in Brussels. Her statements of course do not bind the European Commission. On the absence of binding legal effect see also von Graevenitz (2025) p. 30 f.

[9] Cf. D'Almeida et al. (2024), p. 58.

transactions signed on or after that date cannot be completed without FSR clearance.

The FSR's review procedure for concentrations mirrors many aspects of merger control under the EUMR. Once a notifiable transaction is formally notified via the Form FS-CO (for more see below Sect. 4), a standstill obligation applies (Article 24 (1) FSR). The parties must suspend the implementation of the concentration until the Commission's review is complete and clearance is granted, or time for phase I lapsed.[10] Implementing a notifiable concentration without clearance could expose companies to fines (Article 26 (3) b) FSR) and the risk of invalidity (Article 24 (7) FSR). The Commission's review is divided into two phases. The initial Preliminary Review ("phase I") lasts up to 25 working days from notification.[11] By the end of this 25-working-day period, the Commission must decide whether the transaction warrants an In-depth investigation ("phase II"). If the Commission does not open an In-depth investigation within that time, the FSR review is deemed complete. According to Article 10 (4) FSR,[12] the Commission closes the preliminary review, informs the undertaking under investigation and in certain cases also the Member States. No formal decision will then be adopted. In such a case, the standstill obligation will cease to apply at the end of the preliminary phase and the transaction can proceed thereafter to completion. If, however, the Commission has concerns that the foreign subsidies in question may distort the internal market, it can decide to open an In-depth investigation according to Article 10 (3) FSR. An In-depth investigation under the FSR can last up to 90 working days, extendable by an additional 15 working days if the parties offer commitments to alleviate the Commission's concerns.[13] At the conclusion of an In-depth investigation, the Commission will adopt a decision with commitments, a no-objection decision or a decision prohibiting a concentration (Article 25 (3) FSR). The Commission clearly commits to speeding up the process. The fastest procedure took two months.[14]

In addition to the mandatory notification requirement, the FSR grants the European Commission "call in" powers to investigate other concentrations involving the suspicion of foreign subsidies, even if they fall below the notification thresholds.[15] Therefore, the Commission can call in a concentration for review on its own initiative if it suspects that a foreign subsidy may be involved. This ad hoc review serves as a safety net to capture potentially distortive subsidised concentrations that escape the thresholds. It is generally expected that this power will be used judiciously and only in mergers of major significance.[16] For example, if a transaction is significant in strategic sectors but just below the thresholds, or if information from

[10] Cf. Weiß (2024), p. 93.

[11] Cf. Articles 10 and 25 FSR.

[12] Cf. the reference to Article 10 in Article 25 (1) FSR.

[13] Cf. Article 25 (4), Article 24 (1) b) FSR.

[14] Kaukiel (fn. 8).

[15] Cf. Article 21 (5) FSR; see Weiß (2024), p. 91.

[16] Cf. Oberländer and Sickinger (2024), p. 108.

other sources (such as Member States or competitors) suggest that substantial foreign subsidies are involved, the Commission may require the companies to notify the deal *ex post*.[17] To date, the Commission has not publicly reported on the use of the call-in power in the first few months of FSR enforcement, focusing instead on dealing with the influx of mandatory notifications.[18] However, guidelines on how the Commission will exercise this call-in power are expected in due course (as discussed in Sect. 6), providing more clarity on the scenarios that might trigger the call-in power.

3 Initial Experiences with the Merger Tool: Initial Figures and Procedural Development

As mentioned before, the notification obligation for concentrations under the FSR became effective on 13 October 2023. According to data provided by the European Commission on the initial implementation, the uptake of the FSR notification regime has been significant. As of April 2025, 179 transactions were submitted for pre-notification review, out of which 145 cases proceeded to formal notification. This indicates that most deals that entered pre-notification eventually resulted in a full notification. In fact, the Commission noted that 134 cases were closed after the Preliminary investigation, while 8 cases were closed before formal notification. On average, since October 2023 the Commission has been receiving around 8 notified concentrations per month under the FSR.[19] This level of activity underscores the substantial impact of the new regime on transaction planning: many global deals involving EU businesses now routinely trigger an FSR assessment in parallel to merger control.[20] Many FSR filings to date correspond to transactions that were also subject to EUMR review and a few were under review by one or more EU Member State merger control authorities. Additionally, roughly one-third of the FSR-notified cases were also subject to at least one national foreign direct investment (FDI) screening procedure in the EU. The Commission has highlighted that these cases span a variety of sectors, reflecting that foreign subsidies can play a role across industries.[21] There also has been a notable presence of investment funds and private equity firms among the notifying parties.[22] Recognising this, the Commission's

[17] Ibid.

[18] Cf. Commission, FSR Policy Brief of 22 February 2024, available at https://competition-policy.ec.europa.eu/document/download/22197012-2036-4b1e-8b02-0eb8b2d6e666_en?filename=kdar24001enn_competition_FSR_brief_1_2024_100-days-of-FSR-notification-obligation.pdf.

[19] Data presented by Kaukiel (fn. 8).

[20] Cf. Zonta (2025), p. 7; D'Almeida et al. (2024), p. 61; Reinhold and Weck (2024), p. 34.

[21] See Commission, FSR Policy Brief of 22 February 2024 (fn. 18).

[22] Ibid; D'Almeida et al. (2024), p. 60.

implementing rules (discussed in Sect. 4.2) include specific provisions to streamline notifications for investment fund structures.

Hence, many high-value concentrations now trigger a trio of reviews: competition, FDI, and foreign subsidy.[23] The European Commission thus coordinates internally and with national authorities to the extent possible, to avoid contradictions. In managing this influx of cases, the European Commission's Directorate-General for Competition (DG Competition) set up a dedicated Foreign Subsidies Directorate to handle FSR matters (Directorate K).[24] Given the novelty and complexity of the FSR regime, the European Commission has placed great emphasis on pre-notification consultations and proper timing of notifications.[25] The goal is to ensure that filings are complete and timely, preventing delays in the review process that could hold up transactions. The unit has thus developed procedures to ensure efficient case allocation and review.[26] Companies are advised to approach the Commission sufficiently early before the planned formal notification of a concentration.[27] Typically, this outreach takes the form of submitting a case team allocation request (CTAR),[28] which briefly outlines the transaction and the parties involved, including an initial indication of the foreign financial contributions received. This triggers the swift assignment of a case team who will oversee the file. The Commission's case team then reviews this filing and engages in discussions to clarify any outstanding issues.[29] Pre-notification periods have been used effectively to iron out complexities, such that once formal notification is made, the 25-working-day preliminary review clock can start on the basis of a sufficiently complete filing. As mentioned before, of the 145 notified cases, 133 were cleared after the preliminary investigation with no In-depth investigation. Thus, the vast majority (around 92%) of notified concentrations were resolved at Phase I, with the European Commission not finding it necessary to open a detailed Phase II investigation.

---

[23] Börnsen and Pollakowsky (2024), p. 606.

[24] See Commission Organisation Chart, available at https://competition-policy.ec.europa.eu/document/download/82bca9b5-7a94-45bc-9d51-ae24c09cf71c_en?filename=organisation-chart-dg-comp_en.pdf.

[25] D'Almeida et al. (2024), p. 58.

[26] Ibid.

[27] Ibid.

[28] See Commission Website, available at https://competition-policy.ec.europa.eu/foreign-subsidies-regulation/practical-information_en; see also Weiß (2024), p. 91.

[29] Information about the procedure provided by Kaukiel (fn. 8).

4 Reporting of Foreign Financial Contributions in Concentrations

4.1 Disclosure of Foreign Financial Contributions

A cornerstone of the FSR's operation in merger cases is the requirement for companies to disclose foreign financial contributions (FFCs) in the notification. The scope of what needs to be reported is broad,[30] but the Commission in the notification forms annexed to its Implementing Regulation (EU) 2023/1441[31] has delineated between different categories of contributions, imposing a more detailed reporting for those considered most likely to distort competition. Understanding the criteria for the different requirements of reporting FFCs is crucial for compliance.

The term foreign financial contribution is defined expansively by the FSR.[32] It includes any transfer of funds or liabilities, any foregoing of revenue, or the provision and purchase of goods or services by a third country that provides a benefit to an undertaking. In practical terms, this can encompass grants, loans, loan guarantees, fiscal incentives, the setting off operating losses, compensation for financial burdens. In principle, all such contributions must be reported in the FS-CO form so that the Commission can assess them.

The European Commission distinguishes between foreign financial contributions "most likely to distort the internal market" according to Article 5 FSR and other foreign financial contributions.[33] Under the FSR Implementing Regulation's notification form (Form FS-CO),[34] if an individual foreign financial contribution falls within one of the Article 5 FSR categories and its amount is at least EUR 1 Million, it must be reported in detail in the notification. Each such financial contribution must be described with detailed information: the nature of the subsidy, the granting authority, the amount and date, the conditions attached, and the purpose or use of the funds.[35] For each such foreign financial contribution, the notification form requires an explanation as to whether, in the view of the notifying party, that contribution confers a benefit and is hence a foreign subsidy and whether it could impact

---

[30] Cf. Bauermeister (2022), p. 483; D'Almeida et al. (2024), p. 57; Soltész (2023), p. 176.

[31] Implementing Regulation (EU) 2023/1441 of 10 July 2023 on detailed arrangements for the conduct of proceedings by the Commission pursuant to Regulation (EU) 2022/2560 of the European Parliament and of the Council on foreign subsidies distorting the internal market, 2023 OJ EU No. L 177/1 (FSR Implementing Regulation); i.c.w. Corrigendum 2023 OJ EU L 2414; D'Almeida et al. (2024), p. 57.

[32] Cf. Article 3 (2) FSR. For more on this see in this volume Weiß, The Notion of Foreign Financial Contribution and of Foreign Subsidy; D'Almeida et al. (2024), p. 57.

[33] Cf. Schwendinger and Vollert (2023), p. 130.

[34] Annex I to the FSR Implementing Regulation.

[35] Cf. Section 5.2 of Annex I to the FSR Implementing Regulation; Schwendinger and Vollert (2023), p. 130; Reinhold and Weck (2024), p. 26.

the competition in the internal market.[36] This essentially invites the parties to provide their own assessment of the contribution's nature and potential distortion, which the Commission will then evaluate. It is in the parties' interest to argue, where possible, that certain contributions are either not foreign subsidies or are not capable of distorting the internal market.

Not all foreign financial contributions above EUR 1 Million require full details in the notification. Those that do not fall under the likely distortive categories (i.e. outside Article 5 FSR) but are still significant must be reported in a more summary manner.[37] The Commission's notification form requires the notifying parties to prepare a summary table of other foreign financial contributions.[38] In this table, the contributions can be aggregated by type and by granting country, with more limited information.[39] The rationale is to reduce the administrative burden. The FS-CO instructs that only certain totals and basic descriptions are needed for these "other" contributions. However, there is a materiality threshold here as well. The FS-CO specifies that only those third countries where the total aggregate amount of contributions over the past three years is EUR 45 Million or more need to be included in the summary table. This EUR 45 Million per country rule acts as a further filter to avoid cluttering the notification with trivial information, focusing the Commission's attention on substantial flows of foreign financial support. For the summary table contributions, the information is more cursory, often just the total amount per third country and broad category of contribution—without requiring a benefit analysis for each.[40] The Commission retains the right, though, to request additional information on any financial contributions, even those below thresholds, if during the review it suspects something potentially distortive was omitted or needs scrutiny. The FSR allows the Commission to look beyond what is reported if necessary. In practice, the Commission used requests for information to clarify certain contributions and, in one notable case, to dig deeper into a financing arrangement that was initially presented as being at market terms (the e&/PPF case, discussed in Sect. 5).

4.2 *Exceptions from Reporting*

Additionally, the FS-CO carves out certain types of financial contributions that are deemed non-problematic and thus exempted even from the summary reporting. These typically include small contributions under EUR 1 Million, ordinary

[36] Cf. Section 6 ff., of Annex I to FSR Implementing Regulation.

[37] Cf. Section 9 of Annex I to the FSR Implementing Regulation. See also the Commission's infographic on FSR notification, available at https://competition-policy.ec.europa.eu/document/download/772070e7-7512-45d3-9792-7af65e0083d4_en?filename=2023_FSR_notifications.pdf; Schwendinger and Vollert (2023), p. 130; Reinhold and Weck (2024), p. 26.

[38] Section 9 Table 1 A. of Annex I to the FSR Implementing Regulation.

[39] Ibid.

[40] Cf. Schwendinger and Vollert (2023), p. 130.

provision and purchase of goods and services on market terms (except financial services), and general measures like deferrals of taxes or double taxation tax reliefs.[41] By excluding these from reporting, the Commission again aims to concentrate on genuine subsidies rather than incidental or broadly available benefits.

One practical complication in reporting subsidies arises when the acquirer is an investment fund or a legal entity controlled by or via an investment fund. Such entities may have numerous portfolio companies that also receive various subsidies, even if those portfolio companies are not part of the transaction at hand.[42] Requiring disclosure of all those contributions could be unduly burdensome and not particularly relevant if the fund's other portfolios are unrelated. The Commission recognized this and included another exemption for investment funds in the Form FS-CO.[43] When such funds engage in acquisitions of control or create joint ventures, they are not required to include foreign financial contributions granted to other investment funds managed by the same investment company, as long as the following conditions are cumulatively met:[44]

(i) The fund which controls the acquiring entity must be subject to Directive 2011/61/EU of the European Parliament and of the Council on Alternative Investment Fund Managers[45] or to an equivalent third country legislation in terms of prudential, organisational and conduct rules, including requirements aimed to protect investors; and
(ii) The economic and commercial transactions between the fund which controls the acquiring entity and other investment funds (and the companies controlled by these funds) managed by the same investment company are non-existent or limited.

In this regard, one must provide the Commission with evidence of any of such economic and commercial transactions which may have taken place in the three years prior to the conclusion of the agreement, the announcement of the public bid, or the acquisition of a controlling interest. Economic and commercial transactions include but are not limited to the sale of assets (including ownership in companies), loans, credit lines, or guarantees. This carve-out is intended to significantly lighten the compliance load for investment funds and legal entities controlled by or via an investment fund.[46]

---

[41] Section 9 Table 1 B. of Annex I to the FSR Implementing Regulation; Schwendinger and Vollert (2023), p. 130.

[42] Cf. D'Almeida et al. (2024), p. 60.

[43] Section 9 Table 1 B. No. 7 of Annex I to the FSR Implementing Regulation.

[44] Section 9 Table 1 B. No. 7 a) and b) of Annex I to the FSR Implementing Regulation.

[45] Directive 2011/61/EU of the European Parliament and of the Council of 8 June 2011 on Alternative Investment Fund Managers and amending Directives 2003/41/EC and 2009/65/EC and Regulations (EC) No 1060/2009 and (EU) No 1095/2010, 2011 OJ EU No. L 174/1.

[46] Cf. D'Almeida et al. (2024), p. 60.

It is also worth noting a distinction that sometimes caused confusion initially. All foreign financial contributions count towards the EUR 50 Million threshold to determine if a notification is required in the first place.[47] Even if some contributions are exempt from reporting in the form, they still must be counted in aggregate to see if the threshold for triggering the FSR notification obligation applies.[48] The European Commission clarified in its guidance[49] that companies cannot exclude certain subsidies when calculating the EUR 50 Million just because those would not be reported. The threshold assessment is a separate exercise and must consider all financial contributions in the three-year period to the undertakings concerned.

4.3 Commission Practice

The requirement to report FFCs was surely one of the more challenging aspects for companies in early cases. Many undertakings had to institute internal data collection processes to identify any interactions with third countries.[50] The Commission can be perceived to have been understanding in this learning phase, allowing parties some flexibility to correct their FFC lists during pre-notification. Over time, as companies become more familiar with the categories and thresholds, compliance in gathering FFC information is expected to become more routine. Finally, the FSR's reporting regime for foreign financial contributions in concentrations requires careful preparation by notifying parties.[51] The system of detailed notifying for high-risk subsidies and summary reporting for others in the Commission's view strikes a balance between thorough disclosure and manageability. The Commission's initial enforcement has reinforced the importance of accuracy in these submissions, while also showing some pragmatism to focus on what truly matters.

[47] Cf. Question 3 of the FAQ FSR, available at https://competition-policy.ec.europa.eu/foreign-subsidies-regulation/questions-and-answers_en#procedural-and-jurisdictional-issues.

[48] Cf. Börnsen and Pollakowsky (2024), p. 604; Bauermeister (2022), p. 483; Reinhold and Weck (2024), p. 25.

[49] Cf. FAQ FSR, available at https://competition-policy.ec.europa.eu/foreign-subsidies-regulation/questions-and-answers_en#procedural-and-jurisdictional-issues.

[50] Cf. D'Almeida et al. (2024), p. 57; Soltész (2023), p. 176.

[51] Ibid.

5 The First FSR Decision: *e&/PPF Telecom*

The European Commission's first final decision under the FSR concentration tool was rendered on 24 September 2024,[52] conditionally approving the acquisition of PPF Telecom Group B.V.'s telecommunications businesses in several Central and Eastern European countries by Emirates Telecommunications Group Company PJSC (trading as "e&"). This case is instructive as it demonstrates how the Commission applies the FSR to a transaction, from identifying foreign subsidies to imposing remedies. It also illustrates how the FSR's two-stage distortion analysis, first establishing that a foreign subsidy improves the beneficiary's competitive position and then that it negatively affects competition, constitutes a clear departure from the more formalistic State-aid presumption, amounting to a paradigm shift.[53]

The transaction involved *e&*, a major telecom operator based in the United Arab Emirates (UAE),[54] acquiring a controlling stake in the telecom subsidiaries of PPF Telecom Group in Bulgaria, Hungary, Serbia, and Slovakia.[55] The value of the transaction was approximately EUR 2.2 billion, with potential earn-out payments up to EUR 350 million, making it a significant foreign investment into the EU telecom sector. e& is controlled and majority-owned by the sovereign wealth fund Emirates Investment Authority (EIA),[56] which meant that e& potentially benefited from UAE state support. The target businesses were established telecom operators in their respective EU Member States, collectively serving millions of customers, and thus economically important in those markets.

Because of the size of the target's EU operations, generating an aggregate turnover of EUR 1.8 billion[57] and indications that e& had received substantial financing from UAE state-linked entities, the FSR notification thresholds were met, and the parties notified the transaction to the Commission. The case also required EU Merger Regulation notification and was presumably subject to various national approvals.

During the initial 25 working day phase I investigation, the Commission identified several foreign financial contributions to e& that merited scrutiny. The most important of these were an unlimited state guarantee[58] and financing arrangements for the acquisition,[59] including a term loan provided by a consortium of banks, many of which were UAE state-owned banks. Especially the unlimited state guarantee exemplifies the FSR's "most-likely-distortive" subsidies (Article 5 (1) FSR),

[52] Commission, Decision of 24 September 2024, FS.100011. A public version of the decision is available at https://ec.europa.eu/competition/foreign_subsidies/cases/202514/FS_100011_979.pdf.

[53] See Hornkohl and Mattiolo (2025), p. 12.

[54] Commission, Decision of 24 September 2024, FS.100011, para. 2.

[55] Commission, Decision of 24 September 2024, FS.100011, para. 4.

[56] Commission, Decision of 24 September 2024, FS.100011, para. 2.

[57] Commission, Decision of 24 September 2024, FS.100011, para. 9.

[58] Commission, Decision of 24 September 2024, FS.100011, para. 77 f.

[59] Commission, Decision of 24 September 2024, FS.100011, para. 51 f.

triggering a presumption of distortion and shifting the evidential burden to the beneficiary.[60] Additionally, there were possibly some grants or favorable conditions related to e&'s activities in the UAE. The Commission's preliminary analysis raised concerns under Article 3 (2) and Article 5 FSR, as an unlimited guarantee is explicitly one of the problematic subsidy types, and a preferential loan for acquisition could be a subsidy directly facilitating the concentration.

By the end of the preliminary investigation, the European Commission opened an in-depth investigation (phase II) on 10 June 2024, within the initial deadline, signaling that it found the foreign subsidies in question could potentially distort the internal market and that further analysis was required. This move made the e&/PPF case the first-ever phase II under the FSR concentration tool. In this phase, the European Commission looked closely at two main questions: first, whether the financial contributions identified did in fact constitute foreign subsidies; and second, if so, whether they distorted the acquisition process or future competition.

On the first question, e& contended that the term loan received for funding the deal was on market terms. The financing included tranches in different currencies—notably some tranches in UAE Dirham (AED) provided largely by UAE public banks, and a tranche in USD provided by a private international bank.[61] e& provided comparative analyses showing that the loan terms were similar across the tranches and aligned with a previous loan where public and private banks participated equally.[62] This evidence was used to argue that the loan did not confer a benefit, and thus was not a foreign subsidy. After reviewing the data, the Commission agreed that the term loan did not confer a benefit.[63]

Regarding the unlimited State guarantee, the Commission found that under UAE law (Federal Decree-Law No. 9 of 2016) e&, as a partially state-owned enterprise, was not subject to normal bankruptcy rules unless its Articles of Association (AoA) submitted it to such rules. e& had not opted in, implying that creditors could rely on the UAE state's backing for e&'s obligations. The Commission determined that this situation amounted to an implicit unlimited guarantee by the UAE state, which is a clear example of a foreign subsidy conferring a significant benefit, as indicated in Article 5 FSR, and is specific to that company.[64] e& effectively enjoyed a lower cost of debt and higher creditworthiness thanks to this guarantee, a benefit not available on the market. Thus, the Commission deemed this a foreign subsidy that could distort competition.

With the foreign subsidy identified, the Commission then assessed distortive effects. It concluded that this guarantee did not distort the acquisition process

[60] Cf. Hornkohl and Mattiolo (2025), p. 14.

[61] Commission, Decision of 24 September 2024, FS.100011, para. 51, 52.

[62] Commission, Decision of 24 September 2024, FS.100011, para. 53.

[63] Commission, Decision of 24 September 2024, FS.100011, para. 71.

[64] Commission, Decision of 24 September 2024, FS.100011, para. 94 with reference to State aid rules.

itself.[65] Evidence showed that e& was the sole bidder for PPF's assets; no competitive auction was undermined. Moreover, e& had substantial financial resources and likely could have financed the deal even without the guarantee. Therefore, the Commission did not find a distortion in the acquisition phase.

However, the Commission identified likely distortions in the post-acquisition period.[66] The unlimited guarantee effectively gave e& (and thus the acquired businesses) an extraordinary financial safety net. The European Commission reasoned that this could artificially enhance the merged entity's ability to finance its activities in the internal market, making it "risk-indifferent" in undertaking investments or market strategies. Concretely, with a state guarantee, e& could secure financing or capital at more favorable terms without the same risk constraints a normal company would face. Competitors without such backing would be at a disadvantage. The Commission was concerned that this would disrupt the level playing field in the telecom markets of the countries where PPF operated by enabling e& to potentially outspend or undercut rivals. These findings meant that while in the Commission's view the merger itself raised no classic issues, the FSR dimension revealed a serious concern purely related to the foreign subsidy advantage after the transaction.

To resolve the identified distortion, the Commission and e& discussed a set of commitments. The guiding principle was to remove or neutralize the unlimited guarantee and its effects on the merged entity's EU operations. This illustrates that remedies are the other side of the coin to the distortion test, calibrated to extinguish the identified distortion.[67] The commitments that e& offered and the Commission accepted were:[68]

- Amending e&'s Articles of Association (AoA) to align with ordinary bankruptcy law: This meant e& would formally opt into the standard UAE bankruptcy regime, thereby removing the implicit unlimited State guarantee. By doing so, e& would no longer enjoy exemption from bankruptcy.
- Prohibition on certain financing of EU operations by the UAE state or e&: Specifically, e& and its controlling fund (EIA) committed not to use their resources to finance the acquired PPF businesses in the EU in a way that would mean subsidization. This meant that significant new injections of capital or loans from the parent into the EU subsidiaries would be prohibited, except for emergency business needs or non-EU expansions.
- Notification of future acquisitions to the Commission: e& must inform the Commission of any future M&A transactions in the EU telecom sector even if those deals would not meet the FSR thresholds.

---

[65] Commission, Decision of 24 September 2024, FS.100011, para. 285.

[66] Commission, Decision of 24 September 2024, FS.100011, para. 287 f.

[67] Hornkohl and Mattiolo (2025), p. 21, Weiß (2025), p. 110.

[68] Commission, Decision of 24 September 2024, FS.100011, para. 387. Insofar, one might still contest the legality of the Commission's decision under Article 19 FSR requiring the assessment to be limited "to the concentration concerned", see Weiß (2025), p. 114. But see Oberländer and Sickinger (2024), p. 105.

These commitments were set to remain in force for a minimum of 10 years, ensuring a long-term solution. The Commission evaluated that these measures were sufficient and proportionate to remedy the identified distortion. Aligning the AoA essentially cancels the problematic foreign subsidy (the guarantee)—a direct fix. The financing prohibition prevents any workaround that could reintroduce subsidy effects (like funneling cheap capital to the target). And the notification requirement gives the Commission oversight to prevent circumvention or new issues.

With these commitments, the Commission on 24 September 2024 granted conditional clearance to the e&/PPF transaction by adopting a commitment decision under Article 7 (2), Article 11 (3) i.c.w. Article 25 (3) a) FSR. The decision was the first ever under the FSR for a concentration. It confirmed that the Commission is willing to accept behavioral remedies in order to neutralize foreign subsidies, and that such remedies can even reach into corporate governance and ongoing conduct. The e&/PPF decision set an important precedent for how the Commission might handle future cases. It showed that the Commission will analyze whether a financing arrangement is a genuine subsidy or market-based. In this case, the Commission did not overreach and focused on the unlimited guarantee. This demonstrates a careful approach, giving comfort that the Commission will differentiate real distortions from other. The decision underscored that even if a subsidy does not affect the merger transaction price or outcome, it can still be problematic by affecting post-merger market behavior. This broad view of "distortion" means companies cannot assume they are safe just because they paid fair value. If they bring a subsidy-fueled advantage into the market, the Commission may act. The types of remedies accepted indicate the Commission's flexibility. The commitments basically remove the advantage rather than altering the market structure of the deal. In competition merger control, remedies often involve selling parts of the business to keep competition. Here, the remedy was to alter the conditions under which the merged business operates. This is a different toolkit. For other foreign-subsidised investors, the case is a warning that the Commission can and will impose constraints if necessary. An unlimited guarantee like e&'s is rare, but many state-backed firms could face similar scrutiny of implicit support.

Procedurally, the case was completed ahead of the statutory in-depth investigation deadline. This indicates the Commission can manage complex subsidy cases efficiently, likely aided by the parties' cooperation in offering remedies early enough. It also suggests that having commitments in phase II does not necessarily lead to using the full assessment period.

After adopting the decision, the Commission took the step of publishing a Staff Working Document, which provided a public version of the decision's reasoning.[69] This publication, roughly six months after the decision, was eagerly awaited as it

[69] Available at https://ec.europa.eu/competition/foreign_subsidies/cases/202514/FS_100011_979.pdf.

sheds light on the Commission's analytical approach in detail.[70] This transparency is crucial for companies to understand how future cases might be treated.

Thus, the e&/PPF Telecom case exemplifies the Commission's commitment under the FSR to ensuring foreign subsidies do not skew competition in Europe. The case was resolved with targeted remedies that directly addressed the source of distortion, allowing the investment to proceed while safeguarding the internal market's level playing field. In the Commission's view, it balanced the EU's openness to foreign investment with the need to prevent undue advantages. As the first of its kind, this decision sets a precedent that will inform the Commission's handling of subsequent FSR cases and serves as a guide for companies receiving foreign subsidies on how to structure their deals and possible remedies. It has also been observed that the detailed, indicator-based analysis required by the FSR increases informational and procedural complexity for undertakings, underlining the need for clearer and more granular Commission guidance.[71]

6 Guidance and Upcoming Developments

Alongside case enforcement, the European Commission has been actively providing guidance and clarifications to help businesses navigate the new FSR regime for concentrations.[72] Recognizing that the FSR is a novel instrument, the Commission's aim has been to increase transparency, predictability, and understanding of both procedural and substantive aspects.

Early in the implementation, the Commission published a detailed Questions and Answers (Q&A) space[73] on its competition policy website addressing common queries about the FSR. This Q&A covers topics such as procedural and jurisdictional issues, notification timing, the interpretation of key terms, and technical points regarding the notification forms. The Q&A format allows the Commission to update and expand the guidance as new questions arise. These clarifications are invaluable for companies in doubt about whether they fall under the regulation or how to compile their notifications. The Commission has encouraged parties to consult this living Q&A as a first step when assessing FSR obligations.

In 2024, the Commission issued a FSR policy brief[74] which provided insight into its developing approach on certain substantive issues. While not legally binding,

[70] Cf. Hornkohl and Mattiolo (2025), p. 1.

[71] Cf. Hornkohl and Mattiolo (2025), p. 22.

[72] Ibid.

[73] Cf. FAQ FSR, available at https://competition-policy.ec.europa.eu/foreign-subsidies-regulation/questions-and-answers_en#procedural-and-jurisdictional-issues.

[74] Commission, FSR Policy Brief of 22 February 2024, available at https://competition-policy.ec.europa.eu/document/download/22197012-2036-4b1e-8b02-0eb8b2d6e666_en?filename=kdar24001enn_competition_FSR_brief_1_2024_100-days-of-FSR-notification-obligation.pdf.

such clarifications help companies anticipate the Commission's analysis and possibly prepare arguments or evidence for a positive outcome.

The Commission has also provided templates and administrative guidance to streamline interactions. Templates for documents such as the power of attorney[75] (for authorizing legal representatives in FSR proceedings) and the Case Team Allocation Request (CTAR)[76] have been made available. The template CTAR form helps notifying parties include all necessary preliminary information to expedite assignment of a case number and team. There are also templates for the notification forms (FS-CO for concentrations and FS-PP for procurement) with instructions.[77] By standardizing these, the Commission reduces back-and-forth on basic formatting issues and ensures submissions contain what is needed from the outset.

The Commission adopted the FSR Implementing Regulation, which, inter alia, contains the notification forms and detailed procedural rules. This regulation elaborates the procedural rights, time calculations, and information requirements under the FSR. It essentially operationalizes the FSR's provisions. The Implementing Regulation serves as a key reference for practitioners, and the Commission itself refers to it in its Q&A for precise points. Companies are advised to familiarize themselves with Annex I (Form FS-CO) and the accompanying instructions to ensure compliance.

As reported above, the Commission published the non-confidential version of its first FSR decision (*e&/PPF Telecom*) in April 2025. This publication is a form of guidance by example. It shows the reasoning in an actual case and thus provides precedent. It also adds weight to the Commission's interpretation of various FSR provisions, which, absent court rulings, becomes a point of reference.

Looking ahead, the FSR itself envisions that the Commission will issue more formal Guidelines on certain aspects. The Commission has announced that it plans to adopt Guidelines under the Foreign Subsidies Regulation by 13 January 2026.[78] These forthcoming guidelines will likely consolidate and expand upon the interim clarifications given so far. They are expected to cover, among other things:[79]

(i) guidance on distortion, i.e. how the Commission determines when a foreign subsidy distorts the internal market.
(ii) guidance on the balancing Test, i.e. whether positive effects counterbalance the distortive effects of the foreign subsidy; and

[75] Model Power of Attorney for Notifications available at https://competition-policy.ec.europa.eu/foreign-subsidies-regulation/practical-information_en.

[76] Case Team Allocation Request Document available at https://competition-policy.ec.europa.eu/foreign-subsidies-regulation/practical-information_en.

[77] The FS-CO and FS-PP can be found in the Annex of the FSR Implementing Regulation.

[78] See Commission, Commission launches consultations on guidelines under the Foreign Subsidies Regulation, Press Release of 05 March 2025, available at https://ec.europa.eu/commission/presscorner/detail/en/ip_25_685.

[79] Ibid.

(iii) guidance on call-in powers, i.e. criteria or scenarios in which the Commission would exercise its power to require notification of a non-notifiable deal.

The deadline of January 2026 indicates that the Commission is allowing itself approximately two years of enforcement experience before finalizing these guidelines. During this time, it will have reviewed more cases across potentially different sectors, which will help shape the content of the guidelines. These guidelines will be presented as a formal communication from the Commission, and will be subject to consultation with stakeholders before they are finalized. In this context, the Commission has been actively engaging with various stakeholders, including law firms, industry associations, and Member State authorities. A Call for Evidence, which remained open for feedback until 2 April 2025, allowed stakeholders to provide input on areas that may be unclear or problematic in practice.[80]

In conclusion, the Commission has complemented the FSR enforcement with a proactive approach to guidance. Through Q&As, policy briefs, templates, and planned guidelines, it seeks to make the FSR as clear as possible for companies engaging in M&A activities. Upcoming guidelines by 2026 will further solidify the framework and incorporate lessons from the initial wave of cases.

7 Conclusion

The FSR has introduced a new paradigm in EU merger control by addressing the influence of foreign subsidies on concentrations. From the perspective of the European Commission, the first phase of implementation has been pivotal in operationalizing this framework and ensuring its effectiveness in safeguarding the internal market. The European Commission's experience so far demonstrates that the FSR's concentration tool is so far functioning as intended. Major concentration with substantial foreign state support are being identified and reviewed, most are being cleared expeditiously when no harm is found, and in at least one case, significant commitments were secured to neutralize a distortion, thereby protecting fair competition without blocking the investment.

Several key observations can be drawn from the early application of the FSR in concentrations. First, the notification requirement has captured a broad range of transactions, and companies have generally complied by notifying where required.[81] The Commission, through diligent pre-notification engagement, has facilitated a smooth filing process, integrating this new review into the transaction timeline

[80] Ibid.

[81] See Commission, FSR Policy Brief of 22 February 2024, available at https://competition-policy.ec.europa.eu/document/download/22197012-2036-4b1e-8b02-0eb8b2d6e666_en?filename=kdar24001enn_competition_FSR_brief_1_2024_100-days-of-FSR-notification-obligation.pdf.

alongside merger control and FDI screenings.[82] The statistics show robust filing activity (with around 179 cases notified in the first 18 months) but also an efficient clearance of the bulk of cases at phase I, indicating a focused approach on matters of substance. Second, the merger tool's design has been validated in practice. Undertakings have mostly been able to navigate the reporting requirements by disclosing relevant foreign financial contributions in the required detail, while the Commission has filtered out irrelevant contributions, concentrating on those potentially problematic. The case e&/PPF highlights the Commission's capacity to analyze complex financial arrangements and to demand remedies that directly remove distortive foreign subsidies from the equation.[83] Third, the Commission's active guidance and planned future rules indicate that the FSR is a living instrument that will continue to be refined. The upcoming guidelines will further elucidate the Commission's assessment criteria and enforcement policy, providing stakeholders with greater certainty.[84] By around 2026, with more cases and formal guidance in place, the FSR framework in concentrations will become more mature and embedded in M&A practice.

From a policy standpoint, the Commission's implementation of the FSR in merger cases reinforces the EU's commitment to a level playing field. It complements existing tools: where merger control keeps check on market structure, state aid review on competition and FDI screening on public order, the FSR adds an economic fairness check related to internal market distortions caused by foreign subsidies. Together, these ensure that concentrations in the EU proceed on commercial merit rather than distorted by third country subsidies. In conclusion, the FSR's initial chapter in the field of concentrations has been one of institution-building, learning, and decisive action when needed. The FSR in concentrations thus represents a significant evolution in EU competition and market regulation—one aimed at preserving fair competition in an era of global economic interplay, and one of which one can hope that the Commission is committed to carrying out in a transparent, balanced, and effective manner.

References

Bauermeister T (2022) A tool to investigate M&A transactions with regard to foreign financial contributions. Zeitschrift für Europarechtliche Studien ZEuS 25:477–486

Börnsen N, Pollakowsky O (2024) Ein Jahr FSR-Anmeldepflicht: Übersicht, Erfahrungen und Hinweise. Neue Zeitschrift für Kartellrecht NZKart 12:603–608

D'Almeida C, Molestina J, Pommies C (2024) Money falling from the sky? M&A reviews under the EU's Foreign Subsidies Regulation. Antitrust 38:56–62

[82] Cf. Börnsen and Pollakowsky (2024), p. 606.

[83] Cf. Hornkohl and Mattiolo (2025), p. 21.

[84] See Commission, Commission launches consultations on guidelines under the Foreign Subsidies Regulation, Press Release of 05 March 2025, available at https://ec.europa.eu/commission/presscorner/detail/en/ip_25_685.

Hornkohl L, Mattiolo P (2025) The concept of 'Distortion in the Internal Market' in the Foreign Subsidies Regulation – from the legacy of state aid law to the first case practice. ESTALI Spring Forum. Available at SSRN: https://ssrn.com/abstract=5247472: 1–23

Oberländer I, Sickinger C (2024) Commission calling: "Call-In" of transactions under the Foreign Subsidies Regulation – uncertainty and unpredictable risk? Zeitschrift für Wettbewerbsrecht ZWeR 22:103–114

Reinhold P, Weck T (2024) Welcome to the Jungle! Identification of Foreign Subsidies under the new EU Foreign Subsidies Regulation. Eur State Aid Law Q EStAL 23:22–34

Schwendinger G, Vollert CM (2023) Durchführungsverordnung zu Foreign Subsidies Regulation. Zeitschrift für das Recht der Außenwirtschaft, Sanktionen und Auslandsinvestitionen ZASA 1:129–130

Soltész U (2023) Foreign subsidies control: a bureaucratic monster? Eur State Aid Law Q EStAL 22:175–180

von Graevenitz A (2025) Drittstaatliche Subventionen im Fokus der Europäischen Kommission - Die FSR - Verordnung (EU) 2022/2560 über den Binnenmarkt verzerrende drittstaatliche Subventionen, 2nd edn. https://doi.org/10.48701/opus4-474

Weiß W (2024) The regulation on foreign subsidies distorting the internal market. A path to a level playing field? Springer Nature, Cham

Weiß W (2025) Das Konzept der Wettbewerbsverzerrung in der Drittstaatensubventionsverordnung. Neue Zeitschrift für Kartellrecht NZKart 13:108–115

Zonta E (2025) From economic security to legal uncertainty: exploring the impact of the FDI screening regulation and foreign subsidies regulation on mergers and acquisitions in the EU. J Eur Compet Law Pract 16:1–12

Sara-Alexandra Raitner Ass. Iur., LL.M, is research assistant at the Chair of Public Law, EU Law and Public International Law at the German University of Administrative Sciences Speyer.

Wolfgang Weiß is Professor of Law and holds the Chair of Public Law, EU Law and Public International Law at the German University of Administrative Sciences Speyer.

The FSR in Concentrations: A View from Legal Practice

Harald Weiß

Abstract This Chapter offers a practitioner's perspective on the application of the Foreign Subsidies Regulation to concentrations, reflecting on early trends, practical experiences and challenges faced by companies and their legal advisors. It starts with the observation that after two years on, there is a huge discrepancy between the case load anticipated by the Commission and the actual numbers. After some introductory reflections on this phenomenon, including its possible causes and implications, the Chapter focusses on the practical aspects encountered in the various stages or "key moments" of a typical FSR case from a legal practitioner's perspective: From assessing the FSR filing thresholds over preparing the FSR filing, assisting undertakings in the FSR data collection, and navigating them through the (pre-) notification and FSR review process before DG COMP. It contrasts FSR procedures with EU Merger Regulation practice, identifying not only several parallels but also important differences, such as the lack of a simplified procedure, the absence of clearance decisions at the end of phase I, and the possibility for the Commission to decide based on the facts available. The Chapter critically assesses the burdensome data collection requirements, including the broad scope of foreign financial contributions (FFCs) to be detected across global group entities. Drawing on legal practice, the Chapter reflects common industry frustrations and argues for reform. Suggested improvements include the introduction of a simplified procedure, clearer guidance on the Commission's call-in powers, and a more consistent approach regarding the exceptions from FFC reporting requirements, e.g. regarding tax measures and financial services. This contribution provides a grounded analysis of how the FSR's concentration tool operates in practice and outlines practical reforms to streamline compliance, increase legal certainty and reduce red tape.

H. Weiß (✉)
Gleiss Lutz, Brussels, Belgium
e-mail: harald.weiss@gleisslutz.com

W. Weiß et al. (eds.), *The Foreign Subsidies Regulation*, European Yearbook of International Economic Law, https://doi.org/10.1007/978-3-032-23415-5_8

1 Preliminary Remarks

A lot has been said—and written—about the general design of the Foreign Subsidies Regulation, including in this book. This Chapter will not repeat these basics again, but focus on selected practical aspects—in particular: experiences made and challenges faced—in the various stages or "key moments" of a typical FSR merger case from a legal practitioner's perspective: From assessing the FSR filing thresholds over assisting the FSR data collection, preparing the FSR filing, and navigating the parties through the pre-notification and FSR review process before DG COMP. The conclusion will summarize some ideas for potential improvements. For a more general overview about the legal framework of the FSR's merger tool, we refer the reader to the previous Chapter.[1]

1.1 The Big Picture: And How to Read It?

Before turning towards the different stages of an FSR case in practice, it seems to be worthwhile to briefly pause and reflect on the initial figures and statistics which were also presented in the previous Chapter of this book. The significant discrepancy between the case load anticipated by the Commission and the actual numbers that can be derived from the DG COMP case registry is not only remarkable, but also raises questions. Due to the overly wide scope of the notification threshold—which links the filing requirement to the formalistic concept of foreign financial contributions (FFCs) rather than looking at the substantive issue of foreign subsidies (see Sect. 2.2 below)—there are (unsurprisingly) much more cases than initially expected by the Commission. While the Commission anticipated around 30 notifications per year, the actual volume is three times higher, whereas at the same time the personnel resources at DG COMP appear to be roughly three times less than what was initially hoped for.[2] So: Three times more cases for three times less staff members.

This obviously raises the question of how the new system can work in practice. The fact that the new merger notification regime actually works is difficult to deny. From experiences made in several FSR filings as well as regular contacts with DG COMP through the Q&A tool, it must be acknowledged that the Commission has been quite responsive. So, the situation does not seem to have caused major delays to M&A deals. The fact that the Commission has not yet made use in a single instance from its call-in power under Article 21 (5) FSR (see Sect. 2.3 below) suggests that the personnel shortage may affect its capacity to review M&A deals at

[1] See also, for instance, von Köckritz et al. (2023); Weiß (2024).

[2] See European Commission, Staff Working Document – Impact Assessment Accompanying the Proposal for a Regulation of the European Parliament and of the Council on foreign subsidies distorting the internal market, COM(2021) 223 final, Annex 3, section 2.

its own initiative. The question, however, remains as to how it is possible for the Commission to stem a case load so much higher than expected with an FSR team so much smaller. There are obviously several factors which may come into play here, including the fact that DG COMP officials are notoriously very hardworking people, and it is also fair to assume that, especially in the early days, DG COMP's FSR units will have received support from other units and directorates, if needed. In addition, on a more structural level, it is certainly also relevant that the vast majority of the reported FSR cases appear to have been, on substance, either entirely unproblematic or, at least at first glance, clearly no candidates for an intervention.

While the substantive assessment of an FSR case—including its characterization as a "difficult case" or not—will of course always depend on the circumstances of the case and what kind of potentially distortive foreign subsidies the parties may have received (i.e. information which is often not in the public domain), it seems clear that there are especially two types of M&A deals which are likely to draw a closer scrutiny: First, transactions involving a Chinese buyer—it is indeed an open secret that, despite the Commission's repeated reassurances that the FSR applies in a non-discriminative way to all countries (which is correct), its creation was specially triggered by the fear of subsidized Chinese companies flooding the internal market.[3] Second, transactions involving a non-EU state owned enterprise (SOE), which almost by definition, due to its close links with a foreign government, is likely to have privileged access to state resources (e.g. in the form of state guarantees). From that perspective, it is remarkable that, as things currently stand, around 90% of the notified M&A deals involved privately owned purchasers from the EU, the UK and the US. It appears that, to date, only a handful of deals were filed by Chinese purchasers (each of them cleared in "phase I" so far),[4] and another handful of notifications involved non-EU SOEs as purchaser.[5] Two of these non-EU SOE cases (each with purchasers from the UAE) led to the first "phase II" investigations in a merger context and resulted into the first two —and to date: only—published FSR merger decisions (FS.100011, FS.100156).

Does this mean that FSR does not achieve its objectives because, instead of giving the Commission the opportunity to scrutinize M&A deals involving companies from countries which are suspected for heavily subsidizing their businesses, it hits mainly European and US companies with the additional red tape and the far-reaching data collection burden associated with FSR filings (see below Sect. 4)? This is certainly one way to see things—and at least to some extent probably also true. A different interpretation should however be considered as well:

[3] The Commission's Impact Assessment mentions "China" not less than 101 (!) times.

[4] FS. 100045 – Haier/CCR, see https://competition-cases.ec.europa.eu/cases/FS.100045; FS.100159 – Luxshare/Pierer/Leoni, see https://competition-cases.ec.europa.eu/cases/FS.100159; FS.100229 - DSBJ/GMD, see https://competition-cases.ec.europa.eu/cases/FS.100229.

[5] Commission, Decision of 24 September 2024, FS.100011 - Emirates Telecommunications Group/PPF Telecom Group, available at: https://competition-cases.ec.europa.eu/cases/FS.100011; Commission, Decision of 03 September 2025, FS.100156– Adnoc/Covestro available at: https://competition-cases.ec.europa.eu/cases/FS.100156; FS.100049 – Adnoc/Fertiglobe, see; – Adnoc/Fertiglobe, see https://competition-cases.ec.europa.eu/cases/FS.100049.

- For European and US companies (as well as companies from many other jurisdictions that are not known as generous subsidy-givers) the data collection is obviously burdensome. This is perceived as particularly annoying because, for those parties, it is often clear from the outset that the data collection—focusing on foreign financial contributions—will not bring to light anything close to a distortive subsidy. So, in essence, having to do the FSR data collection and FSR filings amounts more to a mere (expensive!) formality, provided that the homework was done properly.
- For those companies, however, that really are in the focus of the FSR (i.e. SOEs, Chinese players and other heavily subsidized non-EU companies), things are obviously quite different: Not only is the data collection much more burdensome and the preparatory effort significantly higher as, beyond the data work, those companies will also need to find substantive arguments based on EU State aid law (showing why the identified critical foreign financial contributions do either not involve foreign subsidies, or, if they do, have no distortive effects in the EU). In addition, especially in the absence of almost any case law or substantive guidance (e.g. on the balancing test),[6] the outcome of the Commission's FSR review will often be a complete black-box. The dissuasive effect of the FSR for mergers which are candidates for a closer scrutiny should therefore not be understated (as is also evidenced by the fact that in the public procurement context, all three phase II cases initiated so far led to withdrawals of the relevant Chinese bidders).

Against that background, it may well be that to some extent, the FSR is doing its job via its mere existence, and even without the Commission having to spend its limited resources on (m)any difficult cases. This could also explain why amongst those who actually had to deal with FSR cases in practice over the last two years—at the Commission, within companies, in law firms—some "FSR fans" may have been a bit disappointed: Instead of having the chance to apply or see the Commission apply fancy new concepts such as the distortive effect or the balancing test, or at least assessing non-EU measures based on EU state aid law standards to identify hidden subsidies, the bulk of the work is about collecting and assessing—largely meaningless—data on foreign financial contributions.

[6] The guidance provided in the e&-decision (FS.100011), which was published in April 2025, and in the Commission's "Initial clarifications on the application of Article 4(1), Article 6 and Article 27(1) of Regulation (EU) 2022/2560 on foreign subsidies distorting the internal market" of 26 July 2024 (SWD(2024) 201 final) is certainly helpful, but leaves many questions open. The same applies to the "Draft Guidelines on the application of certain provisions of Regulation (EU) 2022/2560 of the European Parliament and of the Council of 14 December 2022 on foreign subsidies distorting the internal market" which were published on 18 July 2025.

1.2 Key Moments in FSR Cases: And Timing of Data Collection

For the Commission, an FSR case generally starts at the moment they receive a case team allocation request for a specific merger case, kicking off the so-called pre-notification stage; after one or usually more rounds of requests for information, the formal filing will ultimately trigger the 25 working days deadline for phase I. For companies and their advisors, FSR cases usually start much earlier. Before reaching out to the Commission on a name basis, they will conduct a filing analysis to assess whether an FSR filing is needed. Preparations for the FSR filing—including in particular the data-collection on foreign financial contributions—will often start well before the first contact is made with the Commission, in order to avoid delays for the deal timeline.

From that perspective, the general architecture of an FSR case presents obviously many common features with merger control and also FDI, the "key moments" being the filing assessment, the preparation of the filing (including the data collection), and the (pre-)notification and review phase. There are however also important differences, which may impact not only the timing but also the chronological order of each of these stages. Indeed, unlike in merger control, the bulk of the FSR filing preparation focusses on information (on foreign financial contributions) which is not only very burdensome to collect—as it is normally not available at central level—but which will also be largely if not completely unrelated to the notified concentration. This also means that the most time-consuming part of the preparation of the FSR notification—the FFC data collection—can be front-loaded, i.e. launched well in advance of a specific M&A project. In such a case, when preparing a specific notification, the data will only need to be updated to cover the relevant time period (i.e. three years prior to signing of the notified transaction). As a result, while a typical merger case would normally start with the filing analysis followed by the collection of the data required to prepare the draft notification, it looks like under the FSR, at least in the long run (or in an ideal world), the filing analysis might take place at a moment when the FSR data collection has already been completed (either proactively and completely independent from a notifiable transaction, or in the context of a previous FSR filing). Yet, similarly as in EU merger control, the parties must be prepared to answer follow-up questions of the Commission on reported foreign financial contributions that may go well beyond the "minimal information" to be provided according to the Form FS-CO, and this even in unproblematic cases.

The following sections will comment from a legal practitioner's perspective on the experiences made and challenges faced with respect to each of these key moments, starting with the filing analysis, followed by the (pre-)notification and review phase, and finally addressing the most burdensome part for most of those who had to deal with the FSR in practice, namely the data collection required for the reporting on foreign financial contributions in the FSR filing.

2 Identification of M&A Deals Caught by the Merger Tool

2.1 *Concept of Concentration and Turnover Threshold as Main Filters*

Similarly as under the EUMR, the FSR filing analysis follows a two step-structure: In a first step, it needs to be established whether the M&A transaction qualifies as a "concentration" (in short: transactions involving a change of control on a lasting basis or the creating of a full-function joint venture, as opposed to the mere acquisition of a non-controlling minority shareholding or the creation of a non-full function joint venture). If that's the case (and provided that the target or joint venture has also an establishment in the EU),[7] the parties must check whether the concentration meets the quantitative notification threshold, i.e. if the target or joint venture's EU turnover is above EUR 500 million and if the parties have received foreign financial contributions exceeding EUR 50 million. Despite some initial concerns, the identification of M&A deals caught by these statutory notification thresholds has turned out to be relatively straightforward to handle for companies and their legal advisors. This comes, however, at the price of having to notify a large number of M&A transactions only because of the high target turnover in the EU, and even in the absence of any indications whatsoever that one of the parties may have received foreign subsidies, let alone foreign subsidies with a distortive effect in the EU.

The concept of "concentration" (including the notions of "control", "full-functionality" etc.) as well as the principles governing the turnover calculation (including, for instance, the geographic turnover allocation, the relevant time period, and the reference to the ordinary course of business) correspond in essence—and often literally—to the definitions and rules applicable under the EU Merger Regulation (EUMR). Accordingly, the case law,[8] decisional practice and extensive guidance provided in the Commission's Consolidated Jurisdictional Notice[9] is also relevant under the FSR. In terms of legal certainty and consistency, it is obviously very much to be welcomed that the FSR relies on the well-established concepts of EU merger control when defining the material scope of application of the FSR's merger tool.[10]

There are, however, two important differences regarding the scope of the turnover threshold: First, from a geographical point of view, unlike under the EUMR,

[7] See on that criterion footnote 7 of the Form FS-CO and CJEU, Case C-230/14, ECLI:EU:C:2015:639, paras. 29 et seq. – Weltimmo; CJEU, Case C-39/13, C-40/13 and C-41/13, ECLI:EU:C:2014:1758, paras. 24–27 – SCA Group Holding and Others; CJEU, Case C-196/87, ECLI:EU:C:1988:475, para. 16 – Steymann.

[8] See e.g. CJEU, CaseC-464/23, ECLI:EU:C:2025:478 - EVH/Commission, para. 104, on the concept of single concentration (and its limits).

[9] Commission Consolidated Jurisdictional Notice under Council Regulation (EC) No 139/2004 on the control of concentrations between undertakings, OJ C 95, 16.4.2008, p. 1.

[10] Weiß, in Bungenberg/Soltész (eds), Article 20 FSR, paras. 6 et seq., 12 et seq.

the FSR turnover threshold only refers to the EU turnover (i.e. the worldwide turnover is irrelevant). Second, and more importantly, from a subjective point of view, the FSR turnover threshold only looks at the turnover of the target or joint venture, i.e. it disregards the turnover of the acquirer, or, as the case may be, the joint venture parent companies. As a consequence, the creation of green field joint ventures which, by definition, will not have generated any turnover in the last financial year, is not caught by Chapter 3 of the FSR.[11] The different refence point (target/joint venture only) in combination with the twice as high nominative value (EUR 500m vs. EUR 250m) means that the FSR turnover threshold serves indeed as a relevant filter, excluding a significant amount of M&A deals notifiable under the EUMR from an FSR notification requirement.

2.2 *(In-)Significance of the Foreign Financial Contribution Threshold*

By contrast, the other elements of the FSR filing threshold have proven to be largely meaningless. This applies, in particular, to the foreign financial contribution threshold, which was supposed to filter out high value M&A deals that are not suspected of being subsidized by foreign governments. Indeed, whenever the EU turnover threshold is met, it is almost certain not only that the target or joint venture will also have an establishment in the EU, but also that (unless very special circumstances) both parties together will easily exceed this second limb of the quantitative threshold. Accordingly, the filter function of the foreign financial contributions threshold in Article 20 para. 3 lit. b FSR is, in practice, extremely limited, if not non-existent.[12]

This conclusion is based on a variety of observations:

- First, the excessive scope of the concept of foreign financial contributions, together with the fact that the limitations and exceptions for the FFC reporting requirements laid down in the Form FS-CO (Table 1, para. 6) do not apply when it comes to the assessment of the filing threshold in Art. 20 para. 3 lit. b FSR.[13]
- Second, the relatively low quantitative foreign financial contribution threshold, especially when compared with the relatively high turnover threshold. The following example may illustrate this asymmetry between the two limbs of the quantitative threshold: For a target company which achieves an annual turnover of EUR 500 million or more outside the EU (i.e. an amount at least equal to the amount it must generate within the EU to fall under Art. 20 para. 3 lit. a FSR), it is sufficient that as little as 3.3% of its yearly non-EU revenues (EUR 16.67 million) are generated with sales to non-EU state controlled entities (which count

[11] See DG COMP, FSR Q&A (Questions and Answers - European Commission), point 2.

[12] von Köckritz et al. (2023), 1 (5). See DG COMP, FSR Q&A, point 3.

[13] See Hahn, Weiß, in Bungenberg/Soltész (eds), Article 3 FSR, paras. 20 et seq.

towards the EUR 50 million/3 year FFC threshold, irrespective of whether the relevant transactions are at market terms or not).

- Third, the threshold is based on the combined, aggregate amount, meaning that all foreign financial contributions received by the parties' corporate groups worldwide over the last three years need to be added together (cf. Art. 23 FSR in combination with Art. 22 para. 2 and Art. 22 para. 4 lit. a-e FSR). Consequently, not only the specific companies and legal entities directly or indirectly involved in the deal need to be taken into account, but the acquirer's entire corporate group, as well as the target and all its subsidiaries worldwide; and, in case of a joint venture, the entire corporate groups of the joint venture and its controlling parent companies.
- Finally, due to the relatively high turnover threshold, only very large M&A transactions are captured, which will generally involve large multinationals (or at least one large multinational) that normally should easily meet the foreign financial contributions threshold.[14]

The EU legislator's choice to link the FSR filing threshold to the concept of foreign financial contributions rather than foreign subsidies has been largely criticized—and for good reason.[15] It obviously means that a much higher number of transactions are subject to a FSR filing requirement, including transactions involving not a single (reportable) foreign subsidy. This unnecessarily increases the administrative burden for deals which, from a substantive point of view, are entirely unproblematic. What could be considered as a "birth defect" or accidental mistake in the design of the filing threshold was actually a conscious choice of the EU legislator. The underlying idea is that that the Commission should not have to rely on the companies' self-assessment as to whether a foreign financial contribution involves a selective benefit and, thus, a foreign subsidy. Rather, the Commission wants to have (at least in theory) the possibility to assess the subsidy character itself based on the information on foreign financial contributions that is provided by the parties throughout the notification process. In practice, it is difficult to see how the Commission should manage to perform this mammoth task effectively for a multitude of measures and within the limited personnel and time resources available in the context of the review of M&A deals.

In practical terms, there is at least one positive side-effect of this faulty design. It actually means that the effort required for companies in terms of FFC data collection is normally quite limited at least for the purpose of the assessment of the filing requirement. For the reasons outlined above, it is highly likely for transactions involving a target or joint venture with an EU turnover above EUR 500 million that the FFC threshold will be easily met (and in most cases by the acquirer alone). So normally, there will be no need at this stage (the FSR filing analysis) to identify and

[14] Weiß, in Bungenberg/Soltész (eds), Article 20 FSR, paras. 45 et seq.; Werner et al. (2024), p. 28.

[15] Barbist (2023), p. 247 et seq.; ESALA, Reponse to the Commission Consultation, 22 July 2021, para. 1.8; Köckritz, Weiß in: FG Bechtold, p. 170; Soltész (2023a), p. 176; Zöttl and Werner (2022), p. 477.

add together all the foreign financial contributions received by the different parties. This also means that each of the parties, in particular the acquirer, will normally be able to assess the threshold on its own at a relatively early stage in the deal planning (i.e.: as soon as the target or joint venture's EU turnover is available). Given that the EU is currently the only jurisdiction worldwide with a foreign subsidy control regime for M&A deals, there is also no need to do a multi-jurisdictional filing analysis (which would trigger the need to collect additional information from the parties). Accordingly, it will normally not be necessary to collect any additional information beyond the target or joint venture's EU turnover (e.g. turnover breakdown on a country-by-country basis; detailed information on FFCs) for the filing analysis.

Even though the foreign financial contribution threshold will thus normally be easily met in case the turnover threshold is exceeded, it is, in practice, advisable to check and confirm that this is actually the case. The FSR filing form requires the parties to indicate in section 4.2 whether this threshold is exceeded, and the only possible answer options are "yes" or "no". This means that the parties cannot leave the question open or make the filing based on the hypothetical assumption that the foreign financial contribution threshold is met. If they answer the question with "yes", they must be prepared that the Commission will ask in the pre-notification phase for a substantiation of this response. This applies especially to such cases in which Table 1 of the Form FS-CO with the list of reportable foreign financial contributions does not show any foreign financial contributions, or if their total amount is less than EUR 50 million, which will often be the case due to the reporting exceptions. Experience has shown that confirming the FFC filing threshold can often be done in a way that avoids burdensome data-collection efforts for the parties, e.g. by checking the turnover generated with large projects involving third country governments or state-owned undertakings (quite frequently, the EUR 50 million threshold will be exceeded by a single important contract involving a non-EU state).

Obviously, the relatively straightforward assessment of the FSR filing requirement comes at a high price, namely the need to notify a large number of deals where there are no indications whatsoever for distortive foreign subsidies.

2.3 And, Not to Forget: Unlimited Call-in Powers?

As outlined above, the FSR filing threshold is in most cases relatively easy to handle—especially when compared to the burdensome multi-jurisdictional filing analysis required under merger control and FDI rules. There is, however, an important extension of the scope of the Commission's review powers under the FSR which is unprecedented under EU merger rules, and which may pose an important additional challenge for M&A deal planners: Art. 21 (5) FSR provides the Commission with the power to request, at its own initiative, the notification of concentrations which do not meet the quantitative notification threshold and which are thus normally out of scope of the merger tool. While this "call-in power" is limited to "concentrations" (meaning that the acquisition of non-controlling minority shareholdings is not covered, nor the creation of non-full function joint ventures) and can only be exercised prior to (full) implementation, i.e. closing of the transaction, the general ex officio instrument under Art. 9 et seq. FSR allows the Commission to investigate (and potentially order the parties to unwind) even closed M&A deals as well as M&A transactions that do not qualify as concentrations. Unlike under EU merger control, there is thus no safe harbor whatsoever for below threshold transactions.[16]

Given that, during the first two years after the FSR's entry into force, the Commission has not yet made use of these new powers in a single case, one could consider their practical relevance to be limited. However, the mere existence of such far-reaching call-in powers may obviously have a significant impact on the preparation of M&A deals, and it adds a significant portion of uncertainty. This is especially due to the fact that the substantive scope of the call-in powers is extremely broad. Based on the wording of the relevant provisions, there are basically no or almost no substantive requirements for the Commission to make use of these powers. Art. 21 para. 5 FSR simply requires the Commission to *"suspect that foreign subsidies may have been granted"* to the undertakings concerned in the three years prior to the concentration. The need for certain *"effects in the Union"* may be self-evident, but it is nonetheless remarkable that this additional requirement is only expressed in the recitals of the FSR (recital 36). All this leaves the Commission, at least in theory, with an extremely broad discretion. It is fair to assume that most large companies that are doing business also outside the EU will have received or can at least be suspected to have possibly received any foreign subsidies in the last three years (e.g. a preferential tax scheme that applies to the whole industry). This means that a huge number of deals is potentially affected by this new instrument.

It is regrettable that the EU legislator did not narrow down any further the substantive threshold for the Commission to make use of the call-in power, e.g. by limiting the scope of application to suspicions of foreign subsidies involving significant subsidy amounts—or at least to subsidies exceeding the EUR 4 million threshold in Art. 4 para. 2 FSR. It is even more unfortunate that the EU legislator seems to be of the view that the suspicion of any types of foreign subsidies is sufficient, no matter whether there is any indication for a potential distortion of the internal market within the meaning of Art. 4 and 5 FSR. The lack of any boundaries for the exercise of this call-in power is also somewhat at odds with the Illumina/Grail case law of the Court of Justice: Despite the different contexts and different legal mechanisms, it could be seen as undermining the effectiveness, predictability and legal certainty that must be guaranteed to the parties to a merger,[17] at least as long as there are no further guidelines or clarifications that bind the Commission's discretion in a legally predictable manner. In order to be in line with the general principles of proportionality and legal certainty, the exercise of the call-in power should therefore at least be limited to cases in which the Commission has the (concrete) suspicion that distortive foreign subsidies have been granted.

[16] Oberländer and Sickinger (2024), p. 103.

[17] CJEU, CaseC-611/22 P and C-625/22 P, ECLI:EU:C:2024:677, para. 206 – Illumina/Grail.

The uncertainties surrounding this unprecedented power make it all the more indispensable for the Commission to specify the criteria it is intending to apply in order to select call-in cases. According to Art. 46 para. 1 lit. c FSR, the Commission shall publish, at the latest on 12 January 2026, guidelines regarding inter alia the application of its power to request the prior notification of any concentration according to Art. 21 para. 5. As stated in recital 73 FSR, such guidelines are *"necessary in order to foster the predictability"* of the FSR. The draft guidelines published by the Commission in July 2025 have therefore been eagerly awaited by the stakeholders concerned. They describe a number of possible factors that the Commission intends to take into account when assessing whether a "call-in" is justified. At the same time, however, the draft emphasises that these indicators are not exhaustive and that, ultimately, it always depends on the circumstances of the individual case. As a result, the draft leaves the Commission's broad discretion untouched, thus continuing to give it maximum freedom. It is to be hoped that the Commission will go one step further in the final guidelines and define the new powers in more detail, both in terms of substance and procedure.

Given the Commission's limited resources and the fact that after two years, it has still not made use of its call-in powers in a single case, it seems likely that the Commission will indeed limit—and have to limit—the exercise of its call-in powers to cases of suspicion of *distortive* subsidies.[18] Moreover, while the uncertainties linked to the call-in possibility affect, at least in theory, each and every non-notifiable concentration, in practice, the number of cases in which this risk is a realistic one is certainly limited. For the vast majority of non-notifiable transactions, the possibility of a call-in is only a merely theoretical scenario and can be practically ruled out, so it should normally not overly affect M&A deal planning. By contrast, certain types of concentrations are clearly exposed to that risk, so that it should be taken seriously. This concerns, in particular, M&A deals involving non-EU state owned undertakings, Chinese companies and/or companies which have received significant amounts of foreign subsidies; and especially if such a merger also needs to be notified under the EUMR, if it is publicly announced (prior to closing), and/or if complaints from other market participants are likely.[19]

M&A deals that qualify as a possible "call-in candidate" must reflect this risk in the M&A agreement. The relevant FSR clauses will normally not need to be drafted from scratch, but can be modelled after merger control and FDI clauses, which may have to address similar risks (e.g. in jurisdictions providing for voluntary merger control notification systems combined with a call-in power of the national competition authority). In merger control cases, one way of dealing with such cases is to include a condition precedent requiring the parties to obtain a (soft) comfort letter of the relevant competition authority. In FSR cases, when drafting such a clause, it must be taken into account that it is unclear whether the Commission will accept to give the parties such comfort. So far, public statements made by Commission

[18] In that sense also van Weelden et al. (2024), p. 19.

[19] See also Oberländer and Sickinger (2024), p. 108 et seq.

officials at conferences have indicated that there is no such intention. In the interests of legal certainty, proportionality and good administration, the Commission should re-consider this position and accept to confirm, upon request, whether it intends to exercise its call-in powers in a given case and at a given stage based on the information available at that moment in time.[20]

3 FSR Timeline and Procedure: Some déjà vus and Important Particularities

The FSR notification process is largely modeled after the EUMR, e.g. when it comes to the two phase review structure (preliminary review vs. in-depth investigation), the review deadlines (25 working days for phase I vs. 90 working days, plus extensions, for phase II), the inevitable Commission demand for a pre-notification (which will usually take at least two, some times more rounds of RFIs, so that a minimum duration of 4–6 weeks for the pre-notification stage should better be always counted in even in completely straightforward cases). Until the 25 workings days waiting period has lapsed or, in phase II, a clearance decision has been obtained, the transaction must not be implemented (standstill obligation and prohibition of "gun jumping"). The Commission's investigation measures are also largely inspired by the powers available under the EUMR: The Commission may send requests for information, conduct on-site inspections, "stop the clock" in case of a failure to respond to requests for information, and impose fines for gun jumping or non-compliance with other procedural duties. The FSR notification form (Form FS-CO) also presents many similarities and overlaps with its merger control equivalent (Form CO). Finally, the vast majority of cases requiring a FSR notification will also have to be notified under the EUMR. This means that the deal will in any event need approval from Brussels, so the impact of the additional FSR filing on the deal timeline will often be limited. Since 2025, DG COMP is keeping a public case register of all FSR merger notifications made since the entry into force of the notification regime. This register is similar to the one for merger control cases and adds more transparency and accountability to the system. It also has the positive side effect that the Commission no longer needs to invest its scarce resources into reviewing and responding to complaints from market participants about cases it is actually already looking into.

Despite these parallels, there are also important differences between the filing process under the FSR and the EUMR.[21] To mention just a few:

- To the extent most FSR cases are unproblematic on substance, it appears that the Commission will normally not reach out to market participants to ask for their views on the notified transaction. In practice, once all the questions raised by the

[20] Similarly Oberländer and Sickinger (2024), p. 112 et seq.

[21] Weiß, in Bungenberg/Soltész (eds), Article 21 FSR, paras. 31 et seq.

Commission during the pre-notification have been answered and formal filing has been made, the parties may not even hear anymore from the Commission until (shortly before) the 25 working days period has expired.

- Unlike under the EUMR, the Commission will not issue a clearance decision at the end of phase I. Rather, it will simply confirm in a short letter (without further explanations) shortly before the standstill period has lapsed that there are insufficient indications to initiate an in-depth investigation (Art. 10 para. 4 FSR). The parties may then implement the transaction once the 25 working days waiting period has lapsed (Article 24 (1) (a) FSR). As a consequence, even two years after the entry into force of the FSR filing regime, there is barely any (published) decisional practice. To date, only one single final decision has been published and it may well be that even after several years, only a handful of decisions will be publicly available. From that perspective, the FSR regime is significantly less transparent and predictable than the EU merger system with its abundant case practice. The lack of a clearance decision at the of phase I may also have important implications for the M&A deal deadline. Indeed, even in straightforward cases where it is clear from the moment of the formal notification (or even way before) that the deal will not raise any concerns whatsoever on a substantive level, the Commission will not be in a position to clear the deal before working day 25. Accordingly, if formal filing takes place later than 25 working days before the planned date of implementation (or before the date defined in the share/asset purchase agreement when all conditions precedent must be fulfilled), there will be, in principle, no possibility for the parties or the Commission to speed up things (e.g. by issuing a clearance decision already on day 20, as may happen in merger cases following the simplified procedure). The only exception would be for the parties to obtain a derogation from the standstill obligation pursuant to Article 24 (3) FSR. In EUMR proceedings, this provision has hardly played any role in practice due its strict interpretation by the Commission. According to public statements made by DG COMP officials at conferences, it seems the Commission is not planning to lighten this approach under the FSR. This is regrettable since the lack of a legal basis for the Commission to adopt a clearance decision prior to the expiry of the waiting period even in cases that are entirely unproblematic is obviously an important difference with merger control cases that would justify a more flexible approach.
- No simplified procedure or Short Form FS-CO is available (yet). This means that even though the vast majority of notified concentrations appears to be unproblematic, there are no alleviations for the parties and the Commission in the notification and review process (apart from the fact that waivers may play a more important role in such cases). Pursuant to recital 75 FSR, the Commission should have the possibility to establish a simplified procedure under which it treats certain concentrations on the basis that they appear less likely to give rise to distortions of competition in the internal market caused by foreign subsidies. Accordingly, Article 47 (1) (a) FSR empowers the Commission to adopt implementing acts concerning a simplified procedure, "taking utmost account of the goal of limiting administrative burden for notifying parties pursuant to Article 21

of this Regulation and Article 4 of Regulation (EC) No 139/2004". It is to be hoped that the Commission will make use of that possibility soon, to reduce unnecessary red-tape for M&A deals that are clearly unproblematic.

- Under the FSR, commitment decisions can only be adopted in "phase II". As set out above, Articles 24 and 10 FSR do not empower the Commission to adopt clearance decisions at the end of phase I—including conditional clearance decisions. By contrast, it follows from Article 10 (3) FSR that the Commission must open an in-depth investigation if it has sufficient indications that an undertaking has been granted a foreign subsidy that distorts the internal market. As a consequence, both the balancing test (Article 6 FSR) and commitments (Article 7 FSR) can only come into play in phase II. In practice, it is however to be expected that, where appropriate, the parties will be able to explore already in the pre-notification phase remedy proposals with the Commission. If a suitable remedy can be found that removes all concerns (e.g. by repaying the subsidy), it is to be hoped that the Commission would find a creative solution that allows it to conclude the case without having to open a phase II investigation.
- In case of non-cooperation, the Commission may not only "stop the clock" or impose fines but can also decide based on facts available. The FSR thus provides for a significant lowering of the Commission's burden of proof in situations where the undertaking under investigation and/or the third country concerned fails to cooperate with the Commission, for example by failing to provide requested information. Article 16 FSR states that, in case of non-cooperation, the Commission can take decisions *"on the basis of the facts available"* and that, in such a case, *"the result of the procedure may be less favorable to the undertaking than if it had cooperated."* As can be seen from the e& decision, the Commission does not hesitate to make use of this new power, including in cases in which it is not the acquiring company itself which fails to provide the request information, but its controlling shareholder, i.e. an entity which is outside of the influence of the acquiring company.[22]
- While the FSR timelines and procedural steps are almost identical to those of EU merger control proceedings, it must be born in mind that the FSR proceedings are separate proceedings that are run independently from merger control proceedings (including by different case teams/units within the Commission). As a result, even if notifications under the FSR and the EUMR can be aligned and filed at the same time, and even if there is some form of alignment and exchange also between DG COMP's merger and FSR units, there is a significant risk of diverging timelines for the completion of both proceedings (e.g. in cases which do not raise any FSR issues but pose problems under the EUMR, or the other way round).[23]

[22] See Commission, Decision of 24 September 2024, FS.100011 – e&/PPF Telecom Group, available at: https://competition-cases.ec.europa.eu/cases/FS.100011, paras. 191–193.

[23] von Köckritz et al. (2023), p. 10.

- Finally, with regard to the filing forms, despite many overlaps and similarities, many sections in the Form FS-CO do not find a direct equivalent in the Form CO. Generally, the FSR filing form contains less sections to fill in, and practical experience confirms that for an average FSR case, the filled-in filing form will normally be much less extensive than the Form CO. In addition, much of the information to be provided only in the Form FS-CO (i.e. which has no direct equivalent in the Form CO) has, at least in unproblematic cases, more of a "tick-the-box" character. Notwithstanding the above, companies which need to do a FSR filing have to provide a lot of additional information, which is entirely different from what is required in the context of merger control.[24] Most importantly, the FSR filing form asks companies to provide information on certain (reportable) foreign financial contributions they have received in the last three years prior to signing the M&A transaction, which requires extensive data collection ahead of the filing. This data collection has kept many companies and their advisors busy over the last 2 years, and it was also in the focus of the debate around the unnecessary red-tape introduced by the FSR including for companies that were clearly not in the focus of the EU legislator.

4 Ready to File? FCC Data Collection and Reporting

The data collection required to enable the parties to provide the requested information on foreign financial contributions in section 5 of the FSR filing form and, for notifying parties, Table 1 of the Form FS-CO is certainly the most challenging part of the preparation of most FSR filings.[25] This is essentially due to the fact that the concept of foreign financial contributions is extremely broad, and that the relevant information is normally not stored centrally, but must be collected worldwide from a multitude of different sources and contact persons in the various local entities. Moreover, many of the reporting exceptions provided for in the FSR filing form can only be fully assessed once the data collection has been carried out in its entirety; so the impact of these alleviations on the scope and burden of the data collection exercise has turned out to be limited. Globally active companies are therefore well advised to plan in sufficient time for the data collection ahead of the filing, and potentially to launch this process even irrespective of a specific merger project in sight. Depending on the internal company structures etc., this process can easily take several weeks or even months. Putting all hopes on getting a waiver in the pre-notification stage may be a risky strategy, as the Commission is always good for a surprise and if the waiver is denied this may cause delays to the deal timeline.

[24] See Soltész (2023c), p. 394.

[25] Weiß, in Bungenberg/Soltész (eds), Article 21 FSR, paras. 31 et seq.; see also van Weelden et al. (2024), p. 21.

The initial draft filing form which was published in February 2023 provided for extremely far-reaching disclosure requirements on foreign financial contributions (blanket reporting request with individual reporting of all foreign financial contributions above an amount of EUR 200,000).[26] This excessive approach has been heavily criticized by companies and business associations during the consultation process.[27] This has led the Commission to significantly reduce the reporting requirements for foreign financial contributions in the final filing form that was adopted in July 2023.[28] The Commission has finally opted for a more targeted approach, whereby only foreign financial contributions exceeding (or equal to) an amount of EUR 1 million need to be disclosed, provided that certain other positive or negative criteria are met. In addition, most of the reporting can be done on an aggregate basis and is limited to countries in which the notifying parties have received significant amounts of foreign financial contributions (EUR 45 million). Yet, in practice, as indicated above, the various reporting alleviations only had a limited impact on the efforts required for the data collection: It may indeed well be that due to the various reporting exceptions, some parties will not need to disclose any foreign financial contribution at all in their FSR filing. However, in order to be able to reach that conclusion with the requisite level of comfort (i.e. without having to fear a fine for providing incorrect information in the notification, Art. 26 para. 2 FSR), extensive data collection efforts are still required.[29]

Regarding the scope of the reporting requirements and the structure of the data collection, a distinction must be drawn between what may be called "high risk foreign financial contributions" (or: "high risk FFCs"; sections 5.1 and 5.2 Form FS-CO) and "other reportable foreign financial contributions" (or: "other reportable FFCs"; section 5.3 and Table 1 Form FS-CO). The reporting requirements and data collection efforts also differ depending on whether a company qualifies as notifying party (typically: acquirer) or only as other party (target or seller), as only the former have to provide information on other reportable FFCs.

"High risk FFCs" are defined narrowly (by reference to Art. 5 para. 1 FSR), but trigger far reaching reporting requirements. They must be reported individually, without any exception (provided that they exceed or are equal to the amount of EUR 1 million) and by all parties, including parties other than the notifying parties (such as the target company). The detailed information and supporting documents to be provided for this kind of foreign financial contributions are set out in sections 5.2, 6.4 and 8.1 Form FS-CO. While the scope of the "high risk FFC" concept is generally rather narrow, the Commission has interpreted the specific category of "directly facilitating a concentration" (Art. 5 para. 1 lit. d FSR) in a surprisingly broad way.

[26] See the file available at: https://ec.europa.eu/info/law/better-regulation/have-your-say/initiatives/13602-Distortive-foreign-subsidies-procedural-rules-for-assessing-them_en.

[27] Soltész (2023b), p. 121.

[28] Weiß et al. (2023), p. 580.

[29] Bauer, in: Bungenberg/Heinrich (eds), Chapter 7, Section B.IV, mn. 495.

According to the informal guidance published by DG COMP,[30] this category is supposed to cover all foreign financial contributions that are used to finance the acquisition or from which the transaction benefits. The Commission takes the view that the intention of the granting third country to facilitate a specific transaction is not decisive. This means that a grant, loan or guarantee which was conceded generally for acquisitions may also be considered as directly facilitating it.

This extensive interpretation had important consequences for private equity companies and other investment funds. According to the Commission, foreign financial contributions granted by third countries (including state-controlled entities) in the form of limited partner investments to an acquiring investment fund should in principle be reported as "high risk FFCs". In September 2025, the Commission has changed this approach and clarified that limited partner investments—not only in non-acquiring funds but also in acquiring funds—only need to be reported in Table 1 as "other reportable FFC", which means that they are no longer considered as "high risk".[31] This clarification was overdue, given that these investors typically act on market terms (i.e. pari passu with private investors), so it is unrealistic to assume that they might involve any distortive foreign subsidies. It is positive that the Commission has finally accepted this reality, which will hopefully allow PE funds to avoid the disclosure of highly sensitive information on third country limited partner (LP) investors that is normally useless for the Commission's assessment of the case. DG COMP has also clarified in its Q&As that, despite the broader wording of Art. 5 para. 1 lit. d ("a concentration" instead of "the concentration under investigation"), it follows from Art. 19 FSR that only third country measures are covered that actually relate to the notified transaction.[32] Accordingly, if it can be demonstrated that foreign financial contributions granted generally for acquisitions have not and will not be used for the notified deal, this should normally be sufficient to rule out their high risk character. In any event, the existence of a high risk FFC alone does not say anything about whether the merger might turn out to be a difficult case. If the parties can show that there is no foreign subsidy (e.g. because the contribution has been granted in line with market terms), then the high risk character of the FFC will become irrelevant for the substantive assessment.

The category of "other reportable FFCs" is, at least in theory, extremely broad, as it covers, in principle, *all* foreign financial contributions (with an amount of at least EUR 1 million) that do not qualify as high risk FFCs. There are, however, important exceptions from the reporting requirement. In addition, unlike for high risk FFCs, only the notifying party(-ies) must report "other reportable FFCs". Moreover, the relevant information in Table 1 of the Form FS-CO does not need to be reported individually, but in an aggregate manner and in the form of estimates. Indeed, Table 1 requires the notifying parties to provide the estimated total amount

[30] Moscoso and Stoyanova (2024), Competition FSR brief 1/2024, p. 4.

[31] DG COMP, FSR Q&A, point 26, added on 16 September 2025.

[32] DG COMP, FSR Q&A, point 30. On the required nexus between the foreign state measure and the notified concentration see also von Köckritz et al. (2023), p. 7.

of other reportable FFCs per third country over the last three years in the form of relatively broad ranges.[33] Thus, there is no need to individually report other reportable FFCs, including foreign subsidies. Importantly, no reporting at all (including of foreign subsidies) is required for third countries where the notifying party(-ies) received an estimated total amount of other reportable FFCs of less than EUR 45 million within the relevant time period. However, in cases involving more than one notifying party (i.e. cases of joint control), the assessment of this EUR 45 million threshold must also take into account the other reportable FFCs received by the other notifying parties. In practice, this means that it will be difficult for each of the notifying parties to rule out from the outset certain countries (e.g. with very limited activities/turnover) from the scope of the data collection, as the situation of the other notifying party must also be taken into account. Importantly, unlike for high risk FFCs, there are several important exceptions from the reporting of "other reportable FFCs". The exceptions for tax measures, however, are defined overly narrowly and it is also difficult to see why the exception for market conform sales and purchase transactions should not apply to financial services. Since not only the receipt, but also the provision of financial services is covered by the counter-exception, it places an excessive and unnecessary reporting burden on providers of financial services such as banks, financial institutes and insurances companies, which can hardly be justified. While it is to be expected that waivers will play an important role here,[34] such waivers can only be granted at the pre-notification stage, meaning that the uncertainties will remain until a relatively late stage of the transaction planning. This is regrettable, as financial companies may want to engage in the FSR data collection well in advance of a specific merger project, in order to be prepared for future FSR filings. In addition to these general reporting exceptions, investment funds, including private equity companies, may be exempted from the need for a group-wide reporting of other reportable FFCs and instead provide this information only for the acquiring fund(s) and its portfolio companies, if they can show that a certain number of conditions are met (Table 1, para. 7 Form FS-CO). The efforts required to demonstrate that these conditions are met does not make this exception overly attractive.[35] Moreover, since many investment funds will decide to do the FSR data collection upfront und irrespective of a specific transaction for all active funds which have received LP funding in the last three years (in order to be fully prepared for future FSR filings), the relevant information will need to be collected in any event for all funds and portfolio companies. Accordingly, in practice, the added value of the PE exception appears to be limited.

Even though the final filing form as adopted under the FSR Implementing Regulation requires the parties to disclose significantly less information than under the initial draft, the legal and factual complexity of collecting the relevant data has remained. The references to complex legal concepts with respect to high risk FFCs

[33] Table 1, footnote 8 of the Form FS-CO.

[34] DG COMP, FSR Q&A, point 28.

[35] See also the doubts expressed in van Weelden et al. (2024), p. 21.

(e.g. the notion of ailing undertaking, the assessment of compliance with the OECD Arrangement on officially supported export credits, or the scope of the concept of unlimited guarantees, etc.) and the multi-layered system of exemptions and counter-exemptions for other reportable FFCs (e.g. in relation to financial services and tax measures) has made the FSR data collection in some respect even more challenging.[36] In any event, with the FSR's catch-it-(almost) all approach focusing on foreign financial contributions rather than foreign subsides, the data collection remains a time-consuming and burdensome exercise, including for EU headquartered companies. For the latter, this is particularly frustrating as it is often clear from the outset that they will not have received any distortive foreign subsidies. At the same time, experience has shown that the FSR data collection is feasible in a reasonable time period for these companies. And there is still a glimmer of hope that a simplified procedure for straightforward cases will be available soon, similar to EU merger control. It is difficult to deny, however, that non-EU state owned companies as well as Chinese companies are in a more complicated situation. For those companies, the effort required not only to collect the data but also to assess it from a substantive law perspective (based on EU State aid standards) is obviously much higher. This fact and the uncertainties regarding the chances of success to get the deal through in a reasonable time frame will have certainly dissuaded some non-EU companies from M&A activities in Europe.

In any event, it is clear that the preparation of FSR filings involves significant data collection efforts. The exercise should be kicked of sufficient time in advance to avoid delays for M&A deals, as its duration is difficult to predict and will be different from company to company. Indeed, despite the focus on numbers, the data collection makes it necessary to familiarize the relevant people within the companies with complex legal concepts. And, importantly, the focus on data collection (i.e. numbers) must not distract from the fact that what matters in the end for the Commission is to assess whether any of the foreign financial contributions disclosed in the filing form may involve a distortive foreign subsidy. Therefore, companies must be prepared to be able to show that the foreign financial contributions reported in the Form FS CO either do not qualify as foreign subsidy, or that they would not have a distortive effect, even when considered as a subsidy.[37] If the parties can show that a distortive effect in the internal market can be ruled out (e.g. because the measure could be approved under EU State aid standards, if granted by an EU Member State), the often highly complex question as to whether the measure involves a subsidy element (i.e. a benefit) can be left open. And the same applies, vice versa, for measures where the subsidy element can be excluded easily (e.g. because they are clearly market conform, or non-selective tax measures), so that there is no need to assess their distortive character. Accordingly, it will be crucial for companies to make sure that they do not only have the numbers right, but also prepare for a substantive argumentation based on EU state aid law principles.

[36] Weiß et al. (2023), p. 580.

[37] von Köckritz et al. (2023), p. 6 et seq.

5 Conclusion: Not Everything Is Bad, But There Is (Significant) Room For Improvement

Despite the FSR's fundamental flaws (in particular: its focus on FFCs rather than foreign subsidies, which has far-reaching consequences not only for the number of notifiable transactions, but also for the effort involved in the FSR data collection), there are quite a few things that actually have worked out rather well:

- The FSR merger tool is indeed functioning and DG COMP is able to handle the notifications without significant delays despite the much higher number of cases and the much lower resources compared to initial projections.
- DG COMP has undertaken significant efforts to provide guidance (including via the Q&A tool, by answering questions in or outside the pre-notification, or via the detailed reasoning in the e& decision) and to increase transparency (e.g. via the case registry).
- The reduced scope of the reporting requirements compared to the initial draft filing form has reduced the burden on companies. While the exercise remains very time consuming, experience has shown that the data collection can be done with reasonable efforts, if it is well prepared and kicked of sufficient time in advance.
- The Commission has handled its call-in powers with moderation (which may however also be due to a large extent to the lack of personnel resources).
- Finally, it is fair to assume (albeit difficult to establish empirically) that the deterrent effect of the new notification regime in combination with the Commission's intervention in the e& case has contributed to protect the level playing field against unfair competition from subsidized non-EU-players (even though this comes at a high price, as also EU players are subject to significant red tape).

At the same time, there is scope for improvements, and many of these improvements can be achieved even without touching the Regulation, but by the Commission itself. From a practitioner's perspective, the following points merit to be highlighted (non-exhaustively):

- The FSR Q&As on the DG COMP website have proven as a very useful tool for legal advisors and their clients. While they are updated from time to time, it would be helpful if DG COMP would provide more regular updates and publish a larger number of the answers they have given to companies or legal practitioners which have sought its advice.
- The scope of the exceptions for the reporting of foreign financial contributions in the FSR filing form should be extended. In particular, it is difficult to see why the exception for market conform sales and purchase transactions should not apply to the provision of financial services by notifying parties such as banks or

insurance companies.[38] Moreover, the scope of the exceptions for tax measures is defined overly narrowly (with its limitation to six very specific tax measures) and should be extended to all non-selective tax measures.

- The country specific threshold for the reporting of other reportable FFCs in Table 1 of the Form FS-CO (EUR 45 million) should be calculated individually per notifying party instead of *"cumulatively for all notifying parties"*[39] (which means that in a joint venture setting, the notifying parties currently only know relatively late in the process for which countries they may benefit from the exception). This would allow companies to limit unnecessary burden by focusing the data collection from the outset (i.e. without having to take into consideration the situation of the other notifying parties, if any) on those countries where they have generated a certain minimum amount of turnover.
- Since there are much more cases than expected and given that the vast majority of the FSR notifications handled by the Commission seem to be unproblematic on substance, the Commission should introduce a simplified procedure for cases in which none of the parties have received any "high risk FFCs" within the meaning of Article 5 FSR. In addition, it should consider to make use of its powers under Art. 49 para. 1 FSR to increase the turnover threshold in Art. 20 para. 3 lit. a FSR by up to 20% by way of a delegated act, in order to reduce the excessive administrative burden for companies.
- The Commission should accept to grant exemptions from the standstill obligation in unproblematic phase I cases (Art. 24(3) FSR) as soon as it is clear that there will be no phase II and that waiting for the expiry of the 25 working days would have disproportionate consequences. The strict approach to this exemption under the EUMR is not justified under the FSR given that the Commission has not even the possibility to issue a clearance decision before the expiry of the statutory waiting period.
- The upcoming guidelines should not only lay down specific quantitative and qualitative criteria for the exercise of the Commission's discretion when deciding about the "call-in" of a "below threshold" transaction, but they should also provide for a mechanism that allows the parties to obtain informal comfort that a "call-in" is *not* intended.
- In line with Art. 44 (9) FSR, the Commission should define a "white list" of countries with bilateral agreements and similar state aid control standards as the EU, such as Norway, Switzerland, UK, etc. Any foreign financial contributions or foreign subsidies received from those countries should be considered as irrelevant under the FSR, and—unlike currently stated in point 21 of DG COMP's FSR Q&A—they should also not count towards the filing threshold.

[38] The explanations provided by DG COMP in its FSR Q&A, point 28, are hardly convincing. In particular, they focus on the provision of financial services by third parties, and do not address the opposite situation of a notifying party whose business purpose consists in the provision of financial services.

[39] In that sense, however, explicitly the guidance provided by DG COMP in its FSR Q&A, point 11.

Other more fundamental, conceptual flaws will need to be corrected by legislator itself (e.g. focus on foreign subsidies rather than FFCs; re-consider the introduction of clearance decision at the end of phase I) in order to increase the acceptance of the new instrument.

References

Barbist J (2023) Die Verordnung über den Binnenmarkt verzerrende drittstaatliche Subventionen - Eine Einführung samt kritischer Auseinandersetzung mit den Vorschriften über Zusammenschlüsse. Zeitschrift für Öffentliches Recht ZöR 78:227–250

Bungenberg M, Heinrich H (eds) (2025) Europäisches Beihilfenrecht, 2nd edn. Baden-Baden

Bungenberg M, Soltész U (eds) (2026) Foreign Subsidies Regulation - Article-by-Article Commentary. Baden-Baden (forthcoming)

ESALA (EU State Aid Law Association) (22 July 2021) Reponse to the Commission Consultation on the proposal for a regulation of the European Parliament and the Council on foreign subsidies distorting the internal market available at: https://www.esala.eu/publications/

Moscoso L, Stoyanova I (2024) The Foreign Subsidies Regulation – 100 days since the start of the notification obligation for concentrations. Competition FSR brief 1/2024

Oberländer I, Sickinger C (2024) Commission Calling: "Call-In" of transactions under the Foreign Subsidies Regulations – uncertainty and unpredictable risks? Zeitschrift für Wettbewerbsrecht ZWeR 22:103–114

Soltész U (2023a) Foreign subsidies control: a bureaucratic monster? Eur State Aid Law Rev EStAL 22:175–180

Soltész U (2023b) Drittstaatensubventionsverordnung und Transaktionspraxis – EU-Kommission gibt Vorgeschmack. Neue Zeitschrift für Kartellrecht NZKart 11:121–123

Soltész U (2023c) Die Geister, die ich rief...Drittstaatensubventionskontrolle als Horrorfilm? Europäische Zeitschrift für Wirtschaftsrecht EuZW 34:393–394

van Weelden V, Smela Wolski J, Bickel F (2024) The Foreign Subsidies Regulation's impact on M&A transactions – the third wheel of regulatory reviews. Mededingingsrecht in de Praktijk 1:18–23

von Köckritz C, Weiß H (2021) "Merger control meets State aid law" – Der Vorschlag der Kommission für eine Verordnung über wettbewerbsverzerrende Subventionen aus Drittstaaten. In: Lutz G (ed) Festgabe für Rainer Bechtold zum 80. Geburtstag, Baden-Baden, pp 165–184

von Köckritz C, Weiß H, Winkelmann K (2023) The EU Foreign Subsidies Regulation: what antitrust lawyers should know about the new instrument. AM Online 06:1–13

Weiß W (2024) The regulation on foreign subsidies distorting the internal market. A path to a level playing field? Springer Nature, Cham

Weiß H, von Köckritz C, Winkelmann K (2023) EU-Beihilferecht "goes global": Die Kontrolle drittstaatlicher Subventionen im Rahmen der EU Foreign Subsidies Regulation - Was Wirtschaftsanwälte über die neue Brüsseler Subventionskontrolle wissen sollten. Recht der Internationalen Wirtschaft RIW 69:572–582

Werner P, De La Barre H, Music K (2024) Untangling the Foreign Subsidies Regulation. CoRe 8:23–27

Zöttl J, Werner P (2022) Vive l'Industriepolitik – M&A unter der neuen Drittstaatensubventionsverordnung. Neue Zeitschrift für Kartellrecht NZKart 10:475–486

Harald Weiß Dr. iur, is Counsel at the law firm Gleiss Lutz in Brussels.

FSR: Fit for Purpose?

International Reactions to the Foreign Subsidies Regulation

Jan Wouters

Abstract This chapter examines how the Foreign Subsidies Regulation (FSR) is perceived internationally, considering its position at the intersection of trade and competition law. Initially conceived in response to perceived distortive subsidies from China, particularly in the post-pandemic economic landscape, the FSR has since evolved into a broader instrument operating in a world where many major economies, including the EU and the US (via the Inflation Reduction Act), deploy substantial subsidy programs. The analysis examines third countries' responses to the FSR and presents case studies of the US, China and India, as they are major trading nations. It also considers the United Arab Emirates, as it was the first country to be subject to an FSR decision.

1 Introduction

The EU's increasing reliance on autonomous external relations instruments has not gone unnoticed in the outside world. Some of the recent unilateral initiatives of the Union in the area of international economic and environmental law have been criticized for not being fully consistent with international law.[1] This applies especially to the new Carbon Border Adjustment Mechanism ('CBAM'), of which it is still unclear whether this mechanism is fully compatible with WTO rules and the Paris Climate Agreement. The EU Deforestation Regulation even caused so much controversy that the implementation date was postponed to December 30, 2025, a year later than originally planned. Finally, the increasing "weaponization" of the EU's trade policy within the framework of the EU's push for strategic autonomy, on which professor Wolfgang Weiss and his co-author Cornelia Furculita have pub-

[1] See Wouters (2024), pp. 1–7.

J. Wouters (✉)
KU Leuven, Leuven, Belgium
e-mail: jan.mf.wouters@kuleuven.be

W. Weiß et al. (eds.), *The Foreign Subsidies Regulation*, European Yearbook of International Economic Law, https://doi.org/10.1007/978-3-032-23415-5_9

lished an excellent book with Cambridge University Press,[2] has resulted in the recent development of several unilateral trade instruments, such as the Enforcement Regulation, the Anti-Coercion Instrument and, last but not least, the Foreign Subsidies Regulation ("FSR" or "Regulation"), which all walk a fine line regarding their compatibility with international and WTO law.

Regarding the FSR specifically, it has been noted that there may be a tension within the objectives of the Regulation which may complicate its enforcement: on the one hand the focus is on competition policy and enabling the undistorted functioning of the internal market, whereas, on the other hand, a focus on trade remedies—which has been the traditional approach of the EU, within the multilateral rules of the WTO—is primarily on avoiding damages for particular industries. Margrethe Vestager had to confess that this position of the FSR, on the cross-roads between competition and trade law, makes it "complicated", as the Regulation was proposed in a "simpler time", when the original impetus was mainly in an attempt to deal with the "Chinese model",[3] whereas the post-Covid appetite of major industrial nations to grant huge subsidies, whether or not within the context of a drive to decarbonization, makes that the FSR now may target a much wider range of foreign countries.

That is why this short contribution engages with how third countries have reacted to the Regulation. It starts with the United States, followed by China and then by India, to conclude with the United Arab Emirates, which has been the subject of the first foreign subsidies investigation and decision.

2 United States

The FSR started to apply on 12 July 2023. Interestingly, by that time, it had become widely seen as the European Union's reaction to the United States Inflation Reduction Act ("IRA"). According to the European Commission, the new set of rules *"enables the Commission to address distortions caused by foreign subsidies and allows the EU to ensure a level playing field for all companies operating in the Single Market while remaining open to trade and investment."*[4] The Commission perceived a problem in foreign subsidies that appeared to give their recipients an unfair advantage to acquire companies or obtain public procurement contracts. Within the EU, subsidies granted by EU Member States are subject to strict State Aid rules, but before the FSR subsidies granted by non-EU governments were unmonitored. According to the Commission, these foreign subsidies caused distor-

[2] Weiß and Furculita (2024).

[3] Cf. Frontier Economics, The EU Foreign Subsidies Regulation: what does it really mean? Available at https://www.frontier-economics.com/uk/en/news-and-insights/articles/article-i20093-the-eu-foreign-subsidies-regulation-what-does-it-really-mean/.

[4] Cf. Commission, Foreign Subsidies Regulation, available at https://competition-policy.ec.europa.eu/foreign-subsidies-regulation_en.

tions and undermined the level playing field of the internal market. The FSR therefore extends existing EU state aid rules to jurisdictions outside the EU, including incentives such as those provided by the IRA. As is known, the IRA's State aid instruments are primarily tax credits and tax deductions, but it will also provide grants, and loans as well as offer loan guarantees.

Whether the Inflation Reduction Act will have such negative effects on the EU economy as some fear, is disputed. However, if it does, the FSR may be put to the test here. But targeting American subsidies may revive long-running allegations that European competition law is protectionist, or even anti-American. In addition, targeting the United States or US firms may be particularly sensitive at this time of war on the European continent when the EU's dependence on US military strength is particularly apparent, and even more so in this time when transatlantic relations have been frayed in record speed during the first months of the Trump II Administration.

All of these factors may caution the European Commission towards a too hasty application of the FSR to American subsidies. However, European businesses suffering from distorting American subsidies may want to try to pressurize the Commission to take action—even though the FSR does not grant interested third parties many explicit rights in the enforcement of the FSR. A further complicating factor here is that a confrontational approach toward US or other foreign subsidies may have different effects in different Member States, for example with export-oriented economies being more exposed to potential retaliation from third countries, which may not like their companies being targeted by the FSR.[5]

In the meantime the United States has itself taken action. President Biden signed legislation on December 29, 2022, including amendments to the Hart-Scott-Rodino Antitrust Improvement Act of 1976 ("HSR Act"), requiring the US Federal Trade Commission ("FTC") to promulgate a rule requiring filings under the HSR Act to include information on subsidies received from certain foreign governments or entities that are identified as "foreign entities of concern" in the US Infrastructure and Jobs Act. In passing this legislation, *"Congress determined that foreign subsidies can distort the competitive process or otherwise change the incentives of the firm in ways that undermine competition following an acquisition and are particularly problematic when provided by entities or countries that are strategic or economic threats to the United States."*[6] The FTC's rule of 11 December 2024 now requires information about "subsidies from foreign entities and governments of concern."

While specific countries are not identified, the rule points to the definition outlined in the Infrastructure and Jobs Act. This definition leaves open the possibility for the Secretary of Energy to designate key countries and regions as concerns (read: China, Macau, and Hong Kong).[7]

---

[5] Blockx and Mattiolo (2023), pp. 53–74.

[6] Government Publishing Office, Federal Register Volume 88 Issue 124, available at Federal Register, Volume 88 Issue 124 (Thursday, June 29, 2023).

[7] Perez (2024).

Interestingly, when the FTC published its new rule, it dealt with some of the inputs and comments it had received during the consultation phase. There was one comment on lessons from the FSR:

> Another commenter suggested introducing a de minimis threshold so that the reporting obligation is limited to only those subsidiaries from foreign governments and entities of sufficiently large amounts to potentially distort the competitive process in markets in the United States in which the merging parties compete. Citing the EU Foreign Subsidies Regulation as an example, this commenter claimed that such a threshold would save merging parties the burden of compiling small subsidy amounts that could not be expected to result in competition concerns. The Commission acknowledges that a de minimis requirement may indeed make sense as part of the information required, but Congress did not provide for a de minimis threshold, and the Commission does not yet have sufficient data to make that determination or establish an amount at this time. Once the Agencies have begun to receive information about foreign subsidies, the Commission can revisit this issue, if warranted.[8]

3 China

In the Spring of 2024 the European Commission launched investigations into bids made by Chinese companies for public tenders for trains in Bulgaria and solar panels in Romania.[9] In each case the Chinese company subsequently pulled out of the bid when the Commission started requesting information and documentation, leading the latter to close the investigations. Bulgaria even canceled its railway construction bid altogether. Interestingly, it was part of the wider financing under the EU's post-pandemic recovery funding.

The Commission is currently undertaking investigations into Chinese suppliers of wind turbines in public procurement projects in Spain, Greece, France, Romania, Bulgaria, and Germany. The investigations do not have a concrete timeline and could extend over several years.

China's reaction in the meantime has become very clear. At the MOFCOM Regular Press Conference of 9 January 2025, a question was asked about MOFCOM's release that same day of its final finding of its investigation on trade and investment barriers posed by the EU in its practices under the FSR. The response was fairly clear:

> In response to the application of the China Chamber of Commerce for Import and Export of Machinery and Electronic Products (CCCME), MOFCOM launched a trade and invest-

[8] International Trade Administration, Regulations Improving and Strengthening the Enforcement of Trade Remedies Through the Administration of the Antidumping and Countervailing Duty Laws, available at https://www.federalregister.gov/documents/2024/03/25/2024-05509/regulations-improving-and-strengthening-the-enforcement-of-trade-remedies-through-the-administration?utm.

[9] Borderlex, Romania solar foreign subsidies case: Chinese intra-corporate subsidy channels in focus, available at https://borderlex.net/2024/04/23/romania-solar-foreign-subsidies-case-chinese-intra-corporate-subsidy-channels-in-focus/.

> ment barrier investigation on the practices of the EU under the FSR on July 10, 2024. After filing the case, MOFCOM verified the relevant situation with all stakeholders through questionnaires and field investigations in accordance with the law, extensively listening to opinions to ensure that the investigation is fair, just, open and transparent. During the investigation, the European Commission did not submit any questionnaire or make related comments.
>
> According to the investigation, there are many unreasonable practices in the Commission's FSR investigations on China, which caused restrictions and hindrance to the access of products, services and investments of Chinese enterprises, compromising the competitiveness of Chinese businesses and their products in the EU market. In view of this, MOFCOM has determined in accordance with the law that relevant practices of the EU FSR investigations constitute trade and investment barriers.
>
> According to Article 33 of the Investigation Rules of Foreign Trade Barrier, MOFCOM will, according to the circumstances, take measures such as holding bilateral consultations to request the European side to adjust or change relevant practices, so as to provide an open, fair, just, non-discriminatory and predictable environment for Chinese enterprises to invest and operate in Europe.[10]

The MOFCOM investigation found that the FSR had caused obstacles or restrictions to the entry of Chinese enterprises, products and investments into the EU market. Ninety-eight percent of respondents to the ministry's survey said that the FSR had directly jeopardised the competitiveness of Chinese enterprises and their related products in the EU market. MOFCOM added that the respondents had indicated that EU companies are likely to avoid Chinese investors in their search for international investors due to fear of FSR investigations, or to use them as a bargaining chip to undermine Chinese investors.

According to MOFCOM, some companies also indicated that the FSR investigation would lead to disruptions in the supply chain, affecting their ability to deliver goods and execute projects efficiently. The ministry said that losses for Chinese firms resulting from abandoned bidding projects totaled RMB 7.6 billion (€1 billion) with other affected projects exceeding RMB 8 billion (€1.06 billion). Seventy percent of respondents said that FSR probes also affect a firm's reputation and will "lead to a crisis of trust among customers, which will have a serious negative impact on the company's brand image and market reputation in the EU", according to the MOFCOM report. The ministry accuses some EU Member States, without naming them, of adding requirements to tenders which make it "impossible" for Chinese companies to bid. Some Member States also cite "national security threats" as a motive for not choosing a Chinese firm, according to MOFCOM.

The ministry added that more than 50% of the respondents had indicated that they would comprehensively evaluate and adjust their investment strategies in Europe to avoid triggering FSR investigations. FSR investigations would also delay the process of developing a green economy in the EU and will not be conducive to the realisation of the EU's net-zero emission targets.

[10] Ministry of Commerce People's Republic of China, MOFCOM holds Regular Press Conference, available at https://english.mofcom.gov.cn/News/PressConference/art/2025/art_f85575c40d154cefbb91368ef096af75.html.

The China Chamber of Commerce to the EU ("CCCEU") declared that it supported the view of MOFCOM and added that the FSR "[erodes] confidence in the EU's commitment to maintaining a fair and level playing field for competition". The chamber urged the EU to "promptly rectify its improper measures under the FSR, ensuring a fair, just, and non-discriminatory business environment for Chinese enterprises operating in the EU". "We believe that the EU's FSR practices have significantly undermined the level playing field for foreign firms in the bloc," said the CCCEU. The chamber accused Brussels of violating "key WTO principles" such as non-discrimination and takes aim at the "reversal of the burden of proof, opaque procedures, unreasonable timelines, and a lack of procedural fairness".[11]

The CCCEU said that the FSR has brought "significant and destabilising "uncertainty for Chinese businesses operating in Europe. The FSR, together with the EU's "antitrust reviews" and the EU's investment screening rules, has "significantly raised the risk of "decoupling" between China and the EU, particularly in the digital, green, and high-tech sectors", according to the CCCEU. The chamber said it was "deeply disappointed" at the Commission's "lack of cooperation and failure to respond to the Chinese side's questionnaires during the trade barrier investigation", examples of which are referenced in the MOFCOM report.

The Commission said that it did not have any specific comment to make about this report. On the allegation that it was not cooperating sufficiently with China, spokesperson Lea Zuber said more generally that the EU executive is "very open to exchanging with the authorities",[12] and specifically in the framework of the FSR.

The General Court has started to develop the law in this area, having considered and dismissed a request for interim measures to suspend an ongoing FSR investigation, and upheld the Commission's power to seize China-based mailboxes. On 12 August 2024 the President of the General Court held that EU subsidiaries can lawfully be required to provide access to email accounts and date held by their overseas parent company.[13] The order is interesting for third countries for a number of reasons. First of all, it endorsed rather far-reaching extraterritorial investigation powers for the Commission based on the "effects doctrine". Secondly, it may have implications for other EU autonomous instruments. Thirdly, the order held that there was no evidence that compliance with the Commission's inspection decision would compel the company or the group of companies to infringe Chinese law.

[11] China Chamber of Commerce to the EU, CCCEU Statement on China Declaring EU's FSR Practices Towards Chinese Companies as Trade and Investment Barriers, available at http://en.ccceu.eu/2025-01/09/c_4589.htm.

[12] Cf. Adnkronos, EU: Commission, 'investigations into Chinese subsidies are not discriminatory', available at https://english.adnkronos.com/2025/01/09/eu-commission-investigations-into-chinese-subsidies-are-not-discriminatory/.

[13] GC, Case T-284/24 R, ECLI:EU:T:2024:564 - Nuctech Warsaw Company Limited and InsTech Netherlands v Commission.

4 India

India may be one of the other third countries to be hit by the FSR. As is known, India is currently still negotiating—since many years[14]—a free trade agreement ("FTA") with the EU. Indian negotiators must ensure not to agree to any FTA text that prohibits India from taking action against FSR. India exported goods worth over USD 74.8 billion to EU countries in FY2023. The European Commission can now investigate these products if they have received any incentives like PLI, FAME or export benefits in India. Most vulnerable are smartphones and other IT-related exports of goods and services to the EU. The Commission is already investigating the PLI scheme (which focuses on attracting investment in high-tech industries, strengthening domestic manufacturing capabilities, and enhancing India's global competitiveness), and a decision is expected soon. If the Commission finds the PLI scheme violates WTO rules, it could impose sanctions/fines. The Indian Government may need to be ready for retaliation and a long drawn battle at the WTO.

5 United Arab Emirates

The United Arab Emirates ("UEA") was the subject of the first foreign subsidy investigation and decision under the FSR. The case involved the acquisition of PPF Telecom Group by the UAE-controlled Emirates Telecommunications Group Company ("e&"). The Commission, which suspected that e& had received financial contributions from the UAE that could give it an unfair advantage in the internal market, opened a Phase II investigation in June 2024 and concluded its investigation on 24 September 2024, requiring commitments from the companies, which were published on 4 April 2025. The decision demonstrates the Commission's approach to assessing foreign subsidies and shows the types of commitments it may require to approve a transaction.

The UAE did not issue a public reaction to the decision, as its company, e&, entered into a binding agreement with the Commission to resolve the issue regarding the acquisition of PPF Telecom Group. Instead of a public statement, the UAE's government is cooperating with the Commission, as evidenced by its commitment to the decision. The UAE has recently improved its international standing by being removed from the EU's list of high-risk countries,[15] which may have helped it to resolve the FSR issue without public conflict.

---

[14] Wouters et al. (2014), pp. 848–869.

[15] Uniwide, EU removes UAE from high-risk countries list, available at https://www.uniwide.com/news/eu-removes-uae-from-high-risk-countries-list/.

6 Concluding Remarks

The EU's Foreign Subsidies Regulation stands as a landmark in the Union's broader pursuit of strategic autonomy and fair competition within its internal market. Yet, the international reactions it has provoked reveal the fine diplomatic and legal balance the EU must strike between defending market integrity and maintaining cooperative global trade relations.

From the cautious watchfulness of the United States, to China's formal denunciation and retaliatory investigations, to India's wary anticipation of potential scrutiny, and finally to the United Arab Emirates' experience as the first subject of an FSR decision, a common thread emerges: the Regulation has swiftly become a symbol of the EU's assertive regulatory reach beyond its borders. At the same time, it has raised legitimate concerns about transparency, proportionality, and the extraterritorial application of EU law.

As enforcement unfolds, the FSR's ultimate success will depend not only on the European Commission's ability to apply it in a legally sound and even-handed manner, but also on its capacity to manage the political and economic repercussions abroad. If implemented with restraint, clarity, and genuine engagement with third-country partners, the Regulation could help to promote a fairer global economic order. If not, it risks deepening trade tensions and accelerating the very fragmentation of the international trading system that the EU has long sought to avoid.

References

Blockx J, Mattiolo P (2023) The foreign subsidies regulation: calling foul while upping the ante? Eur Foreign Aff Rev 28:53–74

Perez H (2024) Foreign subsidy regulation – will the United States follow the European Union, or lead from behind? Available at Cardozo International & Comparative Law Review: https://larc.cardozo.yu.edu/ciclr-online/109/: 1–5

Weiß W, Furculita C (2024) Open strategic autonomy in EU trade policy. Assessing the turn to stronger enforcement and more robust interest representation. Cambridge University Press, Cambridge

Wouters J (2024) The EU's efforts to uphold the international rules-based order: mission impossible? Global Policy 15:1–7

Wouters J, Goddeeris I, Natens B, Ciortuz F (2014) Some critical issues in EU-India free trade agreement negotiations. Eur Law J 20:848–869

Jan Wouters is Full Professor of International Law and International Organizations, Jean Monnet Chair ad personam EU and Global Governance, KU Leuven, and founding Director of the Institute for International Law and of the Leuven Centre for Global Governance Studies.

The FSR: A Critical View

Wolfgang Weiß, Albrecht von Graevenitz, and Ulrich Soltész

Abstract This Chapter provides a critical assessment of the EU Foreign Subsidies Regulation (FSR) roughly two years into its implementation. Drawing on the findings of the previous parts of the volume, the Chapter assesses the FSR's overly broad scope, burdensome notification requirements affecting a wide range of undertakings including many EU based ones, and legal and procedural uncertainties. Bases on this, the Chapter questions the FSR's effectiveness in achieving a level playing field, given its conceptual ambiguities, extensive Commission discretion both in interpretation and enforcement, and potential conflict with international obligations. These weaknesses might give cause for a potential misuse of the FSR as a protectionist tool. Furthermore, the Chapter questions the FSR's compatibility with international obligations and warns of possible geopolitical repercussions. The Chapter therefore calls for a judicious application, and for legal and practical reconsiderations and alterations of Commission practice.

W. Weiß (✉)
German University of Administrative Sciences, Speyer, Rheinland-Pfalz, Germany
e-mail: weiss@uni-speyer.de

A. von Graevenitz
Federal University of Applied Administrative Sciences,
Department Adminstration of the Armed Forces, Mannheim, Germany
e-mail: albrecht.vongraevenitz@hsbund-fbbwv.de

U. Soltész
GleissLutz, Brussels, Belgium
e-mail: ulrich.soltesz@gleisslutz.com

W. Weiß et al. (eds.), *The Foreign Subsidies Regulation*, European Yearbook of International Economic Law, https://doi.org/10.1007/978-3-032-23415-5_10

1 Introduction

The aim of the Regulation 2022/2560 on foreign subsidies distorting the internal market (hereinafter the 'FSR')[1] is to protect the functioning of the internal market against distortions caused, directly or indirectly, by foreign subsidies. It aims to ensure a level playing field (Article 1 (1) sentence 1 FSR) and intends to complement pre-existing EU rules of competition and trade defence law which were not capable of gripping the unfair practices by foreign countries' subsidisation.[2]

However, it is subject to doubt whether this regulation is really fit for this purpose. Its provisions are complex and engender significant interpretive and conceptual uncertainties, as the previous Chapters have clearly demonstrated with regard to the core concepts of the FSR (foreign subsidies, competition distortion, balancing). In addition, they are accompanied by a (growing) body of further extensive regulations such as the Commission Implementing Regulation 2023/1441[3] (hereinafter the 'FSRIR') and soft law.[4] The FSR affects significantly more companies outside and in(!) the EU than expected. The bureaucratic burden the FSR brings along do not only affect numerous undertakings, but also the European Commission (hereinafter the 'Commission'), which had and still has to set up appropriate structures with its (new) Directorate K of the Directorate-General for Competition (DG COMP) and certain units of the Directorate-General for Internal Market, Industry, Entrepreneurship and SMEs (DG GROW).

This Chapter summarises the core findings of the preceding Chapters of the book and presents an initial assessment of the FSR's effectiveness after roughly two years of implementation. First, it will critically analyse the scope of application of the FSR, which appears narrower than anticipated due to the necessary respect for the EU's international commitments, despite the extensive notification requirements making it overly broad. It appears that Commission practice still needs to be adjusted insofar. Next, the vagueness of the three substantive core concepts of the FSR's substantive examination and the resulting room for manoeuvre for the Commission flowing from their broad notions will be analysed. Subsequently, the Commission's broad leeway in its decision-making and call-in powers will be explored. Before

[1] Regulation (EU) 2022/2560 of the European Parliament and of the Council of 14 December 2022 on foreign subsidies distorting the internal market, 2022 OJ EU No. L 330/1; i.c.w. Corrigendum 2024 OJ EU No. L 90559.

[2] For the gap-filling function of the FSR see Commission White Paper on Levelling the Playing Field as regards Foreign Subsidies, COM (2020) 253 final, pp. 9 ff and the Explanatory Memorandum to the Commission Proposal for a Regulation of the European Parliament and of the Council on foreign subsidies distorting the internal market, COM(2021) 223 final, 5 May 2021, p. 2 ff; see also Weiß and Furculita (2024), pp. 329 ff.

[3] Commission Implementation Regulation (EU) 2023/1441 2023 on detailed arrangements for the conduct of proceedings by the Commission pursuant to Regulation (EU) 2022/2560 of the European Parliament and of the Council on foreign subsidies distorting the internal market, OJ EU L 177; i.c.w. Corrigendum 2023 OJ EU L 2414.

[4] von Graevenitz (2025), A.V., VI.

going into these details, however, a brief exposition of the theoretical framework for the criteria relevant for assessing the FSR's fitness for purpose will be provided.

2 Identifying the Criteria for Assessing the FSR's Fitness for Purpose

To assess the FSR's capacity to establish a level playing field and ensure fair competition between all undertakings economically active in the EU internal market, the FSR's regulatory content and the concepts it uses must be explored. In this endeavour, a comparison with State aid law or other EU competition or trade defence rules from which the FSR inferred its concepts can be used as benchmark. The premise behind this approach is the idea that the FSR will work as a tool for creating a level playing field if its assessments, where appropriate, reflect the approaches in the application of State aid law or competition law in general. Otherwise, where novel genuine tools and concepts where used, the new instruments enshrined in the FSR may be open to abuse as a protectionist instrument.

Hence, in order to perceive the FSR as an effective tool of levelling the playing field, one should particularly pay attention to its deviations from EU State aid law, as any difference may give cause for raising doubts over the alleged comparable, even equal treatment of foreign subsidies and State aid in EU law.[5] This is all the more relevant as the EU has to respect its non-discrimination obligations under international economic, in particular WTO law. For, the EU counters discrimination blames related to the FSR and its allegedly different concepts by ensuring that the new rules are comparable to EU State aid review and thus non-discriminatory also in view of WTO law.[6] Any difference between State aid and foreign subsidies review thus is able to nurture the discrimination concerns.[7] In this comparative assessment, the challenges the FSR faces with regard to its implementation must be considered, as any leeway for the European Commission adds to the FSR's capacity to be used for unilateral protectionism. The first experiences with the application of the FSR show that the new instrument raises a number of interpretive, conceptual and practical uncertainties, which open up room for manoeuvre for the EU executive.

Besides, the FSR's fitness for purpose may furthermore be assessed by analysing the effectiveness of its instruments, compared to the originally anticipated origin and numbers of cases and uses of review powers.

[5] Weiß (2024), p. 7.

[6] Commission Staff Working Document Impact Assessment, Accompanying the Proposal for a Regulation of the European Parliament and of the Council on foreign subsidies distorting the internal market, SWD (2021) 99, p. 57.

[7] From a formal point of view, one may contend that there is no discrimination as also undertakings based in the EU fall under the FSR's purview, but substantively, de facto, EU undertakings can become beneficiaries of national State aid which is not subject to the Regulation's tools, and EU State aid control may be more lenient. See also Baumann (2023), pp. 214 f.

3 Broad Scope of Application Due to the Notification Obligation

3.1 *Quantitative and Qualitative Bureaucracy*

The FSR's ex-ante review and intervention mechanisms in relation to concentrations (Chapter 3 FSR) and public procurement procedures (Chapter 4 FSR) are triggered by certain thresholds, and their net is particularly broad as the thresholds relate to 'financial contributions' provided by a foreign (i.e. non-EU) country, directly or indirectly; in this respect it is not necessary for such contributions to confer a 'benefit'.[8] Due to the very broad notion of 'financial contributions' under the FSR, notification obligations and waiting periods are easily triggered.[9]

The very broad scope of application is well illustrated by the publication of the first "phase II decision" under the concentration tool in the e& case.[10] The third--country company e& (majority-owned by a sovereign wealth fund of the United Arab Emirates) intended to acquire sole control of the EU telecommunications company PPF. The decision (more than 90 pages), which is partly textbook in style, shows that the Commission is following the established concepts under Article 107 TFEU very closely when interpreting the term "subsidy". In particular, when applying the FSR concepts, the Commission heavily relies on its Notice on the notion of State aid ("NoA"),[11] which reflects the traditional approach by the Commission and the EU Courts, i.e. to interpret the notion of "State aid" as broadly as possible.

This design of the FSR leads to significantly more bureaucracy in terms of quantity than assumed before its introduction: In the context of public procurement (Chapter 4 FSR) already in February 2025, 140 notifications were reported instead of the expected 36 per annum. By October 2024, more than 1000 contacts for more than 200 public procurement procedures had occurred. Under FSR concentration tool (Chapter 3 FSR), after one year, 100 formal notifications are said to have been submitted instead of 30 expected cases.[12] It is becoming increasingly clear that the number of contacts DG COMP and DG GROW have to deal with is and will remain several times higher than predicted, both under Chapter 3 and 4 FSR. However, the

[8] For the concept of financial contributions see in this volume Weiß, The Notion of Foreign Financial Contribution and of Foreign Subsidy.

[9] See in this volume Weiß, ibid, section 2; von Graevenitz (2025), A.VII, B. For the work load created by the notification obligations see in this volume Linke, The FSR in Public Procurement – A View from Industry, section 2.3 and H. Weiß, The FSR in concentrations – A view from legal practice, section 4. There are some exceptions to the broad scope of application of *ex ante* proceedings according to Chapter 4 FSR, e.g. in the context of defence and security issues; cf. von Graevenitz (2025), B.VI., D.IV.3.

[10] Commission Decision of 24.9.2024 (Case FS.100011 – e&/PPF Telecom Group), available at https://competition-cases.ec.europa.eu/cases/FS.100011. For an exposition of the case see in this volume Raitner, Weiß, The Role of the European Commission in the Concentrations Tool, section 5.

[11] 2016 OJ EU No. C 262/1.

[12] For more details on these figures see von Graevenitz (2025), A.VII.

proportion of proceedings in which substantive legal concerns have actually arisen in relation to the total number of proceedings appears to be extremely low. Consequently, many companies—most of which are based in the EU (and not in third countries)—have to deal with the (possible or actual) application of the Chapters 3 and 4 FSR. As even the mere provision or purchase of goods or services is included in the notion of financial contribution (i.e., the full amount of the revenue generated or the sales price), regardless of whether these transactions are conducted at market terms or not, the FSR goes far beyond the notification requirement under State aid law's Article 108 (3) TFEU, according to which only measures that involve an "advantage" have to be notified.[13] Recent practice under the FSR has shown that there is a great number of European players (i.e. companies with activities basically confined to the EU), which only accidentally have some transactions with non-EU governments (smaller services or supply contracts with public bodies or public companies, acquisition of assets, standard tax benefits and/or credits, etc.) which then trigger the relevant thresholds under the FSR. Just because they happen to carry out some smaller business with public players, often at market terms, these companies will have to undergo a burdensome FSR procedure if they acquire an EU target with a turnover of more than EUR 500 million.

In the vast majority of cases, this will only involve problems with the notification, but no substantive legal concerns will arise,[14] which may prompt the question of the added value of the overly broad scope of the FSR. In this regard, it is interesting to have a look at the origin of the notifying parties. In mergers subject to FSR notification under the concentrations tool, private equity firms apparently account for around one third of all FSR notifications. These came mainly from the US. Furthermore, around 90% of the notifying parties under this tool come from the EU, the US and the United Kingdom. In the procurement context, the figures are comparable, as only 7 percent of procurement authorities receive bids from outside EU, and the main share of successful non-EU bids are related to Switzerland, UK and the US.[15] This may not entirely correspond to the original objective of the FSR, which, according to many observers, seemed primarily aimed at state-supported players from Asia (especially China).

The highest number of formal investigation procedures has been opened in the area of public procurement, where most of these cases involved bids from Chinese companies. As a result of the opening of FSR procedures in these cases, all the bidders concerned have withdrawn before the Commission could complete its investigation, so the whole exercise certainly has a deterrent effect.

In addition, it is interesting to note that the "catch all" approach, which leads to very voluminous notifications, is somewhat different from the Commission's recent

[13] CJEU, Case C-345/02, ECLI:EU:C:2004:448, para 31, 33 – Pearle.

[14] See in this volume Linke, The FSR in Public Procurement – A View from Industry, section 6 and H. Weiß, The FSR in concentrations – A view from legal practice, section 4.

[15] See in this volume Linke, The FSR in Public Procurement – A View from Industry, section 6.

policy in the field of merger control under the EU Merger Regulation (EUMR).[16] Here the Commission has successfully managed to "cut red tape" by simplifying and streamlining the Commission's review process, in particular with the introduction of new categories of unproblematic mergers ('simplified cases'). This has reduced the amount of information required for notifying transactions in all cases and to optimize the transmission of documents.[17]

The resulting broad scope of the FSR notification requirement being applicable to countless measures, many of which contain no subsidy element at all, is certainly a fundamental flaw of the new system. This could possibly lead to a flood of notified measures that the Commission simply cannot handle. This effect may not have been so visible until now because the last months were not characterised by very strong M&A activity. However, if transactional activities pick up again and reach previous levels, this could test the capacity limit. As the Commission is aware from its own decision-making practice, State aid investigations can drag on for years, even if only the State aid character is disputed. If cases are brought to the EU courts, they may sometimes even take decades. The Commission cannot seriously expect that a much larger number of measures can be examined more quickly under the FSR. Against this background and given its more than 60 years of experience with State aid cases, it is surprising that the Commission has opted for such a "catch all" system.

In contrast to the high numbers of ex-ante FSR procedures for public procurement and for concentrations under Chapters 3 and 4 FSR, the number of procedures opened *ex officio* under Chapter 2 FSR are clearly lower than expected.[18] The reason for this is probably that the Commission is so busy with the proceedings under Chapters 3 and 4 FSR that *ex officio* activities have not yet been able to take place to the extent hoped for.

In this respect, at this point, the FSR does not meet the expectations placed on it. This is regrettable, as the activities of the Commission *ex officio* under Chapter 2 FSR would be equally important for addressing competition distortions: For example, the *ex officio* procedure might be used to take up concentrations and public procurement procedures that do not fulfil the thresholds or other requirements for *ex ante* proceedings under Chapters 3 and 4 FSR.[19] Scrutinizing also such cases might be important because foreign countries could pursue the strategy of shifting their activities to transactions and public tenders that are below the thresholds of Chapters 3 and 4 FSR. The *ex officio* procedure could also be used to take up greenfield investments as well as mergers that have already been completed or public contracts that have already been awarded; and the *ex officio* tool is the only one applicable to economic activities outside procurement or concentrations. Hence, its potentially broad scope of application is limited by lack of resources due to the also qualitatively demanding notification procedures.

[16] 2004 OJ EU L 24/1.

[17] See Commission press release of 20 April 2023, IP/23/2357.

[18] von Graevenitz (2025), A.VII.

[19] von Graevenitz (2025), D.II.2.

In addition to the high quantity of *ex ante* procedures under Chapters 3 and 4 FSR, these procedures also engender a high level of bureaucracy in qualitative terms. Via the FSRIR with its forms (Form FS-CO and Form FS-PP) and the practice developing thereto, the Commission often expects and requests extremely detailed information, which companies (at least for the time being) often can only obtain with a great deal of effort because the reporting systems are not (yet) set up for such information.[20] Further, the Commission expects the parties to conduct pre-notification contacts similar to its practice under the EUMR. Even though pre-notification contacts between the parties and the Commission do make sense in many cases,[21] in practice, at least in concentrations relevant under Chapter 3 FSR, such a procedure can hardly be avoided and often turn out to be burdensome and involving considerable time, up to several months.[22]

Although the FSR attempts to mitigate such problems through synergies, they may only occur in relation to parallel notifications under the EUMR and the FSR (Art. 47 I lit. a, recital 39 FSR). And even then, there are challenges, particularly because merger control under the FSR and the EUMR are handled by different directorates within DG COMP.[23]

The (correct) handling of the FSR still seems to be anything but easy for many companies and even for some procurement agencies. The high degree of specialisation required by the FSR may be easier to develop in the context of concentrations (where specialist lawyers are often called in anyway) than in the context of public procurement, especially if the companies do not have sufficient specialist resources available or the involvement of such specialists would be disproportionately time-consuming or expensive.

As a consequence of this high level of quantitative and qualitative bureaucracy, it can be assumed that the FSR discourages certain companies, especially SMEs, from participating in public procurement procedures. This effect has already been observed above with regard to Chinese bidders.

3.2 Ways to Reduce Bureaucracy

The above considerations prompt the question of how to reduce the high level of bureaucracy. One solution would be to limit the scope by amending the FSR itself, for example by restricting the scope of the notion 'financial contribution' in narrowing or precising its definition at least for the notification-based instruments or by increasing the notification thresholds, and by providing for more exceptions and

[20] von Graevenitz (2025), D.III., IV.

[21] Osseforth et al. (2025), para 8, 39, 42 seq.

[22] von Graevenitz (2025) D.III.4; Oberländer and Sickinger (2024), p. 106.

[23] Hornkohl (2023), Article 19 para 13, Article 25 para 3.

facilitations for the reporting in the FSR forms.[24] Another way would be to provide for the possibility of a block exemption regulation, as exist in EU antitrust and State aid law (based on Articles 101 (3), 103 (1), (2) b, 108 (4) TFEU). Such block exemption could, for example, provide for *ex-ante* exemptions of certain standard cases in which negative effects normally are outweighed by positive effects.[25] However, such changes in law seem unlikely for the near future.

Against this background, another way to reduce bureaucracy would be offered by the adoption of soft law, in particular by way of Commission guidelines. As a block exemption solely based on soft law would not give enough legal certainty, the Commission could define the term 'financial contribution' in a restrictive manner through its decision-making practice and, above all, its guidelines to be issued by 13 January 2026 (Article 46 (1), recital 73 FSR)[26] or in other non-legislative statements.

However, 'legislating' via soft law is subject to fundamental reservations: The *de facto* significance of such soft law and the *de facto* power it gives to the Commission cannot be underestimated.[27] Once the Commission sets out its view in a soft law document, it is possible, but statistically unlikely, that this position will be challenged at the EU courts[28] and—if challenged—that the courts will then take a different view. Even if the past has shown that the Commission's view in its guidelines can be successfully challenged at the EU courts in individual cases, years may pass before this happens and the Commission's view may take effect in all the time before a court ruling. Therefore, it can be assumed that most companies will adhere to the view set out in the Commission's soft law, as otherwise they will have to fear negative decisions by the Commission, including fines etc. This gives the Commission considerable de facto power, which seems questionable in terms of democratic legitimacy,[29] even more so as the mandate for guidelines under Article 46 (1) FSR does not include clarifications on the notion of foreign subsidy/foreign financial contribution.

In addition, there is the problem of civil law invalidity: The notification requirement under Chapter 3 FSR is linked to a prohibition on implementation that is relevant to validity, Article 24 (7) FSR: If a concentration subject to notification under Chapter 3 FSR is implemented without notification and approval, it is invalid. A similar situation is being discussed for contracts concluded through public procurement against the rules of Chapter 4 FSR, a violation of a prohibition of 'the award of the contract' derived from Article 32 (1) FSR.[30] If companies rely on the

[24] For the latter see in this volume H. Weiß, The FSR in concentrations – A view from legal practice, section 5. For proposals to alter the FSR's notification scheme see in this volume Linke, The FSR in Public Procurement – A View from Industry, section 6.

[25] See in this volume von Graevenitz, Balancing, section 2.8.

[26] Although not explicitly mentioned in Article 46 FSR.

[27] von Graevenitz (2025), A.VI.

[28] I.e. the EU courts in Luxembourg and possibly national courts in their role as functional Union courts; cf. von Graevenitz (2025), C., J.

[29] von Graevenitz (2019).

[30] von Graevenitz (2025), D.IV.5.

Commission's interpretation of the FSR in its soft law, but the courts later take a different view, transactions that have already been completed could prove to be invalid.

However, one has to face the fact that the procedure of regulating essential matters by the Commission via soft law is part of the EU's current legal practice. Thus, it is likely that the Commission will choose and practitioners accept this way.

Finally, besides the Commission's power to alter the FSR notification forms and introduce further simplifications therein, the Commission has the power under Article 47 FSR to adopt by way of implementing act a simplified procedure regarding notifications of concentrations under Article 21 FSR, which would allow to adopt facilitations for the parties and reduce red tape in particular with a view to FFC outside the high risk ones of Article 5 FSR.[31]

4 Narrowing the FSR's Scope of Application Due to Respect for International Commitments

As alluded to, the FSR's scope of application is narrower than anticipated if one considers the international commitments the EU entered into in bilateral free trade or association agreements, due to the respect for international agreements it has entered into demanded by Article 44 (9) FSR. This includes the respect for the EU obligations emanating from the WTO Agreement on Subsidies and Countervailing Measures (ASCM),[32] as Article 44 (9) FSR also provides that no action under the FSR shall be taken which would amount to a specific action against a subsidy within the meaning of Article 32.1 ASCM.

Whereas the latter commitment is capable of reducing the material scope of application of the FSR, depending on the understanding of the notion of specific action under Article 32.1 ASCM, the former, i.e bilateral obligations, may constrain the personal scope of application with regard to undertakings based in EU treaty partners, provided that the pertinent bilateral treaty contains specific rules and disciplines on subsidies which constrain or even prohibit unilateral actions by the EU against those subsidies.

With regard to the material scope of application, the respect for Article 32.1 ASCM means that all instances of third country subsidisation covered by the ASCM may not come under the purview of the FSR. Insofar, much depends on the interpretation of Article 32.1 ASCM, with regard to which diverse meanings are presented in legal literature. If one understands Article 32.1 ASCM in a way that all measures addressing subsidies (including transnational subsidies) in the sector of goods trade have to be understood to fall under the notion of specific action, then the material

---

[31] See in this volume H. Weiß, The FSR in concentrations – A view from legal practice, sections 3 and 5.

[32] 1994 OJ EU No. L 336 p 156.

scope of the FSR is reduced to foreign subsidies in the services sector and in the situations addressed by the specific FSR Chapters 3 and 4 on procurement and concentrations.[33] With regard to foreign subsidies to undertakings active in the sector of goods trade, the FSR is supplemented by the application of the EU's Basic Regulation 2016/1037 on Subsidised Imports.[34]

With regard to the personal scope, bilaterally agreed disciplines on subsidies control enshrined in EU trade or association agreements may be breached if they can be interpreted in a way which prohibits unilateral actions to counteract subsidies from the treaty partner. One has to recall that there is a remarkably wide range of comprehensive trade or association agreements between the EU and third countries which do not only cover purely "classic" trade issues (free movement, etc.) but also contain provisions on State aid and/or address the question of subsidies. A conflict with the application of the FSR by the Commission may particularly occur, if the bilateral agreements explicitly provide for institutions competent for domestic subsidy control, and even more so, if the agreements provide for general or specific dispute settlement procedures in case the parties do not meet their commitments with regard to subsidy control. In such cases, those agreements' commitments which have to be assessed individually might be seen to be violated if the EU still exercises jurisdiction unilaterally over such subsidies. This applies, for example, to the EU's Trade and Cooperation Agreement with the United Kingdom, and to the European Economic Area Agreement (EEA Agreement).[35] The EEA Agreement, contains State aid provisions basically identical with EU State aid law backed up by a strong institutional framework (EFTA Surveillance Authority, EFTA Court). There is no reason whatsoever why the Commission should investigate subsidies from EEA states under the FSR. It seems strange that the FSR system does not explicitly exclude its application to subsidies granted by Norway, Iceland and Liechtenstein. The EU-UK Trade and Cooperation Agreement admittedly does not go as far as the EEA Agreement, but contains extensive provisions on "subsidies" which are, at least in terms of substance, largely similar to EU State aid law. In addition, the EU has concluded several Stabilisation and Association Agreements with an explicit prohibition of State aid (similar to EU law) and an enforcement system exercised by an independent authority.[36] Some "softer" types of free trade agreements contain an explicit prohibition of State aid but without an institutional framework and/or an enforcement mechanism,[37] and some do not contain an explicit prohibition on State aid but a State aid monitoring mechanism.[38]

---

[33] For this understanding see Weiß (2023b), p. 204 seq.; Weiß (2024), pp. 18 ff; Müller-Ibold (2025), Article 44, mn. 36 ff. Contra, as regards transnational subsidies, Hahn (2025), para. 826 ff.

[34] Also called: Countervailing Duty Regulation 2016/1037, 2016 OJ EU. See Börnsen and Pollakowski (2024), p. 603.

[35] For more detail insofar see Weiß and Furculita (2024), pp. 354 ff.

[36] Turkey, Ukraine, Albania, Serbia, Bosnia and Herzegovina, Kosovo, Moldova and others.

[37] Macedonia, Switzerland, Russia, Egypt, Israel, Morocco, Tunisia and others.

[38] Armenia, Georgia, Canada, Japan, Mexico, Singapore, Vietnam and others.

Consequently, it is also debatable whether the subsidies granted from such countries can be considered when calculating the notification thresholds.

Unfortunately, the Union legislator has refrained from providing legal certainty by e.g. enshrining a safe harbour (white) list for relevant trade agreements into the FSR.[39] A safe harbour list could generally exclude the FSR application (and thus any notification requirements) vis-à-vis those third countries that have entered into a comprehensive FTA with substantive and institutional provisions on subsidies (maybe comparable to a block exemption mechanism). Such an approach could be combined with a "grey list" for EU agreements with a more flexible mechanism adapted to the specific provisions in the respective agreement. This would streamline the notification process, allowing the Commission to use its limited resources for the problematic subsidies. In particular, such an approach would encourage third countries to enter into agreements with the EU that include subsidy control provisions, thereby enabling the EU to export its concept of State aid control. The status quo, i.e. the lack of such a "white list" creates flexibility from the Commission's point of view, but of course legal uncertainty for the parties, and the EU runs into the risk of breaching some of its international commitments. The Commission might close this gap, at least provisionally, by means of soft law.

5 The Commission's Substantive Examination: Assessing Foreign Subsidy, Competition Distortion and Balancing

5.1 Introduction

The Commission's assessment is coined by three core concepts of the FSR which apply in all of its tools. The imposition of redressive measures or prohibitions, or the acceptance of commitments on the basis of Chapters 2–4 FSR require foreign financial contributions constituting a foreign subsidy. Such subsidy is at hand in case of a foreign (non-EU) financial contribution which confers a benefit on an undertaking engaging in an economic activity in the internal market and which is limited, in law or in fact, to one or more undertakings or industries (Article 3 (1) FSR).[40] However, the Commission can only intervene, if the third-country subsidy has led to a 'distortion' of the internal market within the meaning of Art. 4, 5 FSR. Here, the FSR provides for an examination of potential or actual distortions of competition on the basis of categories and indicators.[41] Finally, the Commission may have to engage in

[39] Soltész (2023), p. 123.

[40] For more detail see in this volume Weiß, The Notion of Foreign Financial Contribution and of Foreign Subsidy.

[41] For more detail see in this volume Maes, Buts et al., 'Distortion of Competition' in the Age of Industrial Policy: An Examination of Interpretations across EU Competition Instruments.

a balancing test in accordance with Articles 6, 11 (4) lit. b FSR with a view to outweigh the negative competitive effects by the subsidies' positive effects.[42]

At present, there is only scarce practice on the conceptualisation of these core concepts of the FSR laid down in Articles 4 to 6 FSR, which is why there is still a lot of uncertainty as to how the application of these rules will develop. The Commission has a broad room of manoeuvre in conceptualising these notions. In what follows, we will summarize the core findings of the respective Chapters in this volume dealing with these core concepts, identify the challenges one faces with regard to the FSR's implementation insofar, and assess them in view of the FSR's fitness for purpose. A comparison in particular with comparable concepts of EU State aid law will serve as benchmark, as explained above Sect. 2.

5.2 *The Notion of Foreign Subsidy*

As explored above in the Chapter on the notion of foreign subsidies and foreign financial contributions and already mentioned in Sect. 3.1, the notion of foreign subsidy is conceptualized in close proximity to that of State aid in EU law. Substantively, they share concepts such as benefit or selectivity. Despite some differences identified, the closeness can be expected to induce the Commission's implementation practice to be very much guided by the concept of State aid under Article 107 TFEU and hence by most of the pertinent application practice and CJEU case law when applying the FSR with regard to the concept of foreign subsidy, as illustrated in the e& decision.

As shown, despite these parallelisms, significant differences remain. Under the FSR, the requirement of competition distortion plays a genuine role, as this requirement is not part of the notion of foreign subsidy (even though the notion of benefit has an overlap with the first requirement provided in Article 4 (1) FSR). Furthermore, there appears to be a seemingly lower threshold for attributing a financial contribution to a foreign country, compared to the attribution of State aid to an EU Member State, and rightly so, as explained above.[43] Hence, also insofar there is need for further guidance on the exact criteria for attribution.

Another difference related to the lower threshold for attribution is the lack of relevance of State resources. In the view presented here, the financial contribution to an undertaking does not require as a corollary a cost for the foreign country or the involvement of state resources. As mentioned, a brief statement of the Commission in the e& decision might give cause for uncertainties in this regard.[44]

In sum, despite the expectation that EU State aid practice and respective CJEU case law may guide the Commission also under the FSR with regard to the notion

---

[42] For more detail see in this volume von Graevenitz, Balancing.

[43] See in this volume Weiß, The Notion of Foreign Financial Contribution and of Foreign Subsidy.

[44] See Weiß, ibid. section 3.1.

of foreign subsidies, there are several issues of uncertainty about the Commission's course of action already at the level of the meaning of foreign subsidies, i.e. with regard to the requirements for attribution and the meaning of financial contribution in terms of use of state resources. The Commission insofar enjoys considerable leeway to depart from concepts used in State aid and anti-subsidies law.

5.3 The Concept of Competition Distortion

There is even more interpretive leeway for the Commission under the FSR requirement of competition distortion. Under Article 4 (1) s 1 FSR a 'distortion in the internal market shall be deemed to exist where a foreign subsidy is liable to improve the competitive position of an undertaking in the internal market and where, in doing so, that foreign subsidy actually or potentially negatively affects competition in the internal market.' Article 4 (1) s 2 FSR provides for some respective indicators, Article 5 FSR for categories of foreign subsidies most likely to distort the internal market and Article 4 (2)-(4) FSR for some (potential) exceptions.[45] With regard to the negative effect on competition, a mere potential impairment suffices, i.e. an actual impairment of competition is not required. According to the Commission, Article 4 FSR not only addresses distortions that are established with certainty, but also potential distortions.[46] Thus, the notion of 'distortion' is very broad.

Even though Article 4 (2)-(4) and Article 5 FSR make use of concepts familiar from EU State aid law, and the requirement of competition distortion is well-known from EU competition law in general, due to the new context, the Commission has leeway to fill the still remaining uncertainties.

The comparative analysis of competition distortion in this book has demonstrated that the FSR's concept shares similarities, but provides also for differences, as the FSR is distinctive in combining a definition and some presumptions with specific tools.[47]

The Commission Staff Working Document[48] provides little further clarification as its terminology is mostly based on State aid law and shows only some effort by the Commission to limit the almost boundless scope of the FSR terms borrowed from State aid law. It clarifies, for example, that there must be a link between the foreign subsidy and the company's activities in the EU. There is therefore no presumption that a third-country subsidy automatically distorts the internal market—unlike the concept of 'distortion of competition' under Article 107(1) TFEU. Such

[45] See in this volume Maes, Buts et al., 'Distortion of Competition' in the Age of Industrial Policy: An Examination of Interpretations across EU Competition Instruments; von Graevenitz (2025), E.I.4.

[46] Staff Working Document SWD(2024) 201 final, 26.7.2024, 1.

[47] See in this volume Maes, Buts et al., 'Distortion of Competition' in the Age of Industrial Policy: An Examination of Interpretations across EU Competition Instruments, sections 3.4 and 4.

[48] Staff Working Document SWD(2024) 201 final, 26.7.2024, 1.

a link is missing, for example, if a subsidy is actually only used for activities in non-EU countries. However, this will not be easy to prove, as the Commission itself emphasises upfront that there is always a risk of cross-subsidisation within the group. One example of the broad interpretive leeway of the Commission leading to non-anticipated results, at least for some observers, occurred in the e& case. In this case, when assessing competition distortions, the Commission did not only look at the acquisition process (market on which the target's shares were offered and bought) but also at the competitive position of the combined entity post-transaction.[49] This came as a surprise because Chapter 3 of the FSR, in contrast to the EUMR, actually does not address the effects of the merger, but the effects of the subsidy,[50] so that the issue of delineating both areas of EU law came to the fore.

This interpretive issue of the scope of the assessment of competition distortions appears clearer with regard to public procurement, where 'the assessment pursuant to Article 4 of whether there is a distortion in the internal market and whether a tender is unduly advantageous in relation to the works, supplies or services concerned shall be limited to the public procurement procedure in question' (Article 27 s 2 FSR).[51] Thus, in view of the Commission,[52] the assessment pursuant to Article 4 is limited to the public procurement procedure in question.

5.4 Balancing

The highest degree of vagueness comes with the balancing test under Article 6 FSR, as the factors to be included and the way how the balancing shall proceed are not clarified at all. So far, in the Commission's practice the concept of balancing seems not to have played more than a minor role. The exact shape of this test is very much debated.[53] It is expected to become one central focus in arguments to be brought forward by the parties and to be dealt with by the Commission in its decisions.

It appears unfortunate that this test is not yet properly shaped by the FSR. The EU's demand for legal certainty alone would have called for this important instrument to be given more clarity in the FSR itself. Due to this lack in clarity, legal practice will have to observe the development of the test under Articles 6, 11 (4) lit. b FSR by the Commission in its decisions and soft law and possibly in the rulings of the courts in Luxembourg. Conceptualising the exact notion of balancing therefore will be an arduous and lengthy process in which the Commission effectively has much room for manoeuvre.

[49] Commission Decision of 24.9.2024 (Case FS.100011 – e&/PPF Telecom Group), available at https://competition-cases.ec.europa.eu/cases/FS.100011, para. 248 seq.

[50] SWD (2024) 201 final, 26.7.2024, 4. See also Oberländer and Sickinger (2024), pp. 104 f.

[51] von Graevenitz (2025), E.I.2.c).

[52] SWD(2024) 201 final, 26.7.2024, 6.

[53] Weiß (2024), p. 48.

Certainly, some elements of the balancing can already be considered largely secure:[54] The positive effects to be taken into account in the balancing test according to Article 6 FSR should not be deemed reduced to economic or competitive aspects,[55] but might also include policy objectives such as a high level of environmental protection and social standards, the promotion of research and development as well as policy objectives such as creating jobs, achieving climate neutrality and protecting the environment, digital transformation, security, public order and public safety and resilience.[56] Interests taken into account in EU trade defence instruments should be relevant in the context of the FSR as well.[57]

Nevertheless, there are still massive uncertainties: The relationship between the balancing test under Article 6 FSR with its vague wording of Article 6 (1) FSR[58] on the one side and the elaborated State aid law under Articles 107, 108 TFEU on the other side is unclear. Although there seem to be overlaps and references, the substantive law standards are not congruent.[59] The Commission Staff Working Document[60] refers very vaguely to the EU State aid rules, the basic principles of which could be applied.[61] However, this global analogy with EU State aid law is not always helpful, as the rules referred to, e.g. in the areas of environmental protection, regional aid and R&D&I, are characterised by the highly formalised, technically complex regulatory approach which is typical of soft law in the field of State aid law. One example is the Guidelines on State Aid for Climate Protection, Environmental Protection and Energy (CEEAG). Subsidies granted by a third country are generally unlikely to meet the numerous formal and substantive CEEAG requirements (incentive effect, eligibility, application, necessity, citation requirements, proportionality, cumulation, funding gap, consultation, tendering, etc.). As a result, the analogy with EU State aid law may not really work in many cases.

The e& case, the first "phase II decision" adopted under the concentrations tool, provides only little indication of what to expect from the balancing test.[62] In the case in question, the Commission notes that if a foreign subsidy falls under one of the categories of Article 5 FSR, i.e. if it belongs to one of the categories of foreign subsidies most likely to cause distortion, as was the case there, a presumption operates

[54] For more details to the following see in this volume von Graevenitz, Balancing, section 2.

[55] See in this volume von Graevenitz, Balancing, sections 2.4, 2.5; Weiß (2024), pp. 50, 51; Weiß (2023a), p. 827 seq.; Trapp (2023), para 9.

[56] For more detail see in this volume von Graevenitz, Balancing, section 2.4.

[57] Weiß (2024), p. 51 seq.

[58] Herrmann and Ellemann (2024), p. 94.

[59] For more details see in this volume von Graevenitz, Balancing, section 2.8.

[60] SWD (2024) 201 final, 26.7.2024.

[61] Cf. also Draft Guidelines on the application of certain provisions of Regulation 2022/2560, available at https://competition-policy.ec.europa.eu/document/download/a0b557e7-96f8-4231-9ed5-522f13de9065_en?filename=FSR_draft_guidelines_application_of_EU_Reg_2022-2560.pdf, para 108, 123.

[62] Commission Decision of 24.9.2024 (Case FS.100011 – e&/PPF Telecom Group), available at https://competition-cases.ec.europa.eu/cases/FS.100011, para 370–378.

whereby the positive effects of the subsidy are deemed less likely to outweigh its negative effects under the balancing test. This statement reflects recital 21 of the FSR. Furthermore, the Commission requires a causal link between the foreign subsidies and the positive effects, which was denied in this case.[63]

Nevertheless, the balancing test may be the place in the FSR assessment where the Commission has the chance to observe the non-discriminatory treatment of foreign subsidies compared to EU or State aid as required by WTO non-discriminatory rules.[64] Whereas the basic prohibition of State aid in EU law is subject to severe exceptions, there are only few comparable rules in the FSR: The de-minimis exception and some of the exception clauses in Article 107 (2) TFEU have been transferred into the FSR by Article 4 (3), (4) FSR. A presumption against distortive effects of foreign subsidies not exceeding 4 mio € has also been enshrined into Article 4 (2) FSR. Beyond this, the FSR does not contain similarly huge carveouts that allow for the approval of foreign subsidies as under State aid. In EU State aid law, the broad exception clauses contained in Article 107 (3) TFEU allow the Member States to pursue both non-economic as well as economic policy aims such as regional or business development or fostering important projects of common European interest, even though under the scrutiny and direction of the Commission's State aid control policy. Furthermore, the Global Block Exemption Regulation 651/2014 (GBER)[65] establishes rather comprehensive categories of "aid schemes, individual aid granted under aid schemes and ad hoc aid" that are "compatible with the internal market within the meaning of Article 107(2) or (3) TFEU", provided that such aid fulfils all the general and specific conditions laid down in this Regulation, see Article 3 GBER. The GBER is very detailed and comprehensive in its scope and exempts State aid amounts far beyond 4 mio € so that the relatively broad exemption enshrined in Article 4 (2) FSR is far from establishing an alignment with EU State aid rules.[66] Against this background, the broadly conceived balancing test could be used to finally grant non-discriminatory treatment to foreign subsidies.

[63] For a critique see in this volume von Graevenitz, Balancing, section 2.6.

[64] Article III:8 b GATT excludes the payment of domestic subsidies from the scope of the GATT national treatment obligation; consequently, one might consider applying this carve-out from WTO national treatment also to the treatment of foreign subsidies by a WTO Member. One could, however, still deliberate whether – in case one does not share the view presented here that Article 32 ASCM due to Article 44 (9) FSR excludes subsidies in the goods trade sector from the scope of the FSR in general – the national treatment obligation arises anyway as the treatment of foreign subsidies not covered by the WTO ASCM may still be considered subject to the national treatment obligation. Irrespective of this, there is no carve-out with regard to services trade, as there is no comparable exclusion in the GATS. In addition, also Article IV of the GPA 2012 provides for national treatment. For more on the scope of national treatment in the implementation of the FSR see Hahn (2025), para. 843–846; Weiß and Furculita (2024), pp. 349 ff.

[65] Commission Regulation (EU) 651/2014 declaring certain categories of aid compatible with the internal market in application of Articles 107 and 108 of the Treaty, 2014 OJ EU No. L 187/1, as amended.

[66] Hornkohl (2023a), p. 143.

The balancing test allows the Commission to consider positive effects of a foreign subsidy in relation to policy objectives also from foreign countries. For example, if a foreign country also pursues climate protection by funding certain actions, in a way comparable to the EU, such foreign subsidies' distortions should be carefully assessed with regard to whether their negative competitive effects in the EU might be balanced by the overall positive effects of the foreign country subsidisation to mitigating climate change, as the latter is a worldwide concern.[67]

One has to wait and see whether the Commission in its implementation practice will use this step in the assessment of foreign subsidies to observe equal treatment to third country subsidization policies comparable to the EU ones. At least in the Impact Assessment, the Commission expressed the view that it wants the balancing test to follow criteria that "better align the instrument with EU State aid rules".[68] What the EU does not prohibit internally, should not be treated as competition distortive without very sound reasoning if done externally. As Van Damme opines: the standards for FSR review should in such cases be weakened correspondingly.[69]

Also the question as to whether the Commission will need to investigate and observe positive effects of a subsidy *ex officio* is debated.[70] The FSR leaves the question of how the Commission should actually carry out the assessment largely open, so that only general standards can be taken into account such as the principle of proportionality as a general principle of EU administrative law.[71] In the e& decision, the Commission did not consider positive effects beyond those alleged by the notifying party. It stated that it has not received any other information on positive effects and concluded that there are no positive effects.[72]

5.5 Clarification by Guidelines

The guidelines to be issued by the Commission in the latest on 13 January 2026 (Article 46 (1), recital 73 FSR), shall deal *inter alia* with the application of the criteria for determining the existence of a distortion according to Article 4 (1) FSR and the application of the balancing test in accordance with Article 6 FSR. Thus, as in numerous other areas of law, such as competition or State aid law, the FSR is designed in a way that leaves essential questions open. Their clarification is

---

[67] Commission's Draft Guidelines (fn 55) para 112.

[68] Commission, Commission Staff Working Document, Impact Assessment, Accompanying the Proposal for a Regulation of the European Parliament and of the Council on foreign subsidies distorting the internal market, SWD (2021), 99 final, 48.

[69] Van Damme (2024), p. 6.

[70] See in this volume von Graevenitz, Balancing, section 4.

[71] See in this volume von Graevenitz, Balancing, section 5; cf. recitals (22), (48), (70), Articles 7 (3), 32 (7) FSR.

[72] Commission Decision of 24.9.2024 (Case FS.100011 – e&/PPF Telecom Group), available at https://competition-cases.ec.europa.eu/cases/FS.100011, para 376 f.

transferred to the Commission's guidelines or other soft law. For the reasons mentioned above, this is far from ideal, as it gives the Commission much leeway to push ahead with legal developments largely independently of the EU legislature. In the FSR, the Commission is even mandated by the EU legislative to issue and regularly update Guidelines and bring necessary clarification in this way, reflecting the implementation and enforcement experiences. The EU legislative at least prescribed for some procedural stipulations in their drafting, Article 46 (2) FSR.

Here again, the procedure of (provisionally) regulating essential matters by the Commission via soft law is confirmed as being part of the EU's current legal practice. Thus, it is understandable that it is hoped for that the Commission's guidelines expected for the beginning of 2026[73] will bring more clarity, especially with regard to the aspects of distortion and balancing under the FSR.

Unfortunately, the Draft Guidelines on the FSR, as published by the Commission services in July 2025,[74] which were eagerly awaited, did not yet fully meet the private sector's expectations:

- On the question of "distortion of competition" (Article 4 FSR), the paper (unsurprisingly) favors a broad interpretation of this criterion. The Commission's attempt to identify certain categories of cases in order to clarify the concept of distortion of competition is indeed helpful. The factors to be taken into account are specified in the Draft Guidelines. They include the specific form and conditions of the third-country subsidy (as this can prevent cross-subsidization), the ownership structure of the beneficiary, existing agreements with third parties (which may also reduce the risk of cross-subsidization), the legal framework and the economic situation of the undertaking, and many others. The Draft Guidelines also contain numerous criteria, e.g. purpose, amount, type, company size, sector-specific characteristics and the regulatory environment and deals with the most important scenarios (subsidized M&A activity, low-price strategies, investment decisions, etc.). However, this does still not change the virtually limitless scope of the FSR. In practice, it will rarely be possible to rule out a distortion of competition on the basis of this assessment alone.
- Under the balancing test pursuant to Article 6 FSR, i.e. whether the positive effects of a subsidy outweigh the negative effects of distortion, the Commission seeks to give this concept certain contours by primarily identifying the positive effects on the development of the subsidized economic activity in relation to other relevant policy objectives. These effects must be clearly linked to the third-country subsidy under investigation. The Draft Guidelines contain certain clarifications on the types of positive effects that can be taken into account, e.g. the correction of a market failure and contributions to the competitiveness and resilience of the EU economy. They also confirm that the Commission may rely on positive effects recognized under the TEU, the TFEU, the GRC or the EU state aid acquis. Furthermore, the Draft Guidelines clarify that the positive effects may

[73] Cf. as to the consultation process for these guidelines Ref Ares (2025) 1757107, 5.3.2025.

[74] Commission's Draft Guidelines (fn 55).

also occur outside the EU. The Commission is therefore taking a fairly broad approach and even considers foreign subsidies that contribute to global prosperity or promote global public goods to be potentially relevant, e.g. by supporting high environmental standards (such as climate protection measures in a third country or the protection of biodiversity), upholding human rights or promoting R&D, etc.). However, at the same time the Commission sees the burden of fully with the undertakings concerned and preserves a broad leeway whether to accept the view of sufficient positive effects.

Despite their length (35 pages!) and the Commission's obvious efforts to provide guidance to the stakeholders concerned, the issues addressed in the Draft Guidelines remain difficult and highly uncertain from a legal perspective. Unfortunately, the Commission can ultimately only provide limited assistance on these issues, as the fundamental problem lies in the design of the FSR itself, which has an extremely broad scope and contains only very vague criteria for substantive assessment. The Commission cannot override this fundamental legislative decision. In order to improve the system in the long term, the regulation would have to be reformed by the Parliament and the Council.

In any case, it is to be expected that the Commission's guidelines cannot and will not be conclusive; soft law such as guidelines must never limit the application of primary and secondary EU law. Rather, it is to be expected that for each and any case to come, a detailed assessment of the very circumstances of the case will be necessary.

6 The Commission's Broad Leeway in Its Decision-Making

As a particular concern with regard to the ability of the FSR to be abused for protectionist purposes relates to the broad leeway the Commission has in the implementation of the FSR; the broad leeway the Commission enjoys due to the considerable uncertainties, even vagueness of the basic FSR substantive concepts explored in the previous section is only one aspect of it. The other one pertains to the Commission's use of its decision-making and procedural powers under the FSR. The FSR provisions on the Commission's decision-making and investigative powers explicitly grant further discretion to the authority, as will be explored in more detail here.

It starts already with the decision to enter into an *ex officio* preliminary examination. According to the wording of Article 9 (1) FSR, the Commission "may" examine the provided information, which implies a margin of appreciation and of manoeuvre for the Commission to initiate proceedings.[75] The Commission's leeway in taking action neither is restricted by any rules on a complaints procedure or on procedural rights of complainants, as such do not exist in the foreign subsidies

---

[75] See Luja (2021), p. 194.

review,[76] unlike in State aid or trade defence law. The Commission therefore has a great deal of leeway as to how it treats information about allegedly competition distortive foreign subsidies, and as to how intensively it examines allegations, or whether it decides to collect further information or initiates a preliminary review under Article 10 FSR. Despite, since any party can call on the Commission to act, competitors and other interested parties could still use the FSR instrument to bring foreign subsidisation of a company to the attention of the Commission.[77]

The opening of phase II again is subject to Commission assessment. If it confirms sufficient indication of competition distortive foreign subsidies (see Article 10 (3) FSR), then the Commission "shall adopt a decision", i.e. at this level, the Commission no longer has a choice. The relevant leeway for the Commission therefore lies in its assessment during the preliminary review of the information gathered with regard to whether they allow for the conclusion that there are sufficient indications. It's for the Commission to determine what is sufficient. However, it remains to be seen whether the CJEU will significantly restrict the Commission's room for manoeuvre in deciding whether to open the in-depth investigation, as in State aid law. For the time being, implementation practice indicates a certain reluctance in initiating phase II investigations.

At the end of phase II, the Commission may accept commitments. The Commission again has discretion in this respect, which includes, as in the practice of antitrust or merger law, the further development by the Commission of an initial draft commitment tabled by the undertaking in dialogue with it. It remains to be seen whether the Commission's discretion goes as far as it does in antitrust law (Article 9 Antitrust Procedure Regulation 1/2003[78]), where the CJEU explicitly recognized a wide margin of appreciation on the part of the Commission regarding the acceptance of a commitment.[79] The situation is not entirely comparable to that in antitrust proceedings. While in antitrust proceedings the Commission can leave open the question of whether an antitrust infringement has actually occurred in commitment decisions,[80] out of considerations of procedural economy, it is obliged under Article 11 (3) FSR to determine in its assessment whether a foreign subsidy distorts competition and whether the commitment offered completely and effectively eliminates the distortions. The balancing test has to be addressed as well. Some argue that the recitals of the Regulation give priority to a commitment decision over a remedial decision.[81] However, recital 23 does not contain any binding

[76] Article 29 (7) FSR does not give any special status to persons delivering information about foreign subsidies or communication suspicions about false declarations to the Commission.

[77] Soltész (2023), p. 123.

[78] Council Regulation (EC) 1/2003 on the implementation of the rules on competition laid down in Articles 81 and 82 of the Treaty, 2003 OJ EU No. L 1/1, as amended.

[79] CJEU, Case C-441/07 P, ECLI:EU:C:2010:377, para. 94 – Alrosa.

[80] See recital 13 of Regulation 1/2003, 2003 OJ EU No. L 1/1: "Commitment decisions should find that there are no longer grounds for action by the Commission without concluding whether or not there has been or still is an infringement."

[81] See Trapp (2023a), para. 12.

language in this respect, as it only provides that the Commission, if it considers the commitment to fully and effectively remedy the distortion, "could accept them… the Commission should not impose redressive measures". This wording is rather soft and merely exhortatory. It even implies that it is not completely ruled out that a redressive measure could be combined with a commitment decision if this is the only way to effectively and fully eliminate the distortions of competition. The implementation practice so far, however, points towards a Commission approach that might prefer resolving problematic cases through commitments, as is the case in EU merger control. Only in rare cases one might see prohibitions and other redressive measures to be imposed.

Thus, in comparison to EU State aid, where the Commission may either adopt a positive or a negative decision about the State aid measure (admittedly, the positive decision may be subject to conditions, Art. 9 (4) Procedural Regulation), the Commission has quite a broad leeway when it comes to the substantive content of a decision under the FSR, all the more as the Commission has to ensure that the distortion caused by the subsidy is completely and effectively eliminated, having to consider also the result of a balancing test.

Admittedly, also under the EU State aid rules, the Commission has a room of manouvre when deciding about approval of State aid. The Commission effectively has an important role as a rule-maker in determining the conditions under which State aid may be approved.[82] The conditions are pivotally related to what the EU perceives as necessary for its political objectives of coherence, industrial and economic development, but have little to do with avoiding competition distortions. Only the practically negligible rule of Article 107 (3) d) TFEU refers to competition effects, and Article 107 (3) c) TFEU to effects on trading conditions. Once the objectives of Art 107 (3) TFEU are met, distortions may be perceived to be usually outweighed by the State aid's positive effects for the EU's objectives which are broadly conceived in Article 107 (3) TFEU, and which in practice are determined by the Commission, under control of the CJEU. In State aid review, the balancing of the negative, competition distortive effects against the State aid measure's positive effects is highly relevant and may lead to certain conditions and restrictions for the State aid beneficiary in the Commission's positive decision.

Despite these similarities to EU State aid law, it still appears that the Commission enjoys a broader leeway in its discretion under the FSR. This difference in decision-making by the Commission can easily be explained by the different subjects of the procedures. While EU State aid review deals with approving or prohibiting State aid, FSR review is concerned with offsetting their adverse effect on competition in the internal market. The form of an effective measure required for this purpose depends on the kind of subsidy measure and its effects on the internal market. Furthermore, unlike under EU State aid law, the Commission cannot effectively prohibit a foreign country from granting aid, but can only adopt compensatory measures. And these measures must be tailored precisely to the distortion of competition

---

[82] See Micheau (2016), pp. 23 ff.

caused by the subsidy, which is why the Commission needs a wide margin of maneuver in its decision-making power to adjust the content of its measure accordingly. In the same way, one may understand that the Commission needs to have investigative powers which are more robust under the FSR than under State aid.[83] Establishing a case of foreign subsidization, assessing their distortive effects on the internal market, and addressing these effects by effective countermeasures is an endeavor which requires a more powerful executive that enjoys flexible powers and effective investigative competences for enabling effective review and counteraction. Even though the differences thus may be fully understandable given the different contexts, the problem remains that with these broader powers and greater leeway there comes the greater capacity of the FSR to be misused for protectionism.

7 The Commission's Call-in Powers

As mentioned above, the Commission so far has made little use of its powers to open ex officio proceedings under Chapter 2 FSR. Nevertheless, the mere possibility that such proceedings could be opened *ex post* is a sword of Damocles for the companies (potentially) concerned, as they must fear that investment decisions will be called into question retroactively.

In addition, the Commission has call-in powers. In cases of public procurement, instead of an *ex officio* proceeding, the Commission, where it suspects that an economic operator may have benefitted from foreign subsidies in the three years prior to the submission of a tender or request to participate in the public procurement procedure, may before the award of the contract request a notification under Chapter 4 FSR (Article 29 (8), recital 40 FSR).[84] The latter also applies where a public procurement procedure falls within the scope of Article 30 (4) FSR, i.e. where the Commission had terminated a preliminary review under Chapter 4 without adopting a decision, and later receives information about an incomplete or omitted notification or declaration.[85]

With regard to the concentration tool, the Commission can order a concentration to become notifiable under Chapter 3 FSR even if it does not meet the requirements of Article 20 (3) FSR, if the 'Commission suspects that foreign subsidies may have been granted to the undertakings concerned in the three years prior to the concentration' (Article 21 (5), recital 36 FSR).[86] As a result, M&A deals that did not meet the filing threshold at any time prior to the concentration's implementation, i.e. before lasting change of control or lasting creation of an autonomous economic entity,[87]

[83] See for details Weiß (2022), p. 140 f.

[84] von Graevenitz (2025), D.IV.4.b).

[85] For this situation see the Commission's Draft Guidelines (fn 55), para. 155 f.

[86] von Graevenitz (2025), D.III.2.c).

[87] See Commission's Draft Guidelines (fn. 55), para. 157.

can suddenly turn into notifiable concentrations. This unique "call-in-tool" is very different from the merger control rules in most jurisdictions. It creates a "limbo situation" for the parties of a transaction which seems difficult to reconcile with the principle of legal certainty, also given the fact that Article 21 (5) FSR does not contain any meaningful requirements in terms of substance, the only condition being the Commission's "suspic[ion] that foreign subsidies may have been granted". Thus, the Commission enjoys great leeway. One may limit the discretion by requiring suspicion based on specific indications, and by a ban against fishing expeditions, as under EUMR.[88] As recital 36 alludes, the Commission should make use of the call-in powers only if it considers that the concentration or the tender "would merits ex ante review given its impact" in the EU, from which one can infer a limitation to the Commission's discretion. In the Draft Guidelines the Commission has set out more details on factors to be considered in this assessment.[89] The Draft Guidelines describe a bundle of possible factors that the Commission intends to take into account (economic activity or sector concerned, relevant value chain, strategic importance, market influence or presence, characteristics of third-country subsidies, etc.). This gives the Commission maximum freedom.[90] From the point of view of planning security, this is not very reassuring for the companies concerned.

In contrast to these call-in powers of the Commission, a voluntary notification with the Commission, which could provide security against fines, revocations or invalidity under civil law, is not possible under the FSR.[91] While the Commission has a number of options to step in, the undertakings do not have a formal option to get a relief *ex ante*. This leaves them with only the option of informal consultations with the Commission, as mentioned in recital 38 FSR. This recital states with a view to an *ex ante* review mechanism for concentrations that "undertakings should be able to request pre-notification consultations with the Commission based on good faith, with the aim of receiving guidance on whether the thresholds for notification are met".

In such cases, it would be helpful if the Commission was willing and able to issue some kind of comfort letters reducing the risk of *ex post* measures from the Commission. However, at present, it seems rather unlikely that the Commission would be ready to issue such letters.[92] Further, even if the staff of the Commission

---

[88] Oberländer and Sickinger (2024), p. 108. The Commission's Draft Guidelines (fn. 55) are silent in this regard.

[89] See Commission's Draft Guidelines (fn 55), para. 164 ff.

[90] See also in this volume H Weiß, The FSR in concentrations – A view from legal practice, section 2.3.

[91] Hornkohl (2023), Article 21 para 24.

[92] See e.g. the Q&A 34 on DG COMP's web page (https://competition-policy.ec.europa.eu/foreign-subsidies-regulation/questions-and-answers_en?prefLang=de, answering the question 'Does Regulation (EU) 2022/2560 provide for the possibility to consult the Commission on whether a transaction is to be considered a notifiable concentration?' with 'It is for the notifying parties to assess whether the conditions for a transaction to be considered a notifiable concentration under Article 20 of Regulation (EU) 2022/2560 are met. Notifying parties are invited to discuss during pre-notification the information that needs to be included in the notification.'

would be willing to issue such comfort letters, such letters would very likely—as experience from EU competition law shows—prove not very helpful as such letters neither bind the Commission as an institution nor offer full protection against risks of invalidity under civil law.[93]

Thus, from today's perspective, the FSR provides for a considerable risk for companies that the Commission may intervene even if a notification under Chapter 3 or 4 FSR is neither necessary nor possible. The call-in powers come along with considerable leeway on the part of the Commission. Luckily the Commission has not made use of these exceptional instruments yet. It remains the hope that it will only be used in exceptional cases.[94] Nevertheless, this sword of Damocles hangs not only over companies from third countries, but also—due to the broad scope of application of the FSR—over EU companies.

Against this background, even undertakings taking the view that the FSR is not applicable on a specific activity, may feel pressed to invest in a proper assessment and documentation to be prepared for cases in which the Commission may wish to intervene retrospectively based on the FSR, e.g. by way of an *ex officio* procedure or by fining proceedings.[95] Therefore, the FSR seems to lead to increased uncertainties and thus bureaucracy even for companies with activities actually not covered by the FSR.

8 Summary and Outlook

The rationale for this new legislative instrument is perfectly understandable. The FSR provides the Commission with a comprehensive instrument to counteract distortions of competition on the internal market caused by foreign subsidies, enables the EU to respond effectively to the growing trend towards state protectionism by subsidies (might be used for other purposes such as protecting EU technology from a foreign buy-out)[96] and thereby closes regulatory gaps to protect fair competition in the internal market. The FSR procedures providing for substantial material and procedural powers in the hands of the Commission subjects undertakings operating in the EU to a fairly intensive scrutiny of competition distortion by foreign subsidies.

Nevertheless, there are still considerable doubts as to whether this Regulation is the right way to achieve a level playing field. The FSR is very extensive and complex, and the FSR's redressive measures are based on comprehensive and intricate assessments. The weaknesses in the FSR construction may constrain its ability to ensure a level playing field, and these weaknesses are confirmed when looking at

[93] von Graevenitz (2025), D.III.2.e).

[94] See in this volume Raitner, Weiß, The Role of the European Commission in the Concentrations Tool, section 2, and H. Weiß, The FSR in concentrations – A view from legal practice, section 2.3.

[95] Osseforth et al. (2025), para. 40.

[96] Mattiolo (2025), p. 178 f.

the analyses of the first two years' implementation practice as presented in this volume: The FSR only achieves its objective by creating considerable, very burdensome bureaucracy that causes an extensive workload on the companies affected and even the companies potentially affected by the FSR, including many EU based undertakings. Furthermore, the FSR grants the Commission comprehensive powers implying extensive discretion and wide margins of appreciation in countering foreign subsidies. The FSR represents an entirely new set of rules which even though drawn from pre-existing concepts in competition and trade defence law, have a new context and thus involve considerable ambiguity with regard to the policies to be adopted.[97] The proliferate use of undefined legal terms results in considerable legal uncertainty and unpredictability of Commission action. Despite its Article 44(9), the FSR neither is free of objections with regard to EU compliance with obligations under international and world trade law.[98] In addition, as the EU and its Member States are themselves very extensive subsidisers, they can easily be blamed by foreign countries for causing the very same competition distortions in their domestic market that the EU aims to address by the FSR. At least, it is capable of undermining the EU's level playing field narrative.[99] It will not come as a surprise when foreign countries respond to the FSR with corresponding national legislation to investigate the competitive behaviour of EU companies benefitting from State aid or EU aid on their markets. As the EU's own aid is not subject to comparable supervision, the accusation of discrimination against foreign countries is obvious. A further spiral of discriminatory treatment is therefore to be feared instead of creating a level playing field worldwide or inducing other countries to adopt similar instruments,[100] which then might be used specifically against EU undertakings. The Chinese responses give a hint to a likely backlash which might increase the risk of new trade distortions that could particularly harm EU companies' activities in foreign markets.

As a consequence of the Commission's great leeway in the application of the FSR, and given the very sensitive character of the FSR's subject area of external (economic) relations, redressive measures have the capacity of interfering not only with the commercial relations with undertakings from third countries, but even more so with the EU and its Member States' external political relations with these foreign countries. Foreign policy is not a subject of much EU competence, but is mainly driven by national preconceptions, ideas and understandings. The Commission's measures under the FSR can thus have a significant impact and may induce wider political repercussions.[101] In certain tension with this stands the fact that under the FSR the Commission's application practice hardly is subject to any democratic control in its assessments, as the comitology procedures to be used for

---

[97] Blockx and Mattiolo (2023), p. 73.

[98] Frank (2023), pp. 938 ff; Weiß (2023b), pp. 187, 204 ff.; Weiß and Furculita (2024), pp. 326 ff.

[99] Van Damme (2024), p. 5 f.

[100] Hopes insofar, as expressed e.g. by Kühling et al. (2022), p. 159 appear a bit too positive, as other states might follow the lead of the EU and create similar instruments not for the purpose of levelling the playing field, but with the intention to have a tool at hand that allows for reprisals.

[101] See in this volume Wouters, International Reactions to the Foreign Subsidies Regulation.

the Commission's decision-making are limited to the advisory procedure, so that the Commission can easily assert its draft decisions against Member States' interests and those of the European Parliament, even if the finally adopted redressive measures could have considerable consequences for external policy beyond trade.[102]

As the implementation of the FSR is burdensome and resource-intensive for the Commission, which has limited staff available to apply the FSR—some of whom may already be occupied with handling obligatory notifications and declarations—the decisive question is whether the FSR is worthwhile. If the Commission exercises restraint when using the instruments under the FSR, adopting a judicious approach (not least due to staff constraints and potential international repercussions), and restricts itself to cases of foreign subsidies that heavily distort competition, then the huge administrative burden imposed on so many undertakings active in the EU may be disproportionate. The effort may not be proportionate to the result. At least, implementing the proposals for improving the FSR made in the above sections would contribute to significantly reduce the bureaucracy and legal uncertainty.

Finally, the real problem of the proliferated subsidization practices for competition on a global scale is the position of beneficiaries on the world market, i.e. in other foreign markets. The FSR only is directed towards a level playing field in the EU internal market, but not on foreign markets, not least due to sovereignty restraints. This problem could only be addressed by expanding WTO anti-subsidy rules. The FSR does not address subsidization that aims at increasing local content and hence production at home, which is the most globally proliferate way of subsidizing; insofar, anti-subsidy rules apply as the material scope of the FSR is limited. Though the FSR may be perceived a "unilateral solution for a multilateral problem",[103] it is a very imperfect one.[104]

All in all, the future will show whether the FSR will be a success. The Commission is subject to reporting and review obligations (Art. 52 FSR). It will be interesting to see whether the high level of detail will lead to simple handling with minimal legal disputes or whether the complexity will prevent successful, legally secure handling. For further consideration it will be useful to examine the ratio between the procedures in which substantive concerns actually arose and those that were unproblematic in terms of substantive law. The future will also show how the Commission and the EU courts position themselves on the scope of the investigative instruments envisaged by the FSR.[105]

[102] For the need for greater control over the Commission induced by its broad powers enshrined in the new EU trade policy instruments, see Weiß (2023c), pp. 58 ff.

[103] Nagy (2023) 908.

[104] Van Damme (2024), p. 6.

[105] CJEU, case C-720/24 P(R), ECLI:EU:C:2025:205 – Nuctech.

References

Baumann P (2023) The EU Foreign Subsidies Regulation: The Final Piece of the Regulatory Puzzle to Ensure Competitive Neutrality in Cross-Border M&A? In: Hillebrand Pohl J et al (eds) Weaponising Investments. Springer Nature, Cham, pp. 199–218

Blockx J, Mattiolo P (2023) The Foreign Subsidies Regulation: calling foul while uppending the ante? Eur Foreign Aff Rev Special Issue 28:53–73

Börnsen N, Pollakowski O (2024) Ein Jahr FSR-Anmeldepflicht: Übersicht, Erfahrungen und Hinweise, Neue Zeitschrift für Kartellrecht NZKart, pp 603–608

Frank M (2023) The EU's new Foreign Subsidy Regulation on collision course with the WTO. Common Market Law Rev 60:925–958

Hahn M (2025) Chapter 7, Section B. VIII WTO-Kompatibilität. In: Bungenberg M, Heinrich W (eds) Europäisches Beihilfenrecht, 2nd edn. Nomos, Baden-Baden

Herrmann C, Ellemann T (2024) Die neue Verordnung über den Binnenmarkt verzerrende drittstaatliche Subventionen – Ein Brussels Effect in Zeiten geoökonomischer Subventionswettläufe? Zeitschrift für Europäisches Privatrecht ZEuP, pp 64–104

Hornkohl L (2023) Articles 19 f. In: Krenzler HG, Herrmann C, Niestedt M (eds) EU-Außenwirtschafts- und Zollrecht, 23rd Supplement

Hornkohl L (2023a) Protecting the internal market from subsidisation with the EU state aid regime and the Foreign Subsidies Regulation: two sides of the same coin? J Eur Compet Law Pract JECLAP 14:137–151

Kühling J, Weck T, Reinhold P (2022) Third-country state aid regulation: the European debate on foreign subsidies. In: Chi M, Bungenberg M, Bjorklund A (eds) Asian yearbook of international economic law, pp 149–161

Luja R (2021) The Foreign Subsidies Regulation: countering state aid beyond the European Union. Eur State Aid Law Q EStAL 20:187–199

Mattiolo P (2025) Concordia discors? The Foreign Subsidies Regulation and increased subsidization in the EU under the open strategic autonomy model. In: Fechter, Wiesenthal (eds) The age of open strategic autonomy. Nomos, Baden Baden, pp 157–180

Micheau C (2016) Evolution of state aid rules: conceptions, challenges, and outcomes. In: Hofmann HCH, Micheau C (eds) State aid law of the European Union. Oxford University Press, Oxford, pp 18–35

Müller-Ibold T (2025) Article 44 Relationship to other instruments. In: Bungenberg M, Soltész U (eds) Foreign Subsidies Regulation. A Commentary

Nagy CI (2023) The EU's new regime on foreign subsidies: has the time come for a paradigm-shift? J World Trade JWT 57:889–908

Oberländer I, Sickinger C (2024) Commission Calling: "Call-In" of transactions under the Foreign Subsidies Regulation – uncertainty and unpredictable risk? Zeitschrift für Wettbewerbsrecht ZWeR 22:103–114

Osseforth T, Ackermann C, Sellmeyer M (2025) Meldungen und Erklärungen drittstaatlicher finanzieller Zuwendungen in öffentlichen Vergabeverfahren - Bedeutung und Auswirkung der Durchführungsverordnung (EU) 2023/1441. Neue Zeitschrift für Baurecht NZBau, pp 149–153

Soltész U (2023) Drittstaatensubventionsverordnung und Transaktionspraxis – EU-Kommission gibt Vorgeschmack. Neue Zeitschrift für Kartellrecht, pp 121–123

Trapp P (2023) Art. 6 VO (EU) 2022/2560. In: Krenzler HG, Herrmann C, Niestedt M (eds) EU-Außenwirtschafts- und Zollrecht, 21st Supplement

Trapp P (2023a) Art. 7 VO (EU) 2022/2560. In: Krenzler HG, Herrmann C, Niestedt M (eds) EU-Außenwirtschafts- und Zollrecht, 21st Supplement

Van Damme I (2024) Understanding the Foreign Subsidies Regulation. Univ Bologna Law Rev 9(1):1–6. https://doi.org/10.6092/issn.2531-6133/19378

von Graevenitz A (2019) Wider die Verrechtlichung von soft law der Europäischen Kommission. Zeitschrift für Rechtspolitik p 75

von Graevenitz A (2025) Drittstaatliche Subventionen im Fokus der Europäischen Kommission - Die FSR - Verordnung (EU) 2022/2560 über den Binnenmarkt verzerrende drittstaatliche Subventionen. 2nd edn. https://doi.org/10.48701/opus4-474
Weiß W (2022) Ex officio third country subsidies' review: similarities with and differences to state aid procedure. Eur State Aid Law Q EStAL, pp 132–142
Weiß W (2023a) Die Verordnung über den Binnenmarkt verzerrende drittstaatliche Subventionen: Ein Weg zu mehr Wettbewerbsgleichheit? Zeitschrift für das Gesamte Handels- und Wirtschaftsrecht ZHR 187:809–850
Weiß W (2023b) EU strategic autonomy and rule of law in external affaires: what future for respect for international law and multilateralism in trade policy? In: Hinojosa-Martínez LM, Pérez-Bernárdez C (eds) Enhancing the rule of law in the EU's external action, pp 187–217
Weiß W (2023c) The EU's strategic autonomy in times of politicization of international trade: the future of Commission accountability. Global Policy 14(Suppl 3):54–64
Weiß W (2024) The regulation on foreign subsidies distorting the internal market. A path to a level playing field? Springer Nature, Cham
Weiß W, Furculita C (2024) Open strategic autonomy in EU trade policy. Cambridge University Press, Cambridge

Wolfgang Weiß is Professor of Law and holds the Chair of Public Law, EU Law and Public International Law at the German University of Administrative Sciences Speyer.

Albrecht von Graevenitz is Professor of Civil Law at the Federal University of Applied Administrative Sciences, Department Adminstration of the Armed Forces in Mannheim.

Ulrich Soltész Dr. iur., is Partner at the Law firm GleissLutz in Brussels.

MIX
Papier aus verantwortungsvollen Quellen
Paper from responsible sources
FSC® C105338

If you have any concerns about our products,
you can contact us on
ProductSafety@springernature.com

In case Publisher is established outside the EU,
the EU authorized representative is:
Springer Nature Customer Service Center GmbH
Europaplatz 3, 69115 Heidelberg, Germany

Printed by Libri Plureos GmbH
in Hamburg, Germany